RESTAURANT KID

RESTAURANT KID

KID

A Memoir of Family and Belonging

RACHEL PHAN

PEGASUS BOOKS

NEW YORK LONDON

RESTAURANT KID

Pegasus Books, Ltd.
148 West 37th Street, 13th Floor
New York, NY 10018

First Pegasus Books cloth edition April 2025

Interior design by Maria Fernandez

The author would like to acknowledge funding support from the
Ontario Arts Council and the Government of Ontario for their support.

Library of Congress Cataloging-in-Publication Data is available.

ISBN: 978-1-63936-851-8

10 9 8 7 6 5 4 3 2 1

Printed in the United States of America
Distributed by Simon & Schuster
www.pegasusbooks.com

For Mum and Dad.
It's the greatest honour to be your daughter.

CONTENTS

AUTHOR'S NOTE

The stories you find within these pages are drawn from the threads of my memory and stitched together with as much honesty and care as possible. Memory, of course, has its own way of telling stories—sometimes clearer, sometimes softer at the edges. Although the heart of every moment is true, some names, places, and details have been thoughtfully changed to respect privacy.

In this book, I've chosen to use the Vietnamese spelling for city names to honour the language and culture of Vietnam. However, I've opted to retain the English spelling of "Vietnam" for clarity and familiarity for a wider audience.

Some scenes in this book may be triggering or painful to read. For a full list of content warnings, please visit my website www.rachelphan.com.

Thank you for being here with me and giving me the space to share my story.

PREFACE

I inherit trauma the moment I am pulled, disappointingly female, from my mother's open stomach.

I am never simply just a baby. At birth, I join a new generation of people who will carry the burdensome weight of my family's history on our shoulders and in our bones. After all, mine is a family that has, on multiple occasions, had its land invaded, been caught in the crossfires of war, and been forced to flee.

First, it is the Japanese who come knocking on our doors in the late 1930s, forcing my grandparents out of their original homeland of China and into neighbouring Vietnam in 1938. Then, just a few decades later, there is a war in Vietnam, the fall of a city, and two teenagers fleeing their home with hundreds of thousands of their brothers and sisters. These two teenagers, Hy Phan and Tran Hoang, leave behind everything they know to become displaced boat people, stateless refugees, and citizens of a strange, foreign land called Canada. It will be more than a decade before they become my parents.

This is only a cursory overview of my family's history and the intergenerational trauma I inherit on that June day. But there is literal trauma at my birth, too.

My mother is terrified when she first sees me because, unlike her other children and most babies, I am completely, unsettlingly silent. I have no pinched face, no wailing cries, no angry red cheeks.

Instead, I am unmoving. A purplish corpse blue.

After an excruciating beat, I finally squeal, and relief floods my poor mother's chest. (This relief is later dashed when her mother-in-law—my *ah mah*—expresses disappointment that a daughter has been born rather than the anticipated, expected son. My mother has failed. She will receive no congratulations that day.)

My mother is alone in that hospital room with her near-stillborn daughter.

My father is nowhere in sight. He isn't there to give Mum a loving squeeze of her shoulder as she is cut and pried open. He isn't there, his racing heart matching hers beat for beat, as they wait to see whether I am alive or dead. He isn't there to collapse against my mother as my slow-coming screams ring through the air, anxiety releasing from his body with each of my tiny, laboured breaths.

He isn't there because he is at work. Always, always at work. On that June day, and the hundreds of days before and after, work is his top priority, not a second daughter who should have been a son. His accumulation of cash and experience means security for our family. It means food on the table and assurance that he and my mother will never again starve and that their children will be spared the horrors of their dirt-poor childhoods in bombed-out Vietnam. It means the sacrifice and pain of leaving behind their country, their culture, and their home will be worth it if they can just say they've made it.

Yet a small part of me—a pointy shard within me—always wonders if he would have been there even if it had been his day off. Who is my father, really, outside of work? Who is my mother?

My earliest memory comes two and a half years later. It's not a sunny recollection of loved ones cooing and peering over me with warm, happy smiles.

The setting is the same as my birth. I am alone in a hospital room.

I am a toddler and I desperately need to pee, but I see no washroom, no familiar face, no loving hand to guide me. All around me, the steady *beep, beep, beep* of machines ricochet off the hospital's white, sterile walls. Visiting hours are over. There's no one here to help me.

I'm there because I'm a sickly child, with severe asthma and seizures that terrify my mother every time my eyes roll to the back of my head and my tongue threatens to choke me. But in this memory, all that ails me is my brimming bladder and a heavy feeling of being lost.

I crawl out of my hospital bed and find myself alone in a hallway. The bleached whiteness of the room has followed me to this long stretch of tile with its endless doors to mysterious places. Do any of these doors lead to the *chi so?*

It is overwhelming, this memory. I feel impossibly small and alone in contrast to the seemingly endless expanse of the hallway and its many bizarre and unfamiliar twists and turns. I see no one who looks like me—I see no one at all—and the pressure is mounting, low in my belly.

A tiny, tentative step forward. *Pause. Look up. See that no one is coming to take me to the* chi so. *Squeeze my thighs together to stop the trickle. Alone, alone, alone.*

I continue my aimless, desperate walk before deciding on the door that might take me to where I need to go. The door leads only to a dark, musty broom closet.

Before I have a chance to break down into tears, a nurse appears as if conjured by my growing anxiety. Her shoes squeak against the floor. "What are you doing, honey? Where do you want to go?" she says, lifting me up into her arms. That's when my memory flickers out, not with feelings of hope and relief, but of a stifling, lingering loneliness.

As an adult, I wonder now whether our first hazy memories colour the rest of our lives. Is my life woven from the threads of loneliness and feelings of wrongness that have dogged me from my very first breath, when I arrived not to a celebration but to my mother's painful solitude and jagged grief over almost losing a child who had already failed to live up to expectations?

At not even three years old, I learned that life is all about opening a series of doors and hoping someone is present enough to ask, "Where do you want to go?" If they aren't, then it's up to me to figure it out myself.

1

"MY PARENTS OWN THE CHINESE RESTAURANT."

I am three years old when I meet my replacement.

Instead of a squirmy, red-faced little thing, what comes to consume my parents' already scarce time and attention is a quaint red-bricked building in Kingsville, Ontario—a small town where the people are as friendly as they are pale.

It's a blazingly sunny day in 1991, and our family of five has just pulled up to the back of that red-bricked building in our trusty red Chevrolet Lumina. I remember straining my short neck to look up at this unassuming place my parents kept saying we would make our own.

Like so many other Chinese families who have settled in small towns across Canada, our path toward the elusive Canadian Dream would begin with a family-owned business. This building would be transformed from a generic coffee shop into a humble restaurant serving Chinese Canadian cuisine, with my parents at the helm.

To stake their claim on this building, my parents bestow a name upon it. *My* name. At birth, I was christened Rachel—the Anglo name on my government documents—but to my family, I've always been little May

May. In Chinese, *may* or *mei* can mean "beautiful" or "bright" or "reliant" or even "Chinese plum." It is a name that takes on different meanings and significances depending on the tone, context, and intentions of the speaker.

With such stunning versatility and range, it seemed a natural fit for my parents to name this new building, this new adventure, this new evidence that they'd finally succeeded in Canada, after me, their youngest child.

They name it the May May Inn.

"What do you think, May May?" My dad crouches down low to meet my eyes. My older brother, John, who is ten, grumbles behind him in typical middle-child fashion, envious that it is my name emblazoned on the restaurant. ("How come you named the restaurant after her? Can you name a dish on the menu 'John's jumbo shrimp'?")

It is a monumental day. The turning point for our family. Finally, my parents have something that is all theirs. They can be their own bosses, set their own hours, make even more money. For two kids who survived bombs and starvation during a pointless war in Vietnam, it is a dream come true.

I didn't know it at the time, but that unassuming red-bricked building would become my parents' new baby. I was no longer the only May May in their lives. From that day on, I am a restaurant kid.

———⁓———

The restaurant becomes ours ten years after my parents landed in Canada in 1981, with their infant daughter, Linh, in tow and an unborn baby the size of a plum—my brother, John—in my mother's womb. They finally have a home after two years of waiting in a Hong Kong refugee camp, where my parents landed after fleeing post-war Vietnam on a too-packed boat of disease and despair.

When they land in Quebec, it is a characteristically cold February day. They marvel and shiver at the sight of the unfamiliar white powder that covers everything they see. It is so completely different from Hải Phòng, where they were born. It terrifies them.

"I had tears in my eyes," my dad remembers. "I thought, 'What the hell? We came to Canada and it's all this? It's all white.'" A thousand questions race through Dad's head upon landing in this new place they were to call home. *How do people live here? How do people work? What are we going to eat?* But my dad keeps his anxious thoughts to himself. My parents both speak Cantonese and Vietnamese, my dad can understand Mandarin and some Japanese, but neither know English when they arrive in their new country. What choice do they have but to stay quiet? What choice do they have but to parrot back the same strange words they hear from the same strange people handing them their first-ever winter boots and jackets?

"Snow," someone says, catching the way my parents' wide eyes survey the shockingly white landscape before them.

"Snow," they repeat, feeling how the word wraps heavy and confusing around their tongues.

According to their official landing document, my parents are stateless and the amount of money they had to transfer to Canada was "nil." They have not a single cent to their names and no other home to speak of that would claim them. Canada would be their saviour, their great hope, their land of possibilities. My dad is twenty-two years old and my mother nineteen—just two young, immature kids already parents to a fourteen-month-old daughter, with another child on the way. They are overwhelmed and frightened.

My parents settle in a small town in southern Ontario called Leamington, also known as the "Tomato Capital of Canada" because of its produce-rich greenhouses and the Heinz factory that made the town smell like ketchup chips on windy days. My mum's eldest brother had settled there six months before my parents' arrival.

After the first night in their government-provided apartment, my parents' collective anxieties ramp up to eleven when they discover their front door frozen shut by a particularly nasty overnight snowstorm. "It's like being in jail!" my parents wail, their hearts and bodies longing for humid, familiar Vietnam.

Things don't get much better from there. Following their arrival, my parents pick up odd jobs that no one else seems to want. My mother gets a job sorting through and cutting manure-covered fungi at the mushroom farm, whereas my dad gets a job picking tomatoes and beans. Soon, the days and weeks and years start to quickly blend together—a mix of social assistance, sponsored church visits that end the moment my parents get too busy, and long hours of menial labour.

"Even though we were struggling, we felt really happy," Dad says, a faraway look in his eyes. "We came from a country with war, but Canada was peaceful. We weren't scared of bombs or guns here. Even though we were poor, we were still happy."

Three years after landing, something life-changing happens to Dad: he sees another Chinese person in Canada who miraculously isn't related to him or my mum. Elated by the familiar set of this man's eyes and tanned skin that mirrors his own, Dad goes up to this stranger who, to his immense delight, also speaks Cantonese. What luck! The man, Howard, tells Dad that he owns a Chinese restaurant in town called Happy In. Dad, sensing this was his chance to pivot from back-breaking farm work to back-breaking restaurant work, takes his shot. This way, he'd at least be around other Chinese people.

"Are you hiring?" he asks before the two part ways. He is hired on the spot, becoming Happy In's newest cook.

Dad has to learn everything when he starts his new job because the food he is responsible for making is as foreign to him as it is exotic to the customers. Dishes like the elegantly named "chicken balls," which are chunks of chicken cocooned inside deep-fried breading and smothered in a violently red sweet-and-sour sauce, are so unlike the braised meats, steamed fish, and stir-fried dishes my family eats. There are so many dishes to learn, including more deep-fried fare like chicken soo guy and lemon chicken. My dad, who grew up impoverished and hungry in Hải Phòng, is given a wok and a trial by fire. Over time, he learns that chow mein is a popular, watery dish made of bean sprouts, though Cantonese chow mein is a crispy noodle dish with vibrant green vegetables and sauce-slicked pork, chicken, and shrimp. He also discovers that restaurant work, though a different kind of grind than greenhouse work, is a grind on his body all the same. At the restaurant, he works six days a week, ten hours a day. For his labour, he is paid $180 every week.

With Mum making a similar amount and two young children to feed, clothe, and shelter—I wouldn't arrive for another four years—my dad picks up part-time seasonal work as a worm picker between April and June. During these months, he works at the Happy In until 2 A.M. and then heads over to the manure-rich land outside the mushroom farm where Mum works. There, he trawls through dirt and soil in the dead of night in search of worms to sell as fishing bait or super-secret ingredients in beauty creams. He is paid $30 for each full pail—in reality, old Heinz ketchup cans. On his first night, the ground surges and crawls with moving worms. Dad, scared but brave, grabs them by the handful and fills seven cans with their squirming bodies. At the end of his shift, when he gets his $210 in cash—under the table so he doesn't get taxed—it is like striking gold. The overflow of bills in his pocket makes his fifteen-hour workday and subsequent trek home at 6 A.M. bearable. Once at home, with the early dawn breaking outside, he catches what little rest he can before he is back in the restaurant kitchen again.

—⁂—

I am born in 1988, seven years after my family's arrival in Canada. My parents, feeling more secure in their new country and less-than-stellar but stable jobs, want to try for another boy. We all know how that turns out.

My first three years of life in Leamington are marred by frequent hospitalizations, asthma attacks, and seizures. Aside from my lonely hospital memory, I remember very little from this time. What I can recall comes to me in bits and pieces, some so small that I hesitate to call them real. Did I dream up the memories of my dad crying on the couch after a particularly nasty fight with my mum? Do I actually remember my mother putting her finger in my mouth so I wouldn't choke on my tongue during my seizures? Or are these all stories that have been passed over to me as an adult?

In my mind, my life didn't really begin until the move to the apartment above the new restaurant in Kingsville. When my memories start accumulating for real, the treasure trove that contains them is in the shape of the May May Inn.

After seven years of working in the Happy In kitchen, Dad meets a man named Frank, who owns multiple buildings across Essex County. One of the businesses, a coffee shop in the nearby town of Kingsville, Ontario, has failed and is closing, he tells Dad. Would my dad—who has since taken on his own Anglo name of George—be interested in renting the building and turning it into a Chinese Canadian restaurant? Frank tells him it is an opportunity to get out of someone else's kitchen and own his own business. This is his chance to be a better man, a better provider, for his wife and kids. "Do you want to try it out?" Frank asks.

"Yes," Dad immediately responds, thinking he can try it out for a couple of months. If it doesn't work, there's always the Happy In to fall back on.

On the day of the restaurant's grand opening in 1992, the people of Kingsville flock to the new exotic restaurant on Main Street, with its fiery red sign—very auspicious—and bold white letters in the classic wonton font—very "Chinese"—urging them to try the Cantonese and Szechuan food advertised underneath the name May May Inn. (For years, we'll get calls from confused tourists asking, "Does the May May Inn have any rooms available?")

As soon as my parents turn the "Closed" sign to "Open," it is mayhem. A family friend's daughter is scheduled to help out as a waitress but ends up sleeping in—and my poor mother, who spent ten years working at the mushroom farm, has no idea how to take orders or be a waitress. To make matters worse, neither of my parents has a strong grasp of the English language yet.

The responsibility falls on Dad to make it work. It was, after all, his decision that led our family down this path. That day, he is the cook, the server, and the person fumbling through English and math to settle bills. He is a man possessed, driven by an impossible dream.

"May May was packed that afternoon," he says. "It was hard, but after that day, we knew we were going to make it. Even though we fucked up, we saw the people and the customers, and that gave us hope."

While my parents scramble to learn the ins and outs of running a restaurant, I'm learning lessons, too.

I learn fairly quickly that when you're a restaurant kid, you're never really alone even though you always feel a little lonely. You're constantly trying to get out of the way of your family members who are busy working or you're being doted on by a waitress when she has a moment to spare or you're making polite chit-chat with the regulars who help keep your family's business afloat. Your entire life is marked by the constant thrum of the restaurant's hubbub. The restaurant is always the centre of attention, never you. The restaurant quickly becomes your entire world. It's never just a restaurant—it's evidence your parents, who gave up everything for a chance at a new, safer life, have succeeded. They've made it. The restaurant was, and is, everything.

It is our family room, with the TV blaring in the kitchen during slow hours. We play music videos of Dad's favourite songs—he sings along to "Eternal Flame" by The Bangles on repeat—or make our way through piles of Chinese dramas on VHS tapes. "What's he saying?" I ask, and Dad translates from Cantonese to English while he puffs on a cigarette in between the rushes of lunch and dinner. I love these quiet moments best because it almost feels like I have my parents to myself. I don't have to compete with the customers at table five who are waiting for their dinner for three.

Once, when it is dead inside, Dad takes me outside and asks if I want to sit on his shoulders. I quickly say, "Yes," pleased by the novelty of his attention. But the moment my stumpy little legs bracket his neck, I want off. I am not a child who takes to playing naturally, my earliest years punctuated by so many hospital stays. I never learned how to play freely with a careless, reckless abandon, because I always had to be so careful. Rather than seeking thrills, I learned to prize stability and security.

I am so frightened by my feet parting ways with the ground that I grab fistfuls of my dad's hair and shout, "Down! Down! Down!" The nervous flipping in my stomach prevents me from enjoying even ten seconds atop my dad's shoulders. My dad, laughing, listens to my desperate pleas to be put down before rushing back into the kitchen.

Later, when I'd feel like a ghost in my busy parents' lives, I'd wonder why I didn't relish that moment with my dad more. It wasn't often that he gave me the full weight of his attention, not when there were so many chicken balls to make and the wok to attend to at all hours of the day. In those moments when I'd feel the ache of my parents' absence, I would wish for retroactive bravery and the ability to hold firm to my dad's head and shoulders, trusting that he would never let me fall, willing him to never leave me, believing he would always keep me elevated on a pedestal.

To my horror, the restaurant is also my parents' battleground. When restaurants are busy, the people being run ragged in the kitchen are never at their best. Tensions are high, curse words fly off the tip of your tongue without a thought, and no one's personality is sparkling. That all becomes ten times worse when your spouse is constantly in your space. You never get a break.

When my parents fight, nothing is off-limits. During their frequent kitchen blow-ups, Mum and Dad throw chicken balls hot out of the deep fryer at each other while cursing in Cantonese. A veritable smorgasbord of items are thrown at the other, from the expected—dishes, cutting boards, mushrooms—to the surprising and downright dangerous—knives of various lengths and sharpness, whole plates of cooked food.

"*Diu lei!*" they yell at one another, faces red and forehead veins near to bursting. "*Diu lei lo mo!*" Fuck you. Fuck your mother.

My mother calls Dad a *puk gai*—asshole—and they curse each other's families (*ham ga tsan!*) as if our family unit isn't impacted by such curses thrown out so casually.

My siblings and I cower in the dining room, my sister paralyzed by anxiety and willing herself to disappear while my brother rocks back and forth, his left leg bouncing with nerves. As the baby of the family, I am given the unenviable task of defusing the situation with my charm and elevated status. As the youngest and smallest, I need to be protected and cared for the most. That is the expectation, at least.

"Go in there, May May!" my brother and sister say. "Tell them to stop!"

Pushed into the kitchen, into the eye of the storm, I yell with the full force of my little lungs. "Stop fighting! They can hear you all the way in China!" That is always my go-to line. It usually works and leads to tenuous peace between the two warring factions until the next time a grenade is thrown.

Sadly, we aren't always just collateral damage. Sometimes, the belligerents fix their destructive gaze on us.

There are three early memories I can barely conjure now, partly because of how young I was and partly because of the pain:

I am three or four and my parents are new restaurant owners. There's something I want my mother to see—maybe a drawing or a cut finger—and I pull at the black apron tied around her waist.

"*Mama, Mama*," I plead for her attention. "Look!" My tiny fingers clutch at and grasp for her waist. Each tug is met with an exhausted sigh, but I am undeterred. Persistent. "Look, *Mama*!"

Suddenly, my mother rips her apron from my desperate hands and grabs my delicate wrists.

"*Aiyah*, May May, move!" she snaps. Her tone is harsh, final. She is done with me. I can see it, the way her back is already turned, her attention cast down to the giant colander of rice she is washing free of starch in the sink.

Her dismissal stings, but I take to heart the lesson it brings. I must never get in my parents' way when they are working. Their attention during those many long hours is not mine to take.

Another memory: it's slow in the restaurant and my dad—I still called him *Baba* then—spots me picking at my nails.

"May May, not in the kitchen!" he yells. "Do you need to clip your nails?" I shake my head, feeling obstinate the way children sometimes do. He sighs. "I can see you picking at your nails. Come on, let's go outside and I'll cut your nails for you—they're so long!"

For some reason, the thought of having my nails trimmed fills me with dread and terror. "No!" I cry. "I don't need to, *Baba*!" He ignores my cries and grabs me gently by the hand to lead me outside. "Give me your fingers," he says expectantly. My face twists and contorts in distress, and I shake my head.

"No?" His face, usually a cool river, is also twisting into something new. Dangerous. My mother often talks about how the Phan family is mercurial by nature. She says there is a blackness inherent in our blood that makes us prone to sudden changes in mood. I see that shift in my dad's face too late.

"No?" he repeats. I shake my head and hide my hands behind my back. *My nails are mine! Why do I need to cut them?*

When *Baba* slaps me across the bottom, swiftly and hard, I have no choice but to unclench my resisting fists. When another slap follows, just as hard, I offer him my hands freely without a fight. The pain and shock spreads, and I soon forget why I resisted in the first place. Resistance, I learn, comes with dire consequences.

One final formative memory: *Baba* is at the sink, rinsing a pot. I'm peering up at him, but he doesn't notice I'm there. I am suddenly filled with a reckless desire to do or say something that will get him to divert his gaze from the hot running water to me. *Get his attention, no matter what it takes.*

"I love *Mama* more than I love you, *Baba*," I say. Kids can be unexpectedly cruel and cutting, and I am no exception.

My hurtful words are swallowed by the sound of the water pouring out of the faucet. At least, I assume they are because my dad doesn't bat an eyelash in response. He doesn't look at me at all.

That's how it is for me, living life on the periphery. Since my siblings are old enough to help Mum and Dad in the restaurant, I while away the hours by myself in our apartment. My twelve-year-old sister, Linh, handles the front of the house, from cash to phones to bartending, while ten-year-old John oversees the deep fryer and cuts chicken.

To get to our three-bedroom, one-bath apartment from the restaurant, one has to go outside and walk up a long flight of stairs. Our apartment is technically not above our restaurant, but above the store next to it—a jewellery store called The Jewellery Box. It's where I spend hours marvelling at shining, gem-encrusted trinkets and delicate porcelain figurines, while Mary, the woman who owns the store, patiently tolerates the smudged fingerprints I leave on the glass display cases. I always have too much time on my hands and no one to notice when I'm gone too long.

One day, I am talking to Mary about birthstones and whether Mum would like a necklace proclaiming her to be the "#1 Mom," with all five of our family members' stones casting a sparkling line around a solid gold heart.

"Yes, absolutely," she says. "Your mom is so lucky to have a daughter who loves her so much."

I don't tell her how I feel like I miss my mother all the time even though she is never far from me, frantically scribbling down table number six's order and rushing back to the wok to make their fried rice.

—⁓—

Our fortunes changed when my parents bought and started the restaurant. No longer at the mercy of employers paying them below minimum wage under the table, my parents were suddenly flush with cash, and there was, gloriously, no one swooping in to take a share of their profits. Dad says it was the first time they felt "loose." Mum says it was the first time in their entire lives they had a lot of money. I no longer have to wear my brother's hand-me-downs in their drab, boring boy colours.

My family, like many other Chinese families, is a superstitious lot. Many of my elders place a high premium on luck, fortune, and blessings from our pantheon of gods. We believe in things like auspicious colours—red and yellow—and lucky numbers. It's why Mum will never pick the number four if we're playing a game ("four" and "death" in Cantonese are pronounced similarly: *sei*) and why my birth year of 1988, which has two lucky number eights and is the lucky year of the dragon, is considered doubly fortuitous. My parents were uneducated former refugees from a country that had been torn apart by war, famine, and colonization. Now, as luck would have it, they were the owners of a thriving business in one of the world's safest, most prosperous countries. The gods had clearly bestowed their favour upon us. With so many blessings raining down on our family, it seemed logical to my parents to push the limits of their luck. Just how much would the gods bless us?

Before the restaurant, Mum and Dad had no money or time to go to the casino. This changes after Lady Luck turns her beautiful face in their direction. Not long after the restaurant opens, my parents decide to make the forty-five-minute trek to the casino in Windsor. Their fun doesn't begin until they complete their laundry list of tasks: feeding the last customers, closing up the restaurant, packing away the food, tallying up the bills and counting the cash, making their hungry children dinner, eating said dinner, sweeping and vacuuming the kitchen and dining room, showering their oil-slicked skin, putting on fresh clothes that still always smell like grease, and then, off they go. It's well after one in the morning when they leave.

Three months after my parents' fateful first trip to the casino, Mum wins $17,000 on the slots. They're hooked. They start going for all-nighters once or twice a week to unwind and enjoy their new money. They chase after lightning and try to bottle it.

I didn't know it then, but other kids had large backyards and front lawns and even special rooms devoted just to their play. To them, our small apartment might have seemed like a place of confinement, but to me, it was a sanctuary from the chaos and tension of the restaurant.

Without physical space to take up, I retreat inwards and find adventure and life in my rich interior world.

During those early days—and all the days following—my sister, Linh, who is nine years older than me, becomes my sun, the star around which I orbit. While my parents settle into their routine of working twelve-plus-hour days, I start looking to my sister as the closest thing to an adult in my life. I follow and stay close to her like a shadow, or a parasite, and endeavour to be just like her. It helps that we share a bedroom, so I never have to go long or far without her comforting presence.

Linh, who always has her nose in a book, fills the bookcase in our bedroom with Harlequin romances and book series she quickly outgrows, like The Baby-Sitters Club and Sweet Valley High. One day, when I am four years old, my sister starts teaching me the fundamentals of reading, but we are interrupted when she is called down to work. To pass the time, I make it my mission to complete the lesson on my own. I hole myself up in our room with a ninety-six-page novella from her overflowing bookshelf and will the confusing black lines and swirls to unjumble themselves and make sense. As time passes, I feel fizzy and buoyant each time a cloud of understanding descends over my head. That novella is the very first book I ever read—kickstarting a lifelong obsession with the written word, which would be my form of escapism, play, and companionship. The loneliness I feel living on the sidelines of the restaurant simmers to a dull ache when I go on whimsical adventures with Mr. Tumnus, discover masturbation with Deenie, and join Margaret in asking God if he's there.

I have just adjusted to this quiet life as a full-time restaurant kid when I am suddenly thrust into a new, scary world. Junior kindergarten.

My sister puts me in a tight floral off-the-shoulder dress: a bold, over-the-top choice for a four-year-old. The soles of my feet are imprisoned in the stirrups attached to my leggings. I make a mental note to complain about it to my sister later, so she'll cut them off for me.

I am led down a flight of stairs to the awaiting class, the warm sunlight slowly disappearing behind me as we descend. The sounds of high-pitched singing float up to greet me midstep. When I reach the bottom, thirty new faces stare back at me. These strangers are all wide eyes and bright teeth and white skin. It frightens me.

I want nothing more than to race right back up those stairs and cry into my mother's apron, even though she'll likely just swat me away and say, "*Aiyah*! Go back to school—*Mama* is working," in familiar Cantonese.

"Class, this is Rachel," one of the four teachers says gently, her hands on my bare shoulders. "Can we say hi?"

A shrieking "hi" greets me in unison as I am ushered to a spot on the floor. It is on that floor that I meet the cast of my childhood—the four Ashleys, three Amandas, and a handful of Ryans. But no other Rachels. My little head swims with all the names and faces.

One of the teachers, a white woman with short brown hair and a kind face, crouches down beside me and smiles, her warm brown eyes glinting with something like sympathy.

"Rachel Phan," she pronounces my last name incorrectly, like *fawn*. "What a beautiful name. Welcome to our junior kindergarten class. Is there anything you'd like to share with us?"

I gulp, my little heart racing. When my breathing becomes laboured, my fingers grasp air, reflexively reaching for my puffer that isn't there. Old asthmatic habits die hard.

"Share? With the class?" I stammer dumbly. I am too young to be mortified. Instead, I'm just confused.

The teacher nods. "Something about yourself that you want others to know."

Understanding and relief hit me, and I nod. This is the easiest question in the world. I might have said, "I love to read," or "My best friend is my big sister," but the first thought that crosses my mind is neither of those things.

"My parents own the Chinese restaurant," I announce. Already, the restaurant is a core part of my identity. So many of my waking thoughts revolve around it: *What are my parents doing? Is it busy? Can I go down and sneak a snack? Who is working? Are* Mama *and* Baba *fighting? Can the customers hear them? Do I need to go in and beg them to stop?*

The teacher claps her hands together. "Wonderful!" A boy in my class gasps and shouts, "I love chicken balls!" His vocal eagerness leaves no doubt that he does, in fact, love chicken balls.

I beam and stand up taller, rocking back and forth on the balls of my feet as if pure energy radiates through me. I feel seen, acknowledged. My nerves and fear are replaced with tentative excitement.

Over the coming days, weeks, and months, I learn to relish the chance to get away from the restaurant, with its loud noises and the air of tension that always hangs over us like the filmy layer of oil on a fatty dish. I welcome the chance to be around other children. To play and be a regular kid for a few hours a day. To not have to retreat inwards for escape.

School gives me a glimpse into new worlds and realities I had never known before. I learn that other kids exist, and none of them live in a restaurant like me. I learn that summer camps and after-school dance lessons and swimming in gigantic pools are all real things that people my age get to experience on a regular basis. I learn that families have movie nights together, and that mommies and daddies tuck children in while reading them bedtime stories. I learn that when I ask other kids how often their parents go to the casino, they don't even know what a casino is. I learn that no one else knows what it's like to have to raise their voice above the sound of the sizzling wok or the din of a packed dining room day after day, night after night, just to be heard. To them, going out to eat at a restaurant is a special treat. They envy me and think it's so cool that I get to drink as many pops as I want, whenever I want. But there is nothing special about it to me.

Whereas other children have bedtimes, no one enforces such limits on me. After a long day of working in the restaurant, cooking, and serving, Mum and Dad need to pivot to cleaning, cutting, and preparing for the next day of service. There are no breaks when it comes to the restaurant, not even for parenting. The few rules that are established come from my siblings who, absorbed in their own lives, lack the teeth and spine to strong-arm me into listening. I often stay up well past midnight to watch David Letterman and Jenny Jones with Linh and John, who do not reprimand me.

Waking up is a struggle in the morning. *Why is it always so cold and dark?* Most days, I wake up and watch *Bobby's World* in my brother's room while

enjoying a bowl of sugary Corn Pops cereal before we make the short walk
to school.

But sometimes, I'd squeeze my eyes tight, force a cough, and say,
"*Mama*, I'm sick. I can't go to school." She'd pause, weighing her options
in her head—put up a fight, call my bluff, and force me to go to school;
or take the path of least resistance, cuddling me close and offering to
make me healing congee. She'd usually be too tired to do anything but
the second option.

On those days, I'd crawl into bed with my parents and cuddle with them
as they rested, savouring this unexpected time with them. I don't think
about how odd and sad it is that I need to skip school to spend time with
my parents. I am just a child, happy to have both of my parents' limbs
wrapped around me and luxuriating in the all-too-fleeting safety and
security I find there.

—·—

As the baby of my family, I learn that there are certain allowances I get
that my siblings don't. Although they are expected to devote their weekends and after-school hours to working at the restaurant, my hands remain
unburdened, soft and callous-free. I don't have to puzzle over bills and
make the numbers add up the way my sister does. I also don't have to learn
how to make martinis as a pre-teen the way she does. ("They sent it back
because it tasted like gasoline! I'm only thirteen—what do they expect?")
While everyone works to the bone behind me, I can stand at the bar and
just be charming and useless. I ask customers how they eat their egg rolls
and delight in learning that everyone has their own strategy and vocabulary
when it comes to this cuisine that has brought us all together.

I tell customers all about how I smother mine in Dad's homemade plum
sauce before cutting it in half, eating the insides first, and saving the deep-
fried shell for last.

"You call it a shell? I call it the crust," a customer says.

"The crust? It's the skin!" another chimes in.

"It's very clearly the wrapper," someone else contributes.

While these fiery debates are taking place, my sister is frantically answering phones and my brother is being yelled at in the kitchen by my parents. They're trying desperately to keep up with all the orders. I ignore all that. I'm just happy to be talking to someone.

2

"WHY DO YOU LOOK LIKE THAT?"

By the age of five, my life as a restaurant kid settles into a comfortable, predictable rhythm.

When I'm not reading books at our little employee table in the dining room, where I occasionally help waitresses fold napkins or make wontons, I'm in our apartment, losing myself to TVO and YTV. In between episodes of *Arthur*, *Art Attack*, and *The Hit List*, I'm reading my sister's books and treating her Harlequin romances as personal contraband.

There are endless days when I opt to read my books in the dining room. I learn that hanging out in the restaurant means Mum and Dad are more likely to make a little bit extra when customers order. On very good days, they'll give me little bowls of excess honey garlic spareribs, beef *lo mein*, or fried rice. I eagerly accept these scraps with outstretched hands.

During the seasons when playing outside is possible in Canada, I happily explore the area behind the restaurant. It's a rocky parking space full of dangerous things, like the sharp gravel that skinned my knees when I fell while chasing crickets or the exposed nail that pierced through my flip-flops and taught me the word "tetanus." When I'm not being maimed by my environs, I am digging through the pebbles and grimacing with disgust at the desiccated corpses of flattened frogs that line the street in the spring and summer. My fascination with dinosaurs means I never stop hoping I might get lucky and find a fossil buried somewhere beneath the gravel.

It's out there, on a sticky, hot day, that I make my first real friend.

Being nine years younger than my sister and seven years younger than my brother means that much of my time is spent in my own company. Although my siblings try their best to nurture me and keep me entertained, they just don't have enough time in the day for their little sister—not when there is the cash register and customers to tend to, vegetables to chop, and English homework to puzzle through during their informal, unpaid shifts. Even if they could conjure up more time, I am five years old and they are teenagers. They don't want to spend their free time playing with me when they could be stealing moments with friends at sleepovers or swaying awkwardly at school dances on the rare occasions they don't have to work.

Since my parents neither know about nor think to enroll us in summer camps or extracurricular activities, it is my responsibility to fill the interminably long summer months on my own.

Just a stone's throw away from the restaurant is a four-storey building called the Town Square Apartments, which even then looked archaic. The building's one saving grace was that its apricot trees would grow new life in the warmer months, offering their golden-hued, fuzzy-skinned progeny to us in round, sticky spades.

I find myself on the edge of discovery amongst these tiny stone fruito. With the sun beaming its radiant rays down on me, I chance a look upwards to the sky and am greeted by a pale flash on one of the apartment building's three balconies. *A kid.*

I squint my eyes in the sunlight in an attempt to sharpen the image and inhale sharply at the sight. *A kid!* Her hair is mousy brown and her skin is the sort to easily burn.

I wave up at the girl, who pokes her head over the brick balcony to peer at me with reciprocated curiosity. I shade my eyes with a hand to get a better look.

"Hi!" she shouts, her voice a high, cautious squeak.

"Hi," I reply, my voice cracking from lack of use. I'm so used to speaking with adults at home in alternating Cantonese and English that speaking to someone my own age feels foreign and exhilarating.

"What's your name?"

I know to give my Canadian name to this girl over my Chinese name. "Rachel," I say, leaving May May behind.

"I'm Talia," she responds. "Don't go, 'kay? I'm coming down!"

Sweat trickles down my temples as I wait for her to reappear. A few minutes pass and then she's there, so close I could reach out and grab her bony elbow. She's taller than me and gangly, all limbs and knobbly knees. I'm instantly captivated by the light dusting of freckles that cover her nose and cheeks, challenging me to start counting and daring me to discover as many different shapes and constellations on her face as I can find.

"I'm six," she says. "How old are you?"

I tell her I'm a year younger, and she pauses a moment before nodding, as if to say *Five. I can work with five.*

She gives me an appraising look up and down, and I lean forward to make it easier for her to assess me with her critical eye. I want nothing more than to know what she's thinking when she looks at me. *What does she see?* I suddenly care very much what this girl thinks. *Is she judging the hack-job mushroom cut my sister gave me under the bright bar lights by the restaurant's cash register? Is she as taken by my face as I am hers?*

It turns out she is.

"Why do you look like that?" Talia asks. "Your eyes are different. They're small and like this." She places her fingers at the corners of her eyes and yanks back so they become slits on her face.

I don't know it yet, but it won't be the last time someone does this gesture to me. Because it hasn't become a painful pattern yet and because I don't know how harmful this can be, I just shrug and say, "I don't know. I'm Chinese." I say it simply. I say it without expectation. I haven't yet learned that saying this truth is enough to elicit a barbed response or taunt. I still say it without immediately tensing up. I say it without fear or shame.

And because she's still young and hasn't learned what "Chinese" or "race" is or what it means to be "white" and "not white," she just gives me a shrug back and says, "Oh, okay! Do you want to play?"

That's how the Summer of Talia begins.

Those long days bleed into each other, full of pure golden sunshine. Talia and I play with her dolls in her messy apartment while "Step by Step" and "Please Don't Go Girl" by New Kids on the Block play on cassette tape. One day, Talia drops the volume of her voice to a low, harsh whisper. "There's a song I'm not allowed to listen to, but my mom listens to it sometimes when she thinks I'm sleeping. Do you want to listen?" she asks conspiratorially, eyes looking past my shoulder at the locked door behind me. Her mother isn't home.

I nod my assent, equal parts eager to do something bad and stressed to bits about misbehaving. Talia rifles through the plastic tapes before finding her forbidden treasure. She shoves the tape into the boom box.

A series of "Oh, oooh, ooohs" blasts over the speakers. Talia starts to dance and shout along to the lyrics. She grabs me by the hand and pulls me closer to her. "This song is called 'Let's Talk About Sex,'" she says breathlessly in between her hollering. She's completely tone-deaf, but I love it anyway.

I am five and don't really know what sex is, aside from what I've caught glimpses of on television and in my sister's sex education books. My interest is piqued.

"Rachel, do you know what sex is?" she asks me, while Salt N Pepa raps about how to make any man's eyes pop. I nod shyly.

"It's what husbands and wives do, right?" I ask the question like I'm on a game show. *Is this the right answer?* I look at her earnestly, desperately wanting to learn a new thing I can pull out whenever I need to impress or show off.

Talia smiles at me, showing off the gaps where some of her baby teeth had once been. "Almost, but it's not just husbands and wives," she says. I nod sagely, rich with newfound wisdom. This vital piece of information is logged accordingly in my brain.

"Come on, let's play house." She grabs my hand tightly, undeterred by the clamminess that greets her palm. "We're wives now."

I quickly learn that "playing house" with Talia is my favourite thing to do in the whole world. There's nothing I love more than holding her hand and pretending to be wives. I get a fizzy sensation in my belly whenever we do, a feeling that tells me I never want to play with anyone else or do anything other than this. No Polly Pockets or Barbies could ever, ever compare to the feeling of our palms pressed flush together.

Later in the summer, while we run around the apricot trees behind our apartments with the sun high in the sky, Talia says, "My darling wife, let's play Truth or Dare."

By then, I had learned that whatever Talia says goes. I was happy to let her take the lead on our playtime as long as she never stopped being my friend. Plus, she was older than me by one full year, and I had it drilled in my head that I must listen to my elders. Usually, what she wanted to do was what I wanted to do anyway, so I didn't fight against the expectation.

"Okay," I say, my hand gripped tightly in hers. "Truth."

"Tell me the truth," she says. Her face is covered in an even darker smattering of freckles than when we first met at the start of summer. "Do you want to see my butt?"

Without hesitation, I smile widely and nod my head. I flush with pleasure when she gives me a toothy grin in response. She is pleased with my answer.

"Then I dare you to kiss my butt!" she squeals, releasing my hand to pull her dress up and her underwear down.

It's there and then that I kiss her butt and she kisses mine, and I feel a pure, shocking joy in that warm golden glow of sunlight.

Sadly, our friendship doesn't last. I learn at school that first graders don't play with kindergarteners. We grow apart. I discover that girls shouldn't kiss each other's butts and that wives and husbands are the norm, not wives and wives. I try to forget how buzzy and happy being with her made me feel.

Without Talia's company, I go back to hovering on the sidelines at the restaurant, waiting for delicious leftovers. While there, I get to know our eclectic regulars.

There is John the Tailor, the older man who runs the clothing alterations shop across the street, who talks to me about the books I'm reading and challenges me with riddles and puzzles. Sometimes, he buys me books for the two of us to pore over together. He is impossibly kind and easygoing, always giving Dad "chef's choice" powers over his lunch. Many years later, when a much-older Linh is in a panic because our parents are too busy to drive her back to university, he's the one who steps in to take her the three hours to Waterloo.

There is Janette, a woman who only eats at our restaurant a few times a year. She's from Grand Rapids, Michigan, and takes such a fancy to me that when she visits, she brings me boxes full of toys, games, and letters signed, "Your godmother." She's the most glamorous woman I've ever seen, with highly teased and hairsprayed blonde hair and elegant cursive writing that surpasses the penmanship of even my teachers. I love her and count down the days to when a new box will arrive, just for me. The shine of our arrangement dulls when she starts bringing boxes for my cousins, too. I feel less special after that, hating that this is something I must share.

And then there are the Waldmans. Family patriarch, Jack, and sons Jay, Henry, Peter, and JJ sit at the large round table and drink endless cups of coffee. These men are large and boisterous and fascinating. Even as a child, I take note of how much space they take up—literally, they claim that big, round table in the dining room for hours—and how life to them seems to move at a luxuriously slow pace. They are never rushed or hurried, which is so unlike my parents, whose to-do lists only get longer, never shorter.

Once, while chatting with Peter, I notice a soft, fleshy nub at the base of his neck. Too young to know about decorum or boundaries, I point to it and ask, "What's that?!" Before he can respond, my childlike curiosity gets the better of me, and I grab the lump with my fingers and pull with the force and power of all our gods and ancestors combined. To my horror and awe, the skin gives way, pulling apart from poor Peter's neck in a flash of crimson. His shocked face tells me I have just done something very, very bad, but his good-natured laughter, and the laughter of his brothers and father, ease my anxiety.

"Thank you, Rachel, I was looking to get that removed," he says, patting my head and keeping any pain he feels off his face even though I literally just ripped his skin tag clean off his neck. We give him a Band-Aid and he gives us a tip on the way out, cementing his place in Phan family lore for all time.

Despite appearing rough, with their grease-stained jeans and calloused hands, the Waldman men are kind and soft. I watch them when I should be reading. I am pleased when they ask me questions. Because I am a weird kid, I descend on their table the moment they leave in the hopes that by doing so, I can somehow absorb their way of life—a life where one can sit for hours with family and just talk and enjoy one another. I sniff their seats out of desperation, already missing their presence and hoping for their return. I don't know how to explain why their departure would sometimes cause a piercing ache to run through my gut, except that it felt like my substitute family had also left me behind.

When that inexplicable gnawing pang gets to be too much, I retreat to my books or to my siblings or to the endless number of white women who float in and out of the restaurant as May May Inn waitresses, and in and out of my life as a result. There is Lisa, and Anne-Marie, and Bonnie, and Nathalie, and Michelle, and all of them teach me something about patience and kindness. These temporary mothers show me that parenting needn't always be a full-time job, but one that can be accomplished in shifts.

Instead of camp counselors or piano teachers, these are the adults who shape me and are etched into my memory as I grow up.

—⁂—

As we settle into a routine at the restaurant and Kingsville becomes home, we learn that there are few things people in our town love more than hockey.

Parents will bring their children, most often sons, to the restaurant after their hockey games. Wins are celebrated with incessant, open-mouthed chattering over steaming plates of food, whereas losses are a more sullen, quieter affair.

Customers will come in asking us if we watched the big game. If we say no, we are met with incredulity. Suspicion. Don't we know that hockey is the top way to perform Canadianness? No, of course we don't, just look at us. It isn't long before Mum and Dad's Chinese movies are replaced with *Hockey Night in Canada* and my mother's exasperated cries of "Are you kidding me, Toronto?"

Since we are so close to Windsor, which shares a river with Detroit, most people are part of two warring factions: Toronto Maple Leafs fans and Detroit Red Wings fans. There was never any doubt about which team we'd choose. Even though the Leafs are probably cursed, having gone decades without lifting the Stanley Cup, and even though the Red Wings at the time were the much better team, we never questioned who we would root for.

Toronto's rivals on the ice become our sworn enemies in our hot kitchen as we stand around the TV, our hands clenched into fists, our shoulders hunched toward the screen like it's the North Star. Mum even makes up her own jingle for the Leafs to the tune of "The Muffin Man."

"I hate Detroit!" we say with rabid intensity. We are entranced and invested. Our blood boils with the righteous fury that comes with being long-suffering Leafs fans.

"I hate Boston!" Mum says during other games. She pronounces it "Bossington."

No matter how many first-round playoff series the Leafs lose, we remain committed to them as a symbol of our unwavering commitment to Canada. We commiserate with customers who also foolishly bleed blue and white. We discover the Toronto Raptors and Toronto Blue Jays along the way. We fall in love with tennis, and later, Mum adopts Canadian athletes Denis Shapovalov, Felix Auger-Aliassime, Bianca Andreescu, and Leylah Fernandez as her children. We root for Canadian teams on the international stage.

Although none of us plays sports, we fall in love with the games, the team spirit, the community. We cherish the ability to hold a conversation with our customers, to feel like we belong.

———

The first time a teacher asks me for a parent's signature, I bring the document home, hoping I might catch my parents during a slow moment. I have been raised to respect my elders and their rules, so I feel an excruciating push-pull between not wanting to bother my parents and doing what my teacher asked.

"Just forge it," my brother tells me while I patiently wait for Mum to finish her kitchen prep and clean-up.

"Forge?" I ask. *What does it mean to forge?*

He takes a scrap piece of paper and scrawls an approximate replication of my mother's signature before pushing the paper towards me. "See? Now you don't have to wait for Mum to sign it. She's too busy."

I study the letters he strung together on the paper. There it is. *Tran Phan* in tilted, jagged handwriting, each letter written clearly. I memorize the distinctive shapes and internalize my brother's lesson. It makes me feel free. Now, I don't have to bother my parents with something as inane as a permission slip or homework. They already know I am a good girl from the way I nod, say yes to their demands, and respectfully blend in with the walls. They don't need to see my straight As on report cards to know that to be true. I can forge my mother's signature, look at my own report cards with approval, and give myself permission to go on field trips. It's a small thing I can do for my parents if it means they have one less thing to worry about.

Most of the time, I understand that my parents need me to be good. To never ask for more than what they can give. But sometimes, I rage against the expectation.

Once, with my stomach growling furiously with hunger, I call down to the restaurant, lamenting that I have to starve because my parents are too busy feeding other people and their kids. *What about me? Why do my parents care more about other children than they do about me?*

"I'm so hungry, too hungry!" I cry into the phone. My mother's impatient sigh tells me she has no time for my childish games. She has pork fried rice to make.

"Just wait. We're too busy right now," she says, her voice clipped and tired.

"How can you do this to me? I could call the police! You're starving me," I whine. "All I have to eat is ketchup!"

Without missing a beat, my mother says, "Eat ketchup then" and hangs up. Stunned, I call back and tell them I'm running away.

She hangs up on me again.

I tearfully grab a few of my necessities—my favourite *101 Dalmatians* sweater, a Baby-Sitters Club book, my Polly Pockets—and make a break for it.

When I take my dramatic first steps outside, I am full of bravado and conviction. But it is winter, and it only takes two seconds for the cold, biting wind to humble me. I make it all the way to the bottom of the long wooden staircase before I sheepishly trek back upstairs, my tail tucked and my stomach emitting a low, building rumble.

Of course, I wasn't starved. My entire life has been a delightful feast of umami and abundance and complex flavours. Along with the restaurant, food is the centre of our lives. It has always brought us together.

No matter how busy the restaurant was or how much cleaning up and food prep my parents needed to do, we always built time into the long day for the five of us to spend together. I waited—sometimes impatiently—each day for 10 P.M. to roll around because that was when the restaurant shifted from being everyone's main focus to the backdrop of our family dinners. Someone would say "*Dai gab sih fan*"—which translates roughly to "everyone eat rice together"—and for a too-brief moment in time, we'd focus on each other.

With the *soo guy* and Western fare packed away and refrigerated, we'd sit down to savour the food of our people: Mum's braised pork belly with preserved vegetables in an unctuous sauce I wanted to drink by the salty spoonful; verdant green *choy sum* or *gai lan* stir-fried with garlic; and Dad's lobster prepared traditionally with scallions and ginger or, my favourite, with evaporated milk, butter, and onions.

In none of my memories do I remember what we actually talked about. All I remember is how lit up it made me feel on the inside to be with my family. Even when the memories are bad—like when I was tasked with carrying out a plate of *jiu yim* pork chops for dinner and dropped the whole thing, to my immense guilt and shame—I still remember this dedicated block of family time fondly. No one was sweating over a wok or working the deep-fryer or placating a customer. In those moments, I felt like I belonged to a real family, not just a team of employees. I was truly, fully theirs and they were mine.

The nights I loved best were the ones when we'd have my dad's family over—some from exotic, far-flung places like England or Toronto—and my parents would go into full show-off mode. Look how we made it! Dad would proudly boast about his beloved LaserDisc player that was almost always playing *Top Gun*. Then, once the adults started feeling loose because of the Tsingtao beer or Vietnamese snake wine, Dad would fire up the karaoke machine. My parents, aunts, and uncles would give rousing renditions of the beloved Vietnamese ballads and iconic Chinese songs that floated on the winds of Hải Phòng when they were children. While the adults were transported to the sticky, hot nights of Vietnam, the children were in hell. We'd roll our eyes at their music—"Why does Vietnamese sound like that?"—and wish we were listening to cool music by bands like Bush and Silverchair. Our giant round kitchen table would be laden with an assortment of dishes—stir-fried morning glory, the most tender suckling pig that melted in your mouth, Dad's signature lobster, steamed whole fish with ginger and scallion, and if it was a celebration, a fruit sponge cake from a Chinese bakery in Toronto.

While we ate, my mother would separate the fish from the bones and drop the chunks of white meat on each of our plates.

"I'm full, *Mama!*" I'd say after a while. But she'd keep piling meat and vegetables on my plate, her love for me evident all over her oily fingers and my distended belly. After we finished with the savoury food, Mum would peel us fruit after fruit, dazzling us with how quickly she could strip the fruit of its peel, which was, without fail, always intact. A perfect, long strip. Her love was never more obvious than when she peeled grapes—a seriously tedious chore that she did just for me.

Full of food and unable to keep my eyes open any longer despite my most valiant efforts, I'd go to bed to the sound of the adults cracking jokes and swearing in Cantonese while they played mahjong well into the early hours. The clacking tiles lulled me to sleep better than any soothing lullaby ever could. The comfort of a full house, with everyone present, holding me close and keeping me safe.

I knew customers only in a very specific context—which dishes they loved, what substitutions they made, where in the dining room they preferred to sit, whether they liked me or not. I rarely saw regulars outside of the restaurant.

This changed in December 1994 on what was a typical Friday night for our family. Back then, my parents worked seven days a week, the restaurant staying open until 1 A.M. on Fridays and Saturdays to best cater to the drunken weekend crowd. The three of us children are watching TV in our living room, waiting for Mum and Dad to finish up for the night, when someone bursts through our apartment door. It is 12:45 A.M. There is no frantic knocking, no struggle to get in. This person barrelled into our apartment with a clear purpose.

"Kids?" I hear a strange, yet familiar, adult male voice yell. "Linh? John? Rachel?" Heavy footsteps. Laboured breathing. Suddenly, one of our restaurant regulars, a man named Tom, is inexplicably in our apartment kitchen. Tom is kind and eats at the restaurant often with his partner, Mary-Jo (always a wonton soup with Chinese noodles). They feel like extended family. But that doesn't explain why Tom is in our home at such a late hour.

"You guys need to pack some clothes right now. Hurry! We have to get out of here," he says. His cheeks are flushed. I stare dumbly at him as if he were an impossible mirage. Surely, I have already fallen asleep and this is a dream. "Come on, Rachel. We need to go! There's a fire."

I rub my eyes to clear the hallucination. But my siblings jump into action at the word "fire." I have no choice but to follow. As I rummage through my drawer of clothes—hastily grabbing my Northern Getaway sweaters and underwear with the days of the week on them—I can hear Tom telling Linh and John that he was in the restaurant waiting for Mary-Jo when he saw smoke and heard panic-stricken cries of "Fire! Fire!" The smoke was already coming up through our apartment floor, Tom says, but none of us noticed, our increasingly heavy eyelids glued to the television screen. Other residents in the apartments next to ours were already being evacuated by fellow neighbours and first responders.

In my dreamlike state, I walk out in the hallway. Tom scoops me up in his arms and carries me out into the brisk December night air. I nestle my head on his shoulder, fatigue and confusion keeping my fear and anxiety at bay. He brings us to the side of the road where my parents are. Together, we watch as the fire trucks come and wait for the fire to burn itself out. I fall asleep on someone's shoulder as forty-five firefighters descend on the scene to combat what remains of the blaze.

I wake up the next morning in a hotel—a Quality Inn with scratchy sheets and the smell of cigarette smoke forever trapped in the fabric of the curtains.

"Can we go home today?" I ask no one in particular.

"No, there was a fire," Linh responds. "Dad doesn't know when we'll be able to go back."

"But what about Christmas? Will we be able to go back before Christmas?"

No one tells me anything, not that I would have understood it anyway.

At one point, we go shopping at Zellers to buy replacements for all the things we lost—hand towels, blankets, other housewares. "Buy whatever you want. Insurance will cover it," Dad tells us, as my sister places Santa-themed hand towels in the shopping cart. (Insurance does not cover it.)

Over the coming weeks, years, and decades, I would learn more about that night. First, the fire started in a nearby store that sold sports and trading cards. "I think some loose paper on the heater caught on fire," my sister says, reaching for the memory. At least thirteen tenants were forced out of their apartments, including my family, and four businesses lost everything in the rubble. Although our apartment and restaurant suffered considerable smoke damage—we were closed for a month—we were spared a much worse fate thanks to our neighbour, The Jewellery Box, and its formidable fire wall that stopped the fire's spread.

A whole strip of businesses and homes burned that night, but as I would learn time and again, the restaurant was resilient, the most stalwart member of our family. It would always be there, long after we all started wishing it would actually burn down.

3

"I'M NOT CHINESE.
I'M CANADIAN."

At my elementary school, no one looks like me. There is no one in my class with the same eye shape as mine or the same warm skin tone. There is no one in the hallways or on the playground during recess. When I leave for the day, there is no one on the quiet provincial streets of my small hometown, either. There is no one.

It's not much better when I turn on the television.

As a young child, I fall in love with Disney like everyone else. A family friend records Disney movies on VHS tapes and drops them into my eager little hands whenever he visits. I watch and rewind and rewatch these movies until I know every line and song by heart. But while other girls my age can play and pretend to be Disney princesses, I never feel right doing the same. At four years old, I already know I'm not anyone's idea of a proper princess.

Left with no other options, I pretend to be Maleficent, the dark fairy in *Sleeping Beauty*, who feels most similar to me by virtue of her not being pale-skinned and blue-eyed. I learn to love being the Mistress of All Evil.

I take an old wooden mop handle from the kitchen and pretend it is my staff. I practice my evil laugh when I am alone in our apartment.

(By the time *Mulan* comes out in 1998, I am ten years old and it's too late. My Disney phase is over. I know for certain that life is not a fairy tale.)

When *Mighty Morphin Power Rangers* premieres in 1993, it doesn't take long for me to become obsessed. I see a face that looks like mine for the first time in the form of Trini who is—shocker—the yellow Power Ranger.

But it's not Trini I want to be. I don't look at her and think, "Yes! Finally!" I don't think of her at all. I grimace and reject her as an option immediately.

It's the pink Power Ranger, Kimberly, who I most want to be like. She is pretty and popular and all the boys like her.

My family buys me pink Power Ranger merchandise: T-shirts, sweaters, dolls. She is everywhere with me in my school photos and on our family trips.

I never think about Trini and what she might mean for girls like me. She is easy to ignore. She is not the main character.

A few years later in 1997, the Spice Girls phenomenon sweeps across classrooms, clubs, and convenience stores around the world. I am in the fourth grade, and whenever my friends and I choose which Spice Girl to play, I never feel like I can be anyone but Scary Spice.

When I make my choice—begrudgingly, of course, because who doesn't want to be Ginger or Baby?—my friends nod their heads. They agree this is the only option for me that makes sense. None of them wants to be Scary Spice anyway.

This is the water I am swimming in:

According to the 2016 census of Kingsville, Ontario, less than 3 percent of the town's population is a visible minority. With a total population of around 21,000, just 535 people belong to a visible minority group. One can imagine, then, what it was like in the 1990s. Back then, we were still a tiny town. Back then, people weren't leaving nearby big cities en masse because skyrocketing inflation and red-hot housing markets were pricing them out. Back then, it felt like I could count the number of racialized people on both of my tiny hands.

Back then, the only Chinese people I knew in town were my family and the family that owned the other Chinese restaurant. But because their kids went to a different school, I never actually saw them.

Later, when I dig through archived data on the internet, I see the stark reality in clear, official numbers.

In 1996, when I am eight years old, the population of Kingsville, Ontario is 5,830. There are fifty-five people in total who identify as belonging to a visible minority group: twenty Black, ten Arab/West Asian, ten Latin American, and fifteen Chinese. My immediate family makes up a third of the Chinese population in the whole damn town.

Because of that, I initially strive to be invisible. I hate being remarkable just because I'm so different from everyone else. I hate feeling like an exotic bird to gawk at and not fully understand. It's easier to fade into the walls and be silent. It's easier to not be seen. After all, to be seen would be to invite commentary about my difference.

Still, I'm doomed to stand out.

I am in the second grade the first time a boy takes notice of me.

I am spending recess crouched beside a tree. I find the worker ants walking in the dirt in twos and threes infinitely more interesting than my classmates, who are always so loud and messy. A shadow casts dark over me, making it harder to see my little muses.

I look up to find a boy in the grade above mine standing over me. I have never spoken to him before. His hair shines a tarnished gold in the sunlight.

"What's with your hair?" he asks, pointing a finger at the top of my head. I can see dirt around the fingernail of his index finger. I touch the side of my hair and feel the familiar coarse strands. *Is there something in my hair? Has a fabulous creature alighted on my crown?*

The boy—he's one of the many Matts at my school—twists his face into a sneer. "You look like a boy," is all he says before he turns and walks away. It's my first drive-by insult.

My face flushes hot with embarrassment. His words feel like a sharp blade to my gut. Although I can't articulate exactly why his words feel like acid poured on my skin, I know with certainty that I do not want to look like a boy. I am of an age where I'm starting to notice boys with mild interest. They are the loudest and messiest of us all—how could I not notice them? I shudder to think I look like one.

My hair is still in the roughly chopped but classic mushroom cut from my sister, whose quivering hands lacked confidence and any sense of evenness. My bangs sit at an angle against my forehead. *Is this a boy's haircut? Had my role-model sister somehow made a mistake?* I am seven years old and know boys have cooties, but I also find myself drawn to them. It is the year of my first sexual awakening thanks to Gavin Rossdale, the lead singer of the English rock band Bush. Specifically, Gavin Rossdale shirtless on the cover of *Rolling Stone*, legs spread, fingers teasingly touching his lips, gaze direct and inviting. Before the magazine landed in our mailbox, my only source of titillation had been one very specific scene in *Aladdin* in which Jasmine, enslaved by Jafar, wears a gauzy red two-piece, her thick black hair in a high ponytail. I would rewind the scene over and over again, a confused fire growing in my belly. I chalked it up to loving the colour red and disliking her usual blue garb. Blue, after all, is a boy's colour.

But Gavin is different from the beautiful, spirited daughter of the Sultan in a Disney movie. He is real and breathing, flesh and tousled hair and low growling vocals. Gavin is a boy, which means my singular fascination with him extends to all boys. I imagine an alternate reality where Matt's words—"You look like a boy"—spill out of Gavin Rossdale's lips. I flinch, suddenly remembering my mother's wounded expression when Dad teased her for cutting her hair short after the heat of the kitchen burned up all remaining vanity she possessed. *Nam yun tau*, he'd called her. *Man head.*

Matt pointed a finger at my bowl cut and determined it was the reason for my boyishness. I know immediately it needs to change. I need to be cute and pretty for all the Matts and Gavins who look at me. I need to look like Jasmine, with her lustrous long hair.

My ant friends long forgotten, I commit to browsing my sister's pile of *YM* and *Seventeen* magazines towering high on the staff table at the restaurant. Within those pages, I would learn how to be a real girl.

It's an innate desire to be shaped, moulded, and directed—that is, told what to do—that makes me so keen to learn. It's how I become a bit of a know-it-all and forget my quest for invisibility.

As a young child, I relish knowing the answers to things. I love how often and quickly my hand shoots up in the air when the teacher asks a question. I become addicted to praise and high grades and feel oh-so-smart for knowing how to spell words like "miscellaneous" when I'm just nine years old. When I score high on the province-wide third-grade testing across all subjects, especially in reading and writing, I feel affirmed and worthy. I feel like I have a purpose for the first time in my life. I am a natural. I am born to write. This is who I am.

When I tell my parents, they nod and cast only the briefest momentary glance my way. "Good girl, good job, so smart," they say. Their response doesn't mollify me. It doesn't satisfy. *Don't they know that this is a big deal?*

I push myself to exceed and excel, not because of any parental pressure, but because of the lack of it. If I can just get one more A+, if I can be the top of my class, maybe my parents will notice. Maybe, I hope with every fibre of my being, they will tell me they're proud of me. Maybe they'll even close the restaurant and take me out for a celebratory meal.

As soon as the ridiculous dream crosses my mind, I dash it from my brain. Silly hopes like that are just breeding grounds for disappointment. I'm a child and I've already learned that painful lesson.

I still try. If there's any chance of earning my parents' attention and affection, I am gunning for it. I am ready to seize it with both of my eager hands.

A glittering, undeniable opportunity comes in the fourth grade when we start yearly class speeches. Every year, students must choose a topic, research the hell out of it, write a speech that clocks in at under five minutes, and then present it to their class. We do this every single year until high school.

If that's not enough, it's also a nice friendly little competition for all of us. The student with the best speech in each class gets sent to the second round, where they get to present their masterpiece to the whole school. From there, two winners are selected to represent the school in the third round—a competition with all the other schools in the district.

I am pumped and ready for my moment to shine.

It's a no-brainer what my topic is going to be. I am so proud to be Chinese, and I want my classmates to know just how cool China is, too.

I put on my red *cheongsam* and proudly connect the dots between my pride and my people. I talk about my family and our history as boat people, and even though I don't quite understand the meaning of the words "resilience" and "perseverance," the way I talk about my parents leaves no doubt how grateful I am for what they did to get us on Canadian soil.

I talk about China and excitedly explain to my classmates that we are an industrious and inventive people. I throw out "did you know" facts like my life depends on it.

Did you know that the Chinese invented toilet paper? And gunpowder? And pasta? That's right—your squeaky-clean bottoms, favourite war movies, and spaghetti nights have China to thank. I take the things I know my peers love or depend on and apply a Chinese lens to it. I learn how to be palatable to my friends and classmates while maintaining parts of my heritage and identity.

At the end of my presentation, my class erupts in applause. Multiple people tell me how awesome my speech is. They say they had no idea that China was so cool. I beam with pride. I am so happy to be Chinese.

In the end, I get second place for best speech, but I don't even care. My classmates' enthusiasm for China feels like the most precious prize there is.

Still, some concessions must be made to fit in. To be normal. Unbeknownst to me, my classmates have set limits on how much pride in being

Chinese I am allowed to feel. I can only be proud of the things that have the approval of my peers.

I find this out at lunch because there's always a lunch story.

It's the same one that resonates with countless immigrants and their children the world over regardless of country of origin, language, or skin tone. Mine is not exceptional.

In elementary school, my mother would pack leftovers for me to bring to school for lunch—something savoury and pungent with too many chunks of garlic or *douchi*, which is fermented and salted black beans. I remember noodles slippery with the glorious combo of soy and oyster sauces, Dad's black bean spareribs, and garlicky stir-fried morning glory. I also remember wrinkled noses, craned necks, and the high-pitched squeal of, "Ew, what is that?" I remember faux gagging sounds and the dramatic covering of nostrils.

"I don't want to eat that weird stuff anymore," I say to Mum when I am nine years old. "I want regular food, like everyone else."

Mum looks at me for a beat before throwing her hands up in the air. Later, when she takes me with her to Zehrs, I grasp eagerly for Dunkaroos, Twinkies, and a variety of Lunchables. Finally! I can eat my lunch in peace, without strange looks and bewildered comments. Finally, I have some social capital with which to trade for the really good stuff—the things that always make the kids in my class deliriously happy. The markers of "cool" and "normal."

I have my eyes on the cheese strings my classmates tear into with glee, their fingernails pulling apart the delicate strands of cheese they dangle over their open mouths. When they chew, their eyes glaze over with pure pleasure. I want so badly to experience that same joy.

Cheese is foreign to me. It isn't in our dishes. The only cheese we have in our refrigerators is the Kraft Singles we keep on hand for the customers who order cheeseburgers. I have never eaten it plain and was immediately intrigued by the way my classmates made it seem so delicious and fun to eat.

The time comes when I'm able to trade one of my Twinkies for one of a classmate's prized cheese strings. My eyes widen at the smooth cylinder of cheese tucked cozily in its individual package. I tear it open, excited to finally see what all the hype is about.

I pinch the cheese from the top the way I've seen other kids do and slowly peel it down. The texture is strange—I hate the way it feels under my nail—and the smell is unfamiliar. But I carry on, feeling like this is my initiation into a truly Western childhood. A rite of passage.

When the string cheese lands on my tongue, it's my turn to wrinkle my nose. *What is this?* It's slightly salty and tangy, but mostly, it's just bland. I chew, hoping the taste will miraculously improve, and find myself appalled by the way the cheese sticks to my teeth. I look longingly at the Twinkie half-eaten in my classmate's hands.

Unable to swallow the clumps of cheese, I grab the napkin Mum packed in my lunchbox and discreetly spit out the offending snack. As far as trades go, this was a horrific one. I don't understand why my classmates treasure these rubbery sticks with such rabid intensity. Shaking my head, I throw the rest of the cheese string in the garbage, grateful I didn't bother asking my parents to part with their hard-earned money to buy me a whole bag of such dreadful treats.

The truth is, I never crave the lukewarm Chef Boyardee or the sad Lunchables I beg my mother to pack for me. I much prefer the food we eat at home and count down the hours until 3:45 P.M., when Dad will have my favourite after-school snack of curry chicken ready for me at the restaurant. He'll make it the way I like, with chunks of moist chicken smothered in a fragrant yellow curry sauce and no vegetables in sight. I'll scarf down the mildly spicy chicken, so eager for a proper meal that my poor tongue will become a victim of my haste. On the days I can, I sign out of school for lunch and walk over to the restaurant to eat in the safety and privacy of the kitchen, away from prying eyes and disgusted looks. Yet when Mum tries to send me to school with this food I love and crave, I always resist. "No one likes this food at school," I say. "No one will like me if I eat it."

"So? You Chinese. This what we eat," she responds. At her words, my eyes widen as if she has inflicted a mortal wound on me.

"I'm not Chinese," I reply hotly. "I'm Canadian and this is what Canadian kids eat!" I grab the Lunchables Cracker Stackers and shake the package in her face. "They don't eat smelly shrimp and fatty pork!"

For the longest time, I couldn't understand why my mother looked at me with such sadness in her eyes. Later, I'd wonder if it was the same resignation I felt each time the lunch bell rang and dry, crumbling crackers filled my mouth.

—

That same year, when we're visiting family in Toronto, I see the ugly words spray-painted on the side of a restaurant in Chinatown.

"I HATE ORIENTALS."

The letters are sloppily sprayed, as if the person who hated us knew they were on the clock. There was no time for refinement. They needed to get their message across as quickly and clearly as they could. To them, we weren't even worth the effort.

It's the first time I encounter hate speech. From the moment I cast a glance at those words, something shifts in me. Before then, I didn't know just being Chinese was enough to elicit hatred.

After we get home, I wake up every morning fearing that those same ugly words will be sprayed across our restaurant. I start to wonder if customers or classmates also hate Chinese people.

A few months later, our parents tell us the restaurant is a massive success and that we've outgrown the tiny location on Main Street. As the list of our regular customers grows and we become the more popular of the two Chinese restaurants in Kingsville, my parents find the solution to their problem in the form of a building just a three-minute walk away. The building's dining room is double the size of our existing restaurant, with a much larger kitchen, a back room for a TV, and a spacious two-floor apartment that adjoins the restaurant kitchen.

But what sells me is when Mum says, "It's right across the street from the police station. Much safer."

I think about how their proximity might make people think twice about egging our windows, or dining and dashing after gorging on combination dinners. I think about how the police might deter someone from spray-painting "I HATE ORIENTALS" on the side of our home.

It's enough to convince me even though my heart sinks at the news. The much bigger apartment means I'll no longer have to share a room with my older sister, whose presence has been protection from the terrifying dark and the evenings when my parents' voices rang out a little too loudly.

When it comes time to move our belongings down the street, I do so with a fake smile on my face, but my eyes widen in genuine pleasure when I take in just how much space we now have. The restaurant is big enough that we can finally have a smoking section and a non-smoking section, ignoring how the two spaces are separated only by a small wooden partition that will do nothing to prevent the cigarette smoke from swirling over to the other side. I gleefully welcome the fact that the back room in the kitchen means I have a place to hang out instead of being on full display to customers.

And the apartment! Compared to our first apartment, it's palatial. Although I'm not sold on having my own room, I still squeal when I see it for the first time and feel my chosen carpet—a lush light pink—under my toes. Each of us marvels at having our own space—Linh, at sixteen, finally has the privacy she so desperately wants, and John, always the most rebellious of us, delights when he discovers he can sneak out of his bedroom window to sit on the restaurant's roof.

Although the apartment is different from my friends' houses, with their full decks and sprawling green backyards, this is a home to me. We're conveniently connected to the restaurant by a door, which is excellent for snacking and I'm-bored-and-lonely purposes. My cousins, brother, and I take blankets and slide down the apartment's long staircase, howling over each bump and laughing at whoever had the misfortune of getting carpet burn.

On the days when everyone's working, I spend hours in the tiny back room that's just off the kitchen, hidden in shadows. In there, I read books like *Frankenstein*—it gives me the creeps—and play rounds of MASH by myself, rejoicing when fortune foretells that my destiny is to live in a mansion with the cutest boy at school and curling my nose in resignation when we get the shack.

The new restaurant location comes with a new slate of neighbours in addition to the police. Because I tend to float in and out of nearby stores just for something to do, I soon meet the woman who owns a neighbouring sports store and her kids, who are around my age—one a few years older than me and the other a year younger. It is the older daughter I find most fascinating. When Meredith Brooks's song "Bitch" comes on the radio, she sings the lyrics without any hesitation or shame. I am in awe of how mature and grown up she is.

For a time, I become an honourary member of their family. I sit squished between the sisters in the back of their Chrysler Neon. I spend more time looking at running shoes at their store than I do with my own family at the restaurant. I am invited over to their house for slumber parties, where I sleep in the same bed as the older sister.

One of those nights, as we change into our pajamas, I am rendered speechless when she strips naked right in front of me. Her body looks nothing like mine. Where my chest is still flat, hers is taking shape, and she has hair where I have none. My eyes zero in on the trail of dark hair that marks the place where her legs meet, and I have never been more aware of how immature and young I am. This, I think, is what a woman looks like. I am in the presence of a glorious woman.

The moment is over in a flash—it'd be weird if I just stood there looking at my friend's naked body—but I think of it often in the days and weeks to come. I have never been so achingly curious about the human body. I have never wanted so badly to reach out and touch another person. I want nothing more than to be grown up, too.

I wonder if these thoughts are bad. I can't sleep the night I see her body. It doesn't help that above her bed is a light that shines all night on a statue of Jesus, bloody and in agony on the cross. His eyes seem to follow me no matter how I toss and turn.

"I know what you've seen and what you're thinking about," he seems to say. His face is twisted in anguish and consternation. I turn away from him to face the wall, but I don't sleep much. When my friend wakes up the next morning, I'm already wide awake.

After that, my worries about hateful graffiti fly out my brain to make space for my new obsession: the female form.

How can it be that my body might look like this one day? It seems impossible to me, a trick, a lie. I can't imagine having boobs. I must learn more about what it means to be a woman.

The internet is a relatively new thing at this point, but I navigate it like a pro. Whenever I hear the unmistakable shrill tones of the internet dialling up, I know I am about to embark on a forbidden journey.

At this time, I'm also in the throes of a diehard professional wrestling obsession, which merges beautifully with my new fixation. The women in wrestling, with their unbelievably fit and toned bodies, are often scantily clad. They invite you to look at them, and I am all too happy to accept.

With the internet at my fingertips, I find myself navigating the brutally slow connection to find as many pictures of female wrestlers as I can. I am titillated when the stunning Sable takes off her top to reveal she is wearing nothing but painted handprints on her ample boobs. I scour the internet for images of the moment so I can admire her at length whenever I fancy. When I hear that "Diamond" Dallas Page's wife and ringside valet, Kimberly Page, was once a nude model, I get to work and trawl the interweb for evidence. I am thrilled by her giant breast implants and confused by my own body and the desire that lies heavy there.

I am a ten-year-old girl, but I have the internet habits of a stereotypical teenage boy. It's all too easy to do. There is no one breathing down my neck or monitoring my internet usage. I am free and safe to indulge all my curiosities.

I don't look at the pictures for any real sexual reasons. I'm not touching myself or thinking about anything lewd. I admire. I worship. I see the feminine form as a work of art. I wonder if someone will look at me with this much reverence one day. I hope so.

I experience real joy in those first few years of living in that apartment. If the worst things that happen to me are seeing a one-off message spray-painted on a building and sacrificing taste at lunchtime, I can deal with that. It's not so bad.

———

My pride in being Chinese continues into the fifth grade. I wear my red *cheongsam* in my class photo that year. My smile is wide and genuine.

At home though, I am miserable. My sister moves away to university that same year—I don't yet know that we'll never live together again. If I did, I may have never picked myself back up. This assumed temporary loss feels unbearable enough.

While my parents drive my sister to her new life in Waterloo, I stand in the empty restaurant behind the bar. I've never felt more alone in my life. I sob and wail and ache for my sister. I am getting older and there is still so much I need to learn about how to handle puberty and crushes and school, which is getting increasingly hard. My sister, whom I trust to know everything, is gone and I am on my own to figure everything out.

More than ever, I look to popular media to show me how to be. I rarely see faces like mine, and when I do, we're bit characters. We're stern-faced doctors or nameless students sitting in desks around the main characters, who actually get speaking parts and full personalities. I notice what so many of us look like. Big round glasses, hand up in the air.

I read a lot of The Baby-Sitters Club. I know that Claudia Kishi looks like me, and I know that she's cooler than I'll ever be. She's an artist and style icon who wears quirky things like earrings in the shape of kitchen utensils, Day-Glo high-top sneakers, and seriously distressed jeans. Claudia is truly terrible at school.

Her sister, Janine, on the other hand, is the exact opposite. She wears plain, modest clothing, has almost no friends, uses big words, and takes school very, very seriously. She's smart, studies all the time, and never causes trouble. If

Claudia is the epitome of cool, Janine is the definition of uptight, boring and, according to book seven in the series, "mean."

No one ever wants to be a mean Janine when they can be Claudia. For the first time, I start to wonder whether I should pull back, stop caring so much about school. Be more chill like Claudia. I notice how she has no other friends who are Asian like her. I remember that when a Korean family moves to town and opens a convenience store. Their son is in my grade.

I never talk to him. We are not friends. I refuse to be seen with him. I know that if we are seen together, people will assume we are dating. I know this because, before I even breathed a word to him, my friends gasped and said, "Aw, you and Jonah would be so, so cute together!"

I don't say anything when my classmates whisper about how Jonah's eyes are even smaller than mine. "Can he even see?" Their curiosity about Jonah makes me think of roadside circuses and the way people oohed and ahhed over conjoined twins. I remain silent even when their fascination with Jonah bleeds into questions for me.

"Is it harder to see out of *your* eyes? If I put my hand here, can you see it?"

I can't explain how these questions make me feel. I don't have the vocabulary or knowledge to describe what I'm feeling. I just know I feel bad and wrong. I feel ashamed. I notice how no other kid gets asked this question. Just me and Jonah.

I start to worry that if I am seen with him, I will look even more Asian. My difference will be even more obvious. I decide it's best to keep all my friends and crushes white to not attract attention. It's not hard to do in Kingsville.

I'll do anything to keep from making any unnecessary ripples. I know how fickle the girls in my grade are and how it takes nothing at all to be ousted from the fold. I've seen it happen time and again for reasons as varied as daring to flirt with someone else's crush or giving someone the stink-eye.

I feel too lucky and insecure in my position to ever say anything when my friends decide someone is on the outs. *Better them than me.* To show the Outsider of the Month just how badly they've fucked up, we wait for them to walk over to us during recess. When they get within ten feet of us, we run away from them, laughing. We keep running until they stop and get the hint they aren't wanted. We make sure no one calls them after school. If we do call, it's only so we can use three-way calling to try to catch them saying something bad about someone else—usually the person secretly listening in on the line. (A few years later, when a similar scene plays out in the hit comedy *Mean Girls*, I cringe. That's when I discover three-way calling attacks are a favoured tactic for girls beyond my little school.)

This happens over and over again. We hate each other and treat one another cruelly before we make up and become BFFs once again. Sometimes overnight.

In the fifth grade, it's my turn to be the social pariah.

One of the popular girls in my class discovers her shoes have been thrown into the trash and covered with pencil shavings. No one knows who did it. All I know is that it wasn't me—she's my friend!—but for some reason, everyone says it's me. My friends run away from me at recess and make damn clear that I am completely, utterly alone. I am on the receiving end of a three-way phone call attempt to get me to admit to throwing out the shoes. No one calls to hang out.

Alone and lonely, I start hanging out at a hippy-dippy store close to the restaurant that sells essential oils and crystals. Sue, the old lady who runs the shop, welcomes me—she doesn't have endless customers—and doesn't question why I'm in there every day. What would I have said? "I have no friends"? I'm so lonely that I pretend I'm writing a paper on local businesses just in case she starts getting annoyed by me, too. I actually write a paper and she happily edits it for me. For fleeting moments each day, I have company. I'm not a total loser.

The situation at home is just as awful as it is at school. My parents are fighting with increasing intensity the more successful the restaurant gets.

They fight over money all the time—never having enough of it, the intoxicating quest to get more at the card tables. They fight when Mum forgets an order of sweet and sour wontons in a customer's takeout and when Dad adds onions to a beef and mixed vegetables order that has "NO onions" scrawled in aggressive ink on the bill. They fight when someone fails to order the right amount of chicken from our supplier in Windsor and when Dad lets *ah mah* make a snide comment about Mum.

They fight in front of us in the kitchen. Behind closed doors. In cars. Within hearing of our customers. It successfully distracts me from the pain of being shunned at school but is akin to making a paper cut feel better by getting stabbed instead.

While the wars rage on at home and at school, I discover true freedom in online communities. I learn basic HTML and make Angelfire web pages based on my major interests du jour. I run a shockingly popular site dedicated to World Wrestling Federation wrestler Chyna, whom I feel a connection to because she isn't like the other popular female wrestlers of the day, who are slim, blonde, and conventionally attractive. I also feel a kinship with her because of her name, even though she is not Chinese. When my friends at school tease me and cite my love of wrestling as a reason for my newfound loserdom, I force myself to stop talking about and watching it. I kill all love for the sport entirely. I adopt more acceptable interests and create a fan page for Britney Spears instead.

I discover a completely different universe online, one where no one knows who I am or what I look like. No one knows I'm Chinese. No one can judge me or assume things about me. I am completely anonymous. I am a blank white page.

It's a shame the freedom found online is so fleeting.

The mother of the girl who blames me for her trashed shoes goes to the restaurant one day and talks to my mum about what I've supposedly done. When I tell my mum I didn't do it, she believes me. But no one at school does. It's the first time I learn that I don't stand a chance against a white girl and her tears. It is easier not to trust me, not to believe me.

Then the rumour starts.

The girls say I told them that I masturbate. The girls say I told them that I love to finger myself. The girls say I told them that I finger myself and don't wash my hands. The girls say I told them that I go downstairs to the restaurant to cook with my filthy fingers. The girls say I am dirty and disgusting. By extension, the restaurant is, too.

The truth is, I am a horny kid. With endless time alone, I often find myself mindlessly touching my own body and marvelling at the way a certain graze of a certain body part can feel so good. But the rumour is horrifyingly untrue. I worry endlessly about how this might impact my family's business. *How far will the rumour spread? Will we lose customers because they think we are unhygienic? Will people think I'm a dirty slut? Will people believe I am actually cooking in the kitchen?* None of it is true.

I am not too young to recognize the unfairness of my situation. When others are shunned, they face the cruelty on their own. It mostly stays within the confines of the school's walls. When I am shunned, my family and our restaurant are threatened—the classic case of a whole group of people being cast in a negative light because of the perceived actions of one. When I am shunned, I can't make sense of it. I grasp for reasons why and start to wonder whether my being Chinese is the reason I am suddenly not trusted and why me being such a dirty villain is so believable. I wonder if there is an additional layer to the way people treat and see me. I remember the writing on the side of the restaurant wall.

Do they not like me because I'm Chinese?

Is it easier to bully the Chinese girl?

Is my sexuality as a Chinese girl somehow more threatening? More repulsive?

I think about how one of my cousins once told me that he wished he weren't Chinese.

"It'd be so much easier," he said. "It's just so easy to make fun of us."

It's the first time I really get it. It's easier to ridicule the person whose difference is written plainly all over their face. It's easier to confront someone about their wicked child when they're lowly restaurant workers whose first language isn't English. (Would the girl's mother have stormed into a dentist's office? Or a law firm?)

The situation angers and upsets me, but I don't have time to ruminate over what any of it means. I know I need to make this right. If these girls—my friends—tell their families about this rumour, my parents and the restaurant could lose customers. I stay awake at night, fretting about the potential loss of business.

I come up with a plan.

It's one of the worst things I've ever done. The shame of it still weighs me down, decades later.

I host a belated birthday party at the end of July even though my birthday's in June. This gives everyone time to forget they hate me. I promise a free-for-all with no parental supervision and lots of yummy food. Naturally, my friends decide I'm cool again.

That morning, my parents and brother go into overdrive to make sure the party delivers on the food front. They make heaps of fried chicken wings, egg rolls, and chicken balls. When their part is done, they leave twenty prepubescent kids alone for the rest of the day. We play Seven Minutes in Heaven and pepper each other with water balloons. I have my first awkward kiss with a boy.

"I have an idea," I say, when I feel the energy start to shift. My birthday party has gone on for hours. "Do you want to go over to Kayla's house?"

Kayla is the girl in my class who is currently being shunned. I am already on tenuous footing with my friends, so I didn't invite her to my birthday party even though everyone else in our class is here. It wasn't long ago that my friends were spreading vicious rumours about me and forcing me to spend recesses on my own. I tell myself it can't happen again.

I do the only thing I can think of to prevent it. From watching others who have been shunned and brought back into the fold, I've learned that deflecting and distancing work wonders to get people to like you. I've learned that as long as someone else has everyone's ire and attention, I am safe.

When the others enthusiastically agree to my suggestion, we walk over to Kayla's house—all twenty of us. We knock on her door and ask her mother if she's home. When she comes out, we show her just how cruel we can be. I show her how cruel I can be.

"This is my birthday party. I didn't invite you," I say, lips curling hatefully.

"Do you know why she didn't invite you?" another girl chimes in.

"Because no one likes you," someone else says.

"We know you're the one who actually fingers herself," someone adds. "Disgusting."

Others are standing back. Some are laughing, some are not. I am front and centre of it all, pointing a finger at someone else. *This person*, I am saying, *is the one who deserves all our hate*. I reclaim a little bit of the power I had lost over the school year. I willingly destroy someone else to protect myself. When the guilt and shame hit me later, I tell myself to suck it up and move on. *Better her than me*.

To my surprise, being accepted back into my friend group doesn't make everything better. Ruining Kayla doesn't make everything go back to how it was. The questions and comments return, slowly at first and then in a rush. I constantly have to come up with new ways to protect myself. To blend into the walls.

When a boy in my class sees my full name on my report card—Rachel My Phan—he snickers loudly.

"Ha ha, you're *my* fan? What kind of middle name is 'My'?"

My face flushes a heated, violent red. "That's not my real name. That's my Chinese name. It doesn't count," I shoot back.

"I thought all Chinese people had names like, 'Ching Chong Ching Chong,'" he says in return.

I didn't think skin could grow so hot or so red. My mouth, which fell open after his comment, slams shut. My mind goes blank, searching for a response and finding nothing but racing, incoherent thoughts. When I walk away, it's with the sound of his mocking laughter trailing behind me. Later, I would wonder why I didn't correct him or mention that my actual Chinese name is *Poon May May*. I would wonder why his remark stunned me into such stifling silence and reflect on the confidence with which he said it. *Where did that come from?* I didn't know anyone with a name even close to "Ching Chong." *Why did he think that?*

I decide it is time for a name change and rechristen myself as Rachel Marie Phan. It is an acceptable name, one that doesn't set me on edge whenever someone asks me what my full name is. Instead of teasing or confused looks, the only attention my new schoolyard name gets me is a quick nod and comments like "No way! Mine too," or "That's my aunt's name."

It is unremarkable and mockery-proof. I cling to that name like a safety vest. It is a form of protection that gives me so much comfort, I bestow it upon my mother, too. She is the only one in my family who doesn't have a Western-sounding name. Although my dad, Hy Phan, became George Phan, my mother remained Tran Phan to everyone but the children of her eldest brother, who call her "Aunt Jan."

As I become intimately familiar with schoolyard and playground politics, I realize that "Tran" is a name ripe for snide, snickering comments and agree that "Jan" is much more acceptable. I tell other kids that my parents are George and Jan, and when I forge Mum's signature, I conscientiously take the "r" out of the slanted cursive I write in convincing mimicry of my mother's. In the safety of the restaurant, she can be Tran all she wants, but in public, I decide Jan is best. Jan doesn't invite side-eye glances and open-mouthed howls of "Your mom's a TRANNY?!"

I end up being right. No one bats an eye or makes any remarks about Rachel Marie and Jan Phan. The names are unremarkable in just how normal they are. Our names are acceptable. They are accepted.

After both Kayla and I are eviscerated for committing social suicide by daring to be sexually curious, I decide to keep my growing fascination with sex to myself.

It's isolating trying to find the answers on my own because no one else seems to want to talk about it. There are no talks of the birds and the bees and the ways of our bodies with Mum and Dad. My sister's magazines and books, along with the scenes on the television screen, are my great teachers.

As a young child, I would spend hours reading my sister's bodice rippers when everyone was downstairs working. I was puzzled by what "throbbing member" and "manhood" meant and eager to know what a woman's "rosebuds" could possibly look like. I couldn't visualize it and was desperate to know. When I asked my sister, she seemed to glitch for a moment, her eyes moving this way and that. She opened and closed her mouth and blinked quickly like a robot before telling me not to ask. I was confused. I couldn't quite grasp that some words meant a very specific thing that was out of reach to me. I didn't know why I wasn't supposed to know.

I started to sneak into the living room well after midnight, long after my parents had added up the bills and packed away the egg rolls. While my brother slept off the day's stresses and my parents went off to the casino, I was enraptured by the television screen. I couldn't believe what I was seeing. It looked like the naked people were having a wonderful time, when it didn't look like they were hurting each other. It seemed fun, somehow.

Being bored and unattended was how I learned ways to make myself feel good. I was shocked to learn that quick grazes of my fingers against the front of my underwear made me feel all tingly and floaty. It was a bizarre feeling. It was addictive. It seemed as good an activity as any to help pass the long hours alone at home while the rest of my family worked to earn the cash that kept me fed and clothed.

From there, I learned about sex in stealthy ways. Along with watching television after dark, I read escort ads in the newspaper. Once, when no one was around, I called one of the numbers from those "Pick up the phone!" ads that ran on TV long after David Letterman and Jay Leno signed off. I was stopped in my tracks when I discovered I didn't have this thing called a credit card. I read my sister's magazines and was shocked to the core when Shirley Manson, the lead singer of Scottish-American alternative rock band Garbage, was quoted as saying, "I want a man who will let me pee in his belly button." I thought about her strange words constantly—when eating, putting on my seatbelt in the car, going to the washroom.

Sex became fascinating to me. I was puzzled by why everyone seemed to want it, but no one wanted to talk about it. Like the kid who's told not to touch the hot stove but does it anyway, I became even more interested the more the adults around me seemed intent on keeping this mysterious thing a secret.

At first, my fascination was one of childlike interest and wonder. I hated not knowing things, and this was a huge void. I hated feeling left out more than anything. I prayed for the day to come when I could find out what the big deal was. But as I grew older, my interest changed shape. I'm not just curious for knowledge's sake anymore.

I thought it would get easier to find answers as I got older, but on the cusp of adolescence, the topic is still infuriatingly taboo—at least for girls. I wonder if there'll ever be a day when talking about sex doesn't get me shunned or seen as disgusting.

—∿∿—

I am thirteen years old, and I've just logged into ICQ messenger on my brother's computer when a girl named Stefany messages me.

"Hey, I have a question 4 u," she says.

I am perplexed by the message. This girl goes to another school. We are not friends. But these are the early days of the internet and instant messaging, and we are no longer limited by such things as school buildings and geography.

"Hey!" I type back, before going back to delete the exclamation mark. Too eager, too uncool. "Hey, sure." Perfectly cool and aloof.

"UR chinese, right?" she asks.

When I read her message, my cheeks grow hot and my heart starts hammering wildly in my chest. I am instantly on alert. *Why does she want to know?* I'm less enthusiastic now when I respond. "Yea."

Within a minute, the unmistakable ICQ message alert "Uh-oh!" chimes. I am afraid to read what she's written.

"Is it true u people eat cats and dogs?"

I am so horrified by the question that I respond with rapid-fire messages.
"What! No! That's disgusting!"
"Maybe they do that in fucking China. That's some real Chinese shit."
"Me and my family, we don't do that. We're Canadians :)"

My heart is racing. I want nothing more than to ease myself out of my own skin. I would give anything to be someone else for the day. Someone who isn't asked whether they eat beloved family pets. But since I can't do that, I do what I can. I disavow Chinese people. I separate myself from "them" and canoodle with whiteness. I deflect and distance.

Stefany responds with a smiley face and a, "Good. That shit's fucking nasty. My mom asked if I wanted Chinese food tonight but I told her there's no way I'm eating it if it's cat and dog. U don't sell that at ur restaurant, right?"

When I tell her we do not in fact have cats or dogs on the menu, she sends me another smiley face.

"What about chicken balls? Is that like actual chicken nuts?"

I explain to her that chicken balls are just breaded and deep-fried pieces of chicken breast. As I do so, I wilt on the inside. I suddenly feel abnormal and disgusting. I hate having to be a spokesperson for an identity I never asked for. I'm no longer the Rachel who proudly presented a speech about China. *Why can't they see I'm a true-blue Canadian, just like them?*

"Awesome, I'll tell my mom we can eat it tonight. g2g now, thx!"

Just like that, the conversation is over. But the exchange stays in my mind for a long, long time after she logs off.

It won't be the last time I feel the need to distance myself from people's perceptions of what it means to be Chinese. But it is the first time I learn what, at the time, feels like an important lesson: make the comment or joke before someone else does. I learn to roll my eyes good-naturedly when someone makes a vague remark about my ethnicity.

At thirteen, I'll say things like, "yes, I'm Chinese," before quickly adding, "but no, I don't eat cats and dogs!"

What I would actually be saying is: I'm not *really that* Chinese. See how un-Chinese I am? I can poke fun at my own people and cast them off as savages. I am better than them—better than my ancestors—because I am Canadian. Because all my friends are white. Because I speak perfect English.

As I got older, I learned to embrace my identity as a "Twinkie" or a "banana"—yellow on the outside but white on the inside. That placated my peers, many of whom had known me since we were four. For the most part, I felt safely cocooned. I was not the most popular girl in school, but I was friends with the girls who were. This adjacency was enough for me. I felt lucky to have friends and to be accepted even with my strange foreigner face. I ignored how exhausting it was to have to keep up the act. To edit the words I said before they left my mouth.

4

"I CAME OUT OF MY MUM DOING KUNG FU."

hen you grow up in a town where so few people look like you, you start to notice the flicker. It happens when you cross paths with someone on the street, when you walk into a classroom, when a customer sidles up to the cash register to pay their bill.

It's a fleeting moment when they look at you and you can see the gears in their head turning as they take in your face. You look so different. You *are* so different. The flicker happens when they, without even being aware they're doing it, try to categorize you in their brains to make sense of how you, a living, breathing Chinese person, have found yourself in front of them, in this building, in this town of people. *How did you get here? Who are you? How to make sense of you?*

They don't know what you're like or where you come from, and it's unsettling. You are an enigma. An anomaly. It's thrilling and terrifying in equal measure just to be in your presence. They think of what they know about people like you. They wrack their brains for something, anything, that'll help them classify who you are. They search and recall the Chinese people they've seen on TV or in the movie theatre or what they've read in the news or in history books. And there, there it is! The flicker of recognition when they've successfully found a point of comparison—a thing or memory or archetype they can use to hold you up against. Now, they understand you better. Now, they can slot you into a category that makes sense to them. Now, they know what you are like. Now, they know you.

This is what they might think of when they look at your face:

Papillon Soo as Da Nang Hooker, the Vietnamese woman in Stanley Kubrick's 1987 *Full Metal Jacket*, clad in a hot pink tank top and miniskirt with a daring thigh-high slit. "Me so horny," she says to two white American GIs while gyrating her hips. "Me love you long time." She offers to "sucky sucky" the GIs, who haggle her down from $15 to $10 each. For that amount, she says as she runs her hands all over her body, they can get "everything" they want. Her brief appearance—the scene is just two minutes long—will go on to haunt East Asian women for eternity.

Lucy Liu's Ling Woo in *Ally McBeal*, who is cunning, seductive, and manipulative—the classic dragon lady. She uses her hypersexuality and feminine wiles to get what she wants, when she wants. She's willing to exploit others to advance her own interests, meaning you can never really trust her. She's exotic, inscrutable, and emotionally detached—just another cold, unfeeling Asian woman. You wouldn't dare enter a relationship with such a power-hungry, untrustworthy person. Stripped of any emotional vulnerability and empathy, she's barely human.

Sayuri in *Memoirs of a Geisha*, Cio-Cio San in the opera *Madame Butterfly*, and Kim in the stage musical *Miss Saigon*—all quiet, submissive, and obedient, happily conforming to traditional gender roles and existing solely for the pleasure and service of men. They are sexually available and ripe for the picking, ready to be rescued or enlightened by an often-white protagonist. These delicate flowers, the lotus blossom stereotype, are passive, mysterious, and exotic—perfect for a good time, not a long time. Both Cio-Cio San and Kim fall in love with and are impregnated by white Americans during times of war but are left behind when their respective wars end. Both men return home to marry white American wives. Cio-Cio San and Kim are docile and easy to leave behind, their Asian femininity easily trampled on by Western masculinity. In the end, they both kill themselves.

Mickey Rooney, a white actor, as Mr. Yunioshi, the short-fused nerd in the 1961 film *Breakfast at Tiffany's*. Rooney wears heavy make-up to bring this Yunioshi to life—a clumsy, screaming caricature of a Japanese man with an obligatory heavy accent. Next to the handsome male lead of the movie, he's silly, bumbling, and deeply unattractive, with thick glasses and cartoonishly large buck teeth. He's an absolute joke.

John Cho's Harold in *Harold & Kumar Go to White Castle*, the cast of *Crazy Rich Asians*, and several roles played by doctor and comedian Ken Jeong. These characters are highly educated, affluent, and hardworking. Although these are not inherently bad things, if you look deeper, you'll find the insidious model minority myth that presents Asians as robotic automatons who are exceptionally successful and law-abiding because of their diligence, intelligence, and sheep-like adherence to traditional family values. They're uptight sticks-in-the-mud and not nearly as interesting as the main character, who has a real personality and individuality.

In the same vein, there are Keiko Agena's Lane Kim in *Gilmore Girls* and Gedde Watanabe's Long Duk Dong in *Sixteen Candles*, both nerdy geeks whose intelligence comes at the expense of social skills or physical ability. They're socially awkward, shy, and most definitely losers.

Any number of roles played by Bruce Lee, Jackie Chan, and Jet Li where they're kicking ass. East Asians, especially men, are reduced to being skilled martial artists or fighters, as if there's something inherent in our exotic blood and bodies that gives us otherworldly physical abilities and combat prowess. We're sometimes seen as superhuman, which is to say, we're not really human at all.

Since media representation plays a key role in shaping how we perceive others, what happens when the media we consume perpetuates harmful and reductive stereotypes that fail to show the diverse experiences and identities within Asian communities across the diaspora?

For so many people in my town, my family and I are the first Chinese people they've ever met.

We get put into a lot of boxes.

The hardworking immigrants.

The dutiful children helping their immigrant parents out and sacrificing fun and weekends to do so.

The scary Other here to take your jobs—and your man.

The Yellow Peril right in your own backyard.

The brainy, ambitious nerd.

The hypersexual, unrepentant slut.

The meek and submissive doormat.

The dirty little secret.

I am all of these things. I am none of these things.

As a young Chinese person growing up in a sea of pale faces, I felt confined by the available roles I could play. I was trapped by those boxes. Although others were free to explore their own identities, I felt pressure to fit into specific moulds.

No matter what I did or how much I tried to fit in and be normal, I still felt like I belonged everywhere and nowhere at the same time. I was caught between two cultures. The media I read, listened to, and watched were primarily Western. All my childhood friends were white Canadians. But I never quite felt Canadian enough. My nationality has always had an asterisk beside it or a hyphen right before.

I was raised by parents who were vocal about being proudly Chinese, but since they were too busy trying to keep the lights on and the customers happy, they didn't have time to pass things down to us like language, culture, and traditions. There were no temples or community centres to help make up for the lack. Often, I didn't feel like a "real" Chinese person at all. I responded to my parents in English. I didn't live in a city where I could go to Chinese school, so when my cousins from Toronto visited, I felt like a half-baked Chinese person. I struggled to follow their speech, their mannerisms, their snacks.

I had one foot in each culture, but I never felt like I belonged in either. I operated in the hyphen, the liminal space. No matter where I was, at home or at school, I felt like a fraud.

I later learned the term "third-culture kid," which is used to describe a child who grows up in a culture different from the one their parents grew up in. Third-culture kids often feel confused about where their loyalties lie. Many have no idea who they really are or where "home" is. They often feel ignorant of their parents' home culture and later feel a painful disconnect from it, especially when it comes to the loss of language.

For many third-culture kids like me, it's hard to feel a sense of belonging or identity anywhere. I'm somehow both "too Chinese" and "too Canadian." No matter where I am, I am too much of something to truly fit in. Growing up, I tried to dull my pointy edges, change who I was depending on my circumstances, and become a diluted, murky version of myself. I changed with the seasons. I became whoever the person I was talking to expected me to be. I pretended I didn't notice how lonely it was to feel like I could never be myself.

I discovered later just how common it is for third-culture kids to have a weak sense of self. You can't really know who you are when you don't feel like you belong anywhere. My identity wasn't anchored to anything concrete. Because I didn't know who the hell I was, I didn't put up a fight when others knew better than I did.

I thought: *if this is who they say I am, I need to live up to their expectations.* I thought: *it's so much easier to go with the flow and do what's expected rather than to disappoint anyone.* I thought: *why put up a fight? This is how they see me, so this is who I am.* I thought: *don't make a scene, be a good girl, make them feel good for being right about you all along.*

I learned early on that my only options were to be either the hypersexualized dragon lady, the silent lotus blossom, or the nerdy geek. Without any clear Chinese role models in my community, I cozied up to the stereotypes and became adept at flitting back and forth between each role.

Once, a boy in my class says, "You're Chinese so you probably know kung fu, right?" He positions himself in an exaggerated martial arts stance, his left leg forward and his arms lifted and bent, hands in tight fists. He looks at me expectantly. He's so enthusiastic with his fists that I can tell he wants me to say yes.

"Oh yes," I say, nodding eagerly. "I came out of my mum doing kung fu. I do it after school almost every day." The boy's eyes grow large like dinner plates.

"Cool! I just asked my mom and dad if I can start. So, you can do all the Jackie Chan stuff?"

When I nod, he's practically bouncing on his heels.

"Awesome!" he says, and then he bows to me like a real kung fu master. I am surprised he resists calling me *shifu*, that's how earnest he looks.

I keep the lie going for years. In a time capsule letter I write to myself in the sixth grade, I scrawl, "My ULTIMATE favourite physical activity is karate which I learnt since grade 2. I like karate because I really enjoy contact sports/self defense." Not one lick of these sentences is true. Karate isn't even Chinese! It's Japanese! Even though no one would read this letter but me, I still say it. I feed myself the lies to feel like I'm performing "Asian" correctly.

No one ever asks me where I train or to show them any moves. No one ever asks me to specify what type of martial arts I do. They take my word at face value. I am Chinese. Obviously, that means I do kung fu, too.

In that same grade, my teacher decides to introduce friendly competition into our class to encourage reading. She places a chart at the front of the classroom with everyone's name and says, "For every one hundred pages you read, you'll get a sticker. The person with the most stickers at the end of the month gets a prize!"

Yes, I think, *this is my time to shine*. I am a voracious reader—I practically live at the library! I've got this in the bag. I quickly and easily get six stars on my chart in class, while my classmates struggle to get more than two. I eventually run out of room for stickers.

Later that year, we are each given a sheet of paper with our names in the middle. We are told to walk around to every person's desk and write down a word to describe them. I love this assignment! Who doesn't want to know exactly what people think of them?

I am all excited energy when I get back to my desk and pick up my card. My face falls. I see my teacher has put the word "articulate" at the top, which fills me with warmth, but every other word is the same. All twenty-three of my classmates have used the exact same word to describe me.

Bookworm.

I feel two-dimensional, flat. I feel like no one knows me at all beyond this one thing. I feel deeply, undeniably uncool.

No one wants to be the class nerd, especially when you are twelve years old and starting to develop crushes on your classmates. To make matters worse, I've just discovered I'm nearsighted and have to wear glasses in class. I can't help but feel like this is game over for me. I have fully become the Asian nerd cliché.

I stop raising my hand in class. I ingratiate myself with a group of cool but mean girls who think caring about grades is for nerds and that chasing after boys is a much better use of our time. I keep my love of books and reading a secret, like a clandestine lover.

I strip myself of my voice. I try to hide. I try to be unremarkable the way I did when I was younger. Speaking out in class stops feeling natural to me. I start to second-guess everything I say. *Will this make me sound like a nerd?* My heart thumps wildly in my chest whenever a teacher calls my name. I rehearse everything in my head a handful of times before the words escape my lips.

Despite my best efforts, my seventh-grade speech on disgusting bodily functions is still selected as the best in the class—my first time claiming the honour—and I get to present the speech in front of the whole school.

Fourth-grade me, who just narrowly missed out on the best-in-class prize for my speech on China, would have been overjoyed. But seventh-grade me is mortified. The thought of going up in front of the whole school to talk about burping and flatulence and earwax fills me with dread. *What will they see when they look at me?* There just happens to be one Asian girl in class—of course she's the school nerd!

The morning I am scheduled to present my speech in front of the school, I can't bring myself to get out of bed. My mouth feels sandpaper-dry, and my heart is racing to the point where I feel certain I've developed cardiac arrhythmia overnight. Surely, I am dying. Surely, I cannot speak with hundreds of eyeballs on me.

I am immobilized by anxiety and pinned in place by fears of what others will think of me. When my teacher calls and calls and calls, I don't pick up the phone. It's showtime and I can't bring myself to show up. When I eventually drag myself out of bed, it's after lunchtime and I've successfully skipped my big presentation. I've disqualified myself.

My teacher looks at me with disappointment, but I don't care. I am finally breaking out of the mould. I am not going to be another geeky goody two-shoes.

After that, I embrace playing fast and loose with rules. When I enter my preteens, I start taking advantage of my parents' absence. I take to leaving my house at 11 P.M. armed with a butter knife to meet up with friends and boys in the Becker's parking lot. I treat each instance of sneaking out as a test. Will my parents notice and stop me? They never do.

With my parents away at the casino so often, I have free rein to do things like host sleepovers in the restaurant. My best friend, Ashley, and our friend Shanna push chairs together to form a makeshift bed in the smoking section of the dining room, right outside the swinging doors to the kitchen. To protect us from any would-be intruders and give us peace of mind while we sleep in what's essentially a glass fishbowl, I grab a butcher knife and place it by our heads. We eat fistfuls of fortune cookies until we get sick and Shanna, clutching her stomach, exclaims, "I can't eat another one ever again!"

Even though we barely sleep—the chairs are incredibly uncomfortable—we relish the novelty of the experience. "This is so cool!" Ashley and Shanna repeat throughout the night. "Your parents are the best. It's so cool that they let you do anything you want."

I beam. I always do when friends come to the restaurant with me and stare in wide-eyed awe at the fridges full of pop and juice, and years later, the rows and rows of alcohol. I'm overjoyed when they sit at the bar with me and happily dangle their legs over the tall barstools. It feels so good to just be myself and to show off where I come from. The pain point of my parents' hands-off parenting and absence stings a little less when my friends comment on how cool they are and how much they hate how present their own parents are.

When my parents come home in the early morning hours, they find three girls sleeping in the restaurant, a trail of paper fortunes on the floor. I hadn't asked for permission, but they don't mind. They're just so cool.

During our Canadian winters, when the ground is frozen over and the frigid cold gnaws on our bones, I find myself trapped indoors with nothing but my own imagination to entertain me.

This is before the age of smartphones and social media. In the throes of my cabin fever, I become a nosy child, always poking around where I shouldn't. I rummage through my sister's empty bedroom and flip through her journals. I dig through the top drawer of my parents' dresser and am horrified to find pictures from my *ah gong*'s funeral. I avoid that dresser for the rest of my life.

But it is my brother's closet that brings me the most bountiful treasure. In it, I find a hefty duffel bag tucked in the very back corner. It's a bag I've never seen before. When I zip it open, my eyes widen to the size of planets. Inside are more dirty magazines than I could ever imagine in my wildest dreams. Dozens upon dozens of *Playboy* and *Penthouse* magazines, with hundreds and hundreds of pictures of women in varying stages of undress. I flip through the pages and trace the lines and curves of each woman's body. They are spread before me, mouths open in teasing red pouts, limbs askew, breasts as round as the water balloons we throw at each other at birthday parties.

I see things that astound my senses—pink nipples, erect penises jutting out of unruly curly hair, men and women staring at each other like they want to bite or kill one another. I even see women who look like me, which is rare for me to see in other magazines. There are stories too, but these are unlike anything I've ever read at the library. These stories make my heart race and hands go clammy. People write about having sex in public parks and on desks in their office buildings. They write about being bored housewives who suddenly come back to life when the gardener comes in for a refreshing ice-cold drink of water.

I touch myself in earnest when I read the words and look at the pictures. I close my eyes and trace the lines and curves of my own body and think about the women in those magazines. I wonder if the fizzy lightness I feel when I do so is the same type of coming alive the housewives feel.

I wonder what more could be out there.

In those early internet days, there was nothing like the thrill of entering an online chat room. How exciting! How thrilling! It was hard to believe that we could suddenly find ourselves talking to anyone from any corner of the world. I could be messaging back and forth with Usher for all I knew. That was the beauty and magic of being online—you could be anyone. And the person you were sharing your innermost confessions with could be anyone, too. You could spill your guts to a stranger in some faraway land, and no one could tease you about it at school the next day. You could just be.

I become obsessed with a site marketed to teenagers called Bolt.com. It is one of the first social media sites to pop up on the internet.

I learn on Bolt that "a/s/l?"—age, sex, location—is the most important icebreaker when making new friends online. Of course, I lie. Instead of my actual age of twelve, I say I am a mature sixteen years old, just like the girls I see on *Maury*. I say I'm from exotic places like Orlando or Los Angeles. Sometimes I have brown hair, sometimes I have blonde hair. I never say I am Chinese.

With anonymity being my shield, I am free to be as bold and brazen as I want.

"do u want to cyber?" I ask Conrad from Poughkeepsie. "F yea" he does.

We choose our location—a hot tub—and it's clear that neither of us knows what the heck we're doing. He says he's squeezing the shit out of my big boobs. (I'm not even wearing a training bra at this age.) I tell him I'm rubbing his "hard thing." Now, he's squeezing my butt. There's a lot of squeezing going on. He asks if I'm ready for it. I tell him I am. I tell him I've been waiting for this moment, with him, Conrad from Poughkeepsie. I repeat what I've read in romances. "Make me come," I type.

"Come where?" he says.

I pause. I don't actually know where we're supposed to be coming or going. So I just send him a smiley face. He sends me one back. I feel so grown up. I've had cybersex!

I am less enthused when I press play on our VCR, expecting to find my latest recordings of NSYNC, but instead see an older man wearing a neck brace standing behind a white woman with fluffy blonde hair. They look like they're straight out of the '80s. She's on all fours and pleading with him, "Put it in, Sparky!" I find myself recoiling with disgust.

Sparky is not an attractive man. He has long, stringy bleached blonde hair. His skin is leathery brown. And he's wearing a neck brace! He is repulsive to me. As I watch him touch and feel up this woman with the Farrah Fawcett hair, I feel a creeping sense of shame start in the pit of my belly and spread outwards. Unlike all the other times, I don't feel a heady, hypnotic sensation.

It's the first time I've felt disgusted by sex. I had no idea sex could bring about such negative feelings. I didn't know sex could make you feel bad. I turn off the TV and wish for a lobotomy.

Still, the disgust Sparky inspires in me does little to silence the questions I have about my own body and burgeoning sexuality. Lucky for me, I have the freedom to explore whenever and however I want.

In my early teens, I take to sitting in front of my full-length mirror with my legs spread wide and the sun shining brightly through the window onto my flesh. I poke and prod gently, examining all the parts of my most tender places. I explore with tentative fingers. I learn where everything is and what feels best when touched. I learn who I am in a wholly intimate way. What does that bundle of nerves do? What happens if I rub there, slip a finger here, keep going, don't stop?

Later, when I am older, I am grateful for my strong sense of self-exploration. I am thankful for the many hours of free, unsupervised time I had to explore, to push, to play. I can tell partners exactly what I want and like and where they should touch me. I am astonished when I hear how common it is for women to have never looked at their own vulvas.

My open-minded and inquisitive approach to my sexuality starts in front of that mirror, with my body serving as my playground. In doing so, I learn how to enjoy my own company. I teach myself things about my body that no one else seems comfortable teaching me and that no one dares to discuss at school.

—⁂—

Yet despite my personal exploration of my own sexuality, I never feel beautiful growing up. Like the hum of a refrigerator, I am just there.

In the seventh grade, hormones start to swirl and rage amongst our class. We start to cross our arms self-consciously to cover our chests and wrinkle our noses in disgust at the potent onion sweat emanating from our classmates' underarms. I no longer feel relieved when a boy doesn't notice me.

One day after school, I am hanging out with three friends, each of us taking turns on a skateboard. As the four of us perch side by side on the concrete, one of the boys, Aaron, looks at my best friend with her blonde hair and blue eyes and says, "You're really pretty."

I don't know whether I want to fade into the background, embarrassed that I don't anticipate a compliment for me forthcoming, or throw myself in his line of vision and scream, "What about me? Am I pretty? What if I stood up straight and sucked in my stomach? Am I pretty now?"

I didn't have to worry. A compliment does end up coming my way.

"Rachel, you have good dick-sucking lips."

I am twelve years old and unaccustomed to such attention from anyone, let alone someone of the opposite sex. I am thrilled by the remark.

It is not the first time I have wondered if my sexuality is the only thing I have to offer. After all, when I see women that look like me in the media, if I see them at all, they are usually temptresses, dripping with sexuality.

Even as a young girl, I know they are a source of desire and derision. You want them, but you know they are no good for you. They are beautiful but cold. They are the most desirable of the undesirables. And you better betray them before they betray you.

In that moment, as I am complimented on my lips and the specific act I could do with them, I feel the intoxicating high of being noticed and feeling desirable for the very first time. It registers with me that my body—my sexuality—could be my superpower. I think about how I could give pleasure to a man, specifically these white men in my orbit, and I find some small comfort in knowing that at least my body is desirable to others. It beats being completely alone and ignored.

I let that belief shape me and set my path for the next decade of my life. *Maybe I am not the girl you could love and date, but I can offer you my body. I can finally be noticed, desired, wanted.* This is the one way I can unapologetically take up space because it's what's expected of me.

Over time, I learn how my sexuality—my exotic Otherness—grants me access to an exclusive club, where the ultimate reward is the white man's approval and attention. For years, I chase that exhilarating, miserable high at whatever cost, no matter how much it tears at the very fabric of my being or how many pieces of myself I lose and let degrade over time.

It's not that I actively seek white boys. I just live in a small town where 99 percent of the boys are white.

What other choice do I have? There's Jonah, the Korean boy in my class, but I don't go near him out of fear that the two of us merely breathing in the same space might invite double the "Ching chong ching chongs" in the hallway or the number of requests to help with math homework.

No, white boys are plentiful. White boys are safe. White boys are the ultimate prize. That's what my television screen and the naked male torsos on romance book covers tell me anyway. I'm too young to think critically or question anything. I just follow the crowd.

Plus, I think, how wonderful would it feel to be chosen and protected by a literal white knight? I am impossibly naive and can think of no greater reward, no greater form of security.

I become boy crazy to the point of obsession and madness.

I gravitate toward boys that everyone else likes. Rather than feeling a spirit of competition, my girlfriends and I bond over hushed tones and secret smiles when a popular boy looks at us. I don't want to seem uncool by liking someone no one else wants, so I hop on the bandwagon and obsess over boys with names like Brandon and Jake and Steven.

Occasionally, when I sign in and out of MSN Messenger to make sure they see that I'm online, they'll message me first. But for the most part, they ignore me. Some are even mean to me. I chase and want all the same.

I give up on trying to earn my parents' time and attention. I focus instead on doing everything I can to earn the affection of these boys. I give so much of myself. I get so little, if anything, back.

One day, my friend and I are hanging out at the park with the same two boys who told me I had good dick-sucking lips. We're in the seventh grade and feel so grown. It's June 1st and we're just a few months away from being eighth graders—the top of the school!

When the boys ask us if we want to give them hand jobs, we giggle and demur. A compromise is struck. We will grab and rub their penises over their shorts. The boys seem plenty excited by this. When one of them leads me to a private clearing under a big maple tree, he takes my hand and places it on his erect penis. He squeezes my hand over himself once, twice, and then it's done. He doesn't push for more. He doesn't ask if I want anything.

We blush and smile and whisper about it in classrooms and hallways over the coming year. "I know what you did on June 1st," we say, eyebrows waggling knowingly.

We feel so grown up carrying this spicy secret. I ignore the ache in my chest when the boy doesn't ask me to be his girlfriend.

—※—

At some point my pride in being Chinese starts to conflict with something new: the knowledge that my ethnicity is something that makes me a target, the butt of a joke, the subject of unwanted advances.

Everything I have done to survive and blend in at elementary school stops working once I start high school. Oh, miserable high school.

My high school brings together kids from different schools in the region. That means I am suddenly surrounded by kids who don't know me. Kids who have never had to interact with someone who doesn't share their same alabaster skin. And we all know that kids can be assholes.

I am in a ninth-grade history class when three boys spot me and sit at the desks beside me. Two of them are popular, attractive boys, and the other is their funny friend. While the teacher drones on about some war, the whispers begin.

"You don't belong here," they say with quiet snickers.

"You should get deported," they chime together. "You and your whole family should get deported. Why are you in this class learning about Canadian history? You're not even Canadian."

I am stunned. I try to fight back tears, but embarrassingly, the tears come unbidden anyway. Because the boys don't stop.

"I am Canadian," I say, my voice cracking and my hands trembling. "I was born here."

They just laugh.

"Nah, you need to be deported. There's no space for people like you here."

Their cruel words continue for the rest of class. It doesn't end with the next class either. "Oh, you're still here?"

"Why haven't you been deported yet?"

They recruit a boy from my elementary school who was always so sweet and gentle with me. He was my first kiss when we played Seven Minutes in Heaven during that fateful birthday party years ago. But with these new boys, he is brutal. He joins the chorus telling me I should be deported. He tells me that he hates the food at the restaurant and that the other Chinese restaurant in town is "much better." He says we should be run out of town.

They say to never let your enemy see your weakness. But I break anyway. I cry. They laugh.

—⁓—

What makes someone a "real Canadian" anyway?

If you had asked me as a kid, I would have said something about white skin, blue eyes, light hair, perfect English, and a name like Meghan Marie or Ashley Jean. I was 0/5.

I found myself doing everything possible to get me to that prized promised land: true acceptance as an uncontested Canadian. Although there was nothing I could do about not being white, I could change other things. So I did.

High school is when I become tyrannical about spelling and grammar to showcase my mastery over the English language. I start carrying *The Elements of Style* by Strunk and White in my purse like the most infuriating smug asshole you'd ever meet. I laugh at my mother's pronunciation of words like "blood" and "whatever" and "north" until she learns. My parents stop calling me "May May," preferring "Rachel" instead, and it's not until I'm in my thirties that the change starts feeling like a million little heartbreaks. As a high schooler, it's just a relief to have one acceptable name.

No one is there to talk me out of getting turquoise-coloured contacts, which is how I learn to live with the discomfiting experience of walking through life in a blue-green haze. The contacts make everything look as if I'm peering through a turquoise-lined tunnel, but I think it's a reasonable price to pay for the cool confidence I feel as a blue-eyed girl.

I wear coloured contacts for a long time—years—before my dad notices. It's one of their days off and we've driven forty-five minutes to Windsor to eat at the nearest *phở* restaurant. As we stand on the sidewalk outside, Dad takes one look at me and does a double take. "What's wrong with your eyes?" he asks gruffly. "Why are they that colour?"

I roll said eyes the way all teenagers do when exasperated with their parents. "They're coloured contacts, Dad. Don't they look pretty?"

He gives me a *What the fuck is this kid on?* look and shakes his head with the same intensity he has when watching sports. "Why don't you like your normal eyes? What's wrong with them? I don't like these. You look different. You don't look like you."

I want nothing more than to holler, "You don't know anything about me, Dad!" with the force of all my teenage angst. But all I say is, "I think they're cool and so do my friends. You just don't get it. You're too old and Chinese."

His gaze pierces me while his head continues its slow, disappointed shake from side to side. "There's nothing wrong with being Chinese. You're Chinese. I'm your dad and I think you look stupid."

I roll my eyes one more time for good measure and ignore the sting of his rebuke. I let the angst I feel propel me to make even more changes.

The first time girls like Krissy, Lila, and Maya bring me to a tanning salon, I reluctantly agree, not wanting to be the kind of party pooper they derided in song.

I'm amazed by how relaxing I find being encased in that cozy cocoon, with the fan blowing gently across my lower body and my skin warmed like a rotisserie chicken. When I step out, I gleefully pull the palm-tree-shaped sticker off my upper thigh and marvel at the difference between my natural skin tone and my new nut-brown hue.

"Oh my God, you look amazing," Krissy gushes. "Your tanned skin really makes your blue contacts pop."

I quickly become addicted to tanning. When we aren't at the salon, we slather ourselves in baby oil and lay out on Maya's deck, the sun cooking and toasting our young flesh. "The best time to tan is 11 A.M.," Maya says, her skin glistening with oil. "This is cheaper than going to the salon." I follow her lead, covering myself in the slippery liquid and lying prone in direct, punishing sunlight. Summer is made up of endless days like this.

One day, my mother fixes me with a scrutinizing gaze. As her eyes rove over my turquoise eyes, my darkened skin, and my stark white teeth courtesy of Crest Whitestrips, she steps back, a mix of surprise and confusion spreading across her face.

"Rachel," she whispers. "Why are you turning black?"

I laugh and roll my eyes. It's the only way I communicate with my parents these days. "I'm not turning black, Mum! I'm tanned. Don't I look better?"

"I don't like it. You look dirty," she says as she grabs my cheeks. Her close examination of my skin rankles me. I pull away from her grasp.

"I'm sorry I actually go outside. I don't just stay inside the restaurant all day," I snap.

My mother drops her still-outstretched hands. "Mummy work hard for you," is all she says before her face cools into a hardened mask. "No more black."

It unsettles me. My attempts to fit in with my classmates and dodge that horrific question—"Why do you look like that?"—aren't having the desired effect if the question is still being asked of me at home. Either way, there is always someone looking at me and deciding I'm not quite up to standard.

―――

The thing about teenagers is that they change with the wind. What's seriously uncool one day can suddenly become the hot new trend the next.

You can imagine my surprise when I start high school and discover that trying in school is suddenly cool again. All the hot, popular kids make it no secret they're gunning for the top marks in class. Suddenly, if you don't try, you're seen as a good-for-nothing loser with zero prospects in life.

In high school, the flicker happens all around me, nearly constantly. My peers say things like "I bet you're really good at math" and "I hear you're at an advantage in French because you speak Chinese."

After years of muting myself, I'm still too nervous to raise my hand in class, but I'm no longer afraid of being seen as a geek. Now, I worry about not sounding smart enough. *Oh God, everyone expects me to be smart. What if I sound stupid?*

I work tirelessly but silently to make sure I am consistently at the top of my class.

When I get a seventy-nine in algebra, I am so horrified by my mediocrity that I immediately sign up for private lessons with a math tutor. *Everyone tells me I should be good at math. Why am I not good at math?* That's how the house of a retired math teacher becomes my new after-school hangout spot until I get my grades above eighty. It still feels painfully average to me.

We're sitting in a circle in drama class when our teacher asks us, "Who would play you in a movie?"

My classmates start chattering excitedly. People throw out names like Leonardo DiCaprio, Orlando Bloom, Keira Knightley, Natalie Portman.

I am silently sweating in my chair.

It's 2004 and I have only one name. She's the only Asian actress any of us can name.

"Lucy Liu," I say, even though we look nothing alike. But everyone nods around me like "No duh." Who else could I possibly say?

This is what I know at age fifteen: there are fewer opportunities for people like me on the main stage. We are not the main event. We do not get top billing. Another thing I know: the few of us who do make it are interchangeable. Lucy Liu and I have very few physical similarities, but what does that matter? We're both Chinese. How different could we really be?

In *Rush Hour 2*—a Phan family favourite—Chris Tucker's Carter accidentally punches Jackie Chan's Lee in the face, confusing him with the dozen or so Chinese baddies who have swarmed them at a massage parlour. When Lee grabs for his nose and widens his eyes in betrayed alarm, Carter quips, "All y'all look alike!"

Watching this, I internalize that we are not unique individuals in the eyes of many. We are a monolith, flattened into stereotypical caricatures without nuance. I am as much Lucy Liu as my dad is Bruce Lee, which in reality is not at all. But no one else seems to think this. I hate having only one option, even if that option is as beautiful as Lucy Liu.

Because I never see Asian leads in popular media, I always feel like the invisible sidekick—the girl boys go to when they want me to put in a good word with my blonde-haired, blue-eyed best friend. Because Asian women are seen as exotic, hypersexual temptresses, I begin cultivating a version of this role for myself. With very little direction from my parents or role models in the media and with my sister away at university, I internalize the stereotypes and become my own super trope: The Slutty, Nerdy Best Friend.

But I do fight against the roles I can.

As a surly teenager, I lash out and buck against the submissive "good Asian" stereotype. I party all night, I get high excessively, I sleep over at my friends' places without telling my parents.

I fight against the hated "restaurant kid" role, too. I refuse to be roped into it like my sister and brother were.

Wanting to hang out with friends instead of helping at the restaurant, I force my parents to endure many terrible acts of defiance. I yell and break dishes. Once, I purposely ruin a batch of rice with my cousin for laughs. We oversoak the grains and mash it with our violent hands until it resembles congee. The defeated, tired look on my mum's face when she sees what we've done still splits my heart in two.

If I can't control how others see and treat me, I can at least push back against how my family sees me. They won't run away no matter how hard I push them. They have a duty to stick around. To love me.

As part of this effort to reinvent myself, I start to fall in love with writing. In my stories, I am everything I can possibly ever want to be. I am the heroine. I am the love interest. I am the main character. I am all the things I never feel I can be in real life. There are no boxes placed around me when ink hits paper, so I colour outside the lines. It is the perfect way to create a new reality, an escape.

5

"IT'S OVER."

I never believed in happily ever after. I never dreamed of my wedding day or what my future spouse would look like. I never thought I would get married. It's hard to believe in the institution of marriage when every single marriage modelled for you in real life is miserable.

One of my earliest memories is of Dad crying on the couch. He and Mum are fighting again. *Did she get too close to another man? Is she leaving him?*

I don't know. I don't ask because I'm only three years old. All I know is that this behaviour is out of character for him. My father is usually so unemotional and stoic. The tears on his face are alien. He looks as uncomfortable with the trails they leave behind as I am.

I must remember this memory because of how novel it is. To this day, I've only seen him cry a handful of times.

Of course, my parents don't split up. Instead of a Band-Aid baby, they start a Band-Aid business together.

But it's far from a Band-Aid. Once the restaurant opens, the fights intensify. Dad makes belittling comments to Mum when she's slow to calculate the bills. Mum loses it with Dad when he gives one too many discounts or freebies to his friends. The stress of working non-stop in a steaming hot kitchen with waitresses yelling out orders and the *ding* of the bell when new customers walk in is overwhelming even for me, and I'm just sitting at a table with a book.

The fights in the kitchen are unpleasant, but those make sense. Who isn't stressed out in a kitchen?

It is the fights that spill into our home that are frightening. These are the ones that follow Mum and Dad out of the kitchen and into the sanctuary of our apartment, the place that is supposed to be free of the restaurant's chaos and noise. These are the fights that are so brutal and visceral that the belligerents—my parents—just can't wait until morning to have them. These are the explosive kind of fights that are deemed worthy of putting off precious sleep for. Physical exhaustion be damned, their dukes are up. They become so focused on their battle that they forget they even have kids. We're the collateral damage.

I hate these fights.

One night, after I've fallen asleep in front of the TV, I am awakened by the sound of anguished screaming and crying. The smashing of glass. I squeeze my eyes shut and grip the blanket tightly in closed fists in a childish attempt to drown out the noise of the war happening in my parents' bedroom.

Their tone tells me my parents are saying ugly, cruel things in Cantonese, but I'm so groggy I can't make out the words. I'm sure they're going through the usual favourites. I hear my mother howling, "I hate you! I hate you!"

I run to my bedroom where the ugly words can still reach me, but their potency is dulled. I close the doors and shake in my bed, my hands clasped tightly around my ears. I will the screaming to stop. It doesn't. By the time I feel brave enough to leave my bedroom in the morning, all evidence of destruction from the night before is gone. Their room is empty—they're both already downstairs in the restaurant—and the sunlight streams in, undeterred by the gloom that hangs heavy in this apartment.

Later, I learn what the source of the smashed glass was. My mother had taken a gigantic framed photo of her and my dad—one from a photo shoot in Toronto where she wore a rented puffy-sleeved lace wedding dress and he wore a suit with a red bowtie—and thrown it with all her fury and rage to the floor.

That photo shoot was the closest thing they ever had to an actual wedding. I never saw that photo again.

———

When I'm fourteen, my dad goes on a month-long trip to Hà Nội, Vietnam. My mother doesn't go because she never passed her Canadian citizenship test. Like so many other immigrant women, she never had enough time to study for the test, not while juggling work at the mushroom farm, taking care of us, and all the other mundane tasks that come with settling in a brand-new country. My mother was working on the day most of my dad's family received their citizenship in the late 1980s, after Dad sponsored their move to Canada. Seeing so many of them, the officer passed them all right then and there. It was easier for him than administering the test and grading it. One of Mum's greatest regrets was that she wasn't there that day.

That's how Dad ended up going back to Vietnam without her for a month. When he comes back, everything changes.

The fights between him and Mum get worse. They start spilling into the apartment more and more. The war zone has shifted, changed shape, expanded. Now, nowhere is safe.

As the cracks between my parents widen, I'm left in the dark. *No one tells me anything! No one ever has!* My teenage angst is in its infancy but given plenty of nourishment to grow and fester.

To help me make sense of all the screaming and crying, I start filling in the blanks with my own imagination. Once again, I escape through stories.

I tell myself that my parents are fighting because one of the waitresses has seduced my dad. I convince myself that he and the waitress have gotten way too close. I begin to hate her and treat her cruelly. I don't respond to her when she says hello or asks me how I am. I don't even look at her.

I think if I can just make her life miserable, she'll quit and leave us alone. Then Mum and Dad will be okay again. The fighting will stop. They'll learn how to be together again after their time apart. They'll get back into the routine.

But the fighting doesn't stop. And they never get back into the routine.

It's September 2002 and I'm just finishing my first week of high school. *I'm a grown-up now!* I have a locker and I can choose my own classes and I'm no longer surrounded by annoying screaming kids. We don't get recess anymore, but it's okay because now there are cool kids skateboarding in the parking lot and invites to parties without parents.

It's a Friday and I'm walking home. The sun is shining and I feel accomplished, mature. *I did it! I survived my first week of high school without getting shoved in a locker!*

Walking through the doors of the restaurant, I feel the atmosphere shift. Twist into something deformed. My parents are there and the air around them, which has been so charged and toxic lately, has frozen over and grown icy cold.

I don't hear the words they say. They're forever lost to me. No matter how hard I try to dig through the crevices of my fallible memory, I can't find them. But I get the gist.

My parents are splitting up.

They've sold the May May Inn.

My mum, brother, and I are moving that weekend.

I have to get going and start packing right away.

It's over.

The shock is overwhelming, but I don't have time to process. I need to hastily grab my things and walk them over to our new apartment a block away—the same apartment where my first friend Talia lived, beside the first May May Inn.

An onslaught of questions comes to me all at once.

How can this be? How can there be no more May May Inn? What will happen to my dad? Is this because of the waitress? Does the restaurant still exist? Why? What will happen to us? What will happen to me? The questions fire in and out of my brain. I don't have time to contemplate them, and I definitely don't have time to ask for answers. We're all so busy trying to hightail it out of there that there's no time to process what's happening. What my parents have done. What's been irrevocably broken.

I focus my attention on throwing everything I own and love into boxes and trying my hardest not to cry.

The sun's still shining the next day when I carry my small boxes of things over to the new apartment. My hands are clammy and I'm angry that the sun remains vibrant and warm while my world collapses around me.

The apartment looks exactly the same as when Talia lived there seven years ago. It's run-down and musty. The elevator is slow and makes weird noises, and I wouldn't at all be surprised if it broke down while I was in it. Everything else is already breaking.

The apartment has two bedrooms, one bath. Mum and I have our own rooms, but there isn't a room for John, whose mattress is being set up in the living room next to the TV. It's carpeted except for a section that's been inexplicably torn out outside my room—new carpet will be put in eventually, we're told—and my feet curl from the cold of the exposed concrete floor.

Years of conditioning tell me not to make a fuss. I stay quiet even though I have a thousand questions I want to ask. I force myself to accept that this is my home now. This is my life now. I'm not surprised when no one tells me anything.

<hr>

So much of my identity was being a restaurant kid. I was Rachel, whose parents ran the Chinese restaurant on Pearl Street. I was *the* May May of May May Inn! I don't know who I am if there's no restaurant. I can hardly describe the searing pain I get in my chest when I walk by the restaurant named after me that's inexplicably no longer my home. No longer mine.

I find out that my parents sold the restaurant to one of my maternal uncles. When I think about my cousin enjoying the plush pink carpet I'd chosen for myself all those years ago, my blood boils. My mother tells me that my uncle is upset by how many coats of paint they'll need to cover the years' worth of doodles and scribbles my friends and I made on my bedroom walls. Boys' names and funny quotes and song lyrics.

I wish I could shoot back that he and his family shouldn't even be in our home because it's not theirs. If I had known I'd be so unceremoniously kicked out of my room, maybe I wouldn't have spent so much time lovingly leaving my mark on the walls. I wish I could tell her it's her and Dad's stupid fault for not getting over whatever they were fighting about and letting some usurpers into our home.

But I don't because the sadness and confusion—pure shell shock—is written plainly on my mother's face. If my heart is breaking, how much is hers? She's lost her husband, her home, her life's work. She's no longer her own boss and now has to work at the restaurant under a brother she barely likes. How humiliating it must be to have to return to the scene of your greatest heartbreak day in and day out. If the universe were fair, there would be a limit on how often a person is forced to endure so much loss.

I give her a hug and rest my head on her shoulder. I forget about myself for a while and try to be brave for her. I promise to do everything I can to protect her so her heart will stop breaking.

Because I'm just a child and not grown up at all, I still see the world as cut and dried, black and white. I see sides to choose.

I've chosen a side and it's not my dad's.

Since no one's told me anything about why my parents have split up or why we've sold the restaurant, I lean into my stories. It's easier to speculate than to be confined in the suffocating dark.

Clearly, my dad did something wrong. *Everything's been messed up since he came back from his trip. And what about that touchy waitress? What role did she*

play here? Are the two of them together right now? If they are, are they satisfied
with the mess they've made?

I'm so angry with my dad that I start to hate him. But I can't articulate
why or if any of the stories I'm telling myself are true. I just know that this
is his fault and I'll never, ever forgive him for rashly selling the restaurant
and breaking up our family.

Not long after the separation, Dad starts coming by the apartment.

"Who is it?" I yell into the intercom. When I hear Dad's voice, I tell
him to leave. "Go away! No one wants you here!"

He buzzes and buzzes and buzzes. Sometimes he holds his finger on the
buzzer, so the jarring noise goes on and on for minutes.

I stand my ground and refuse to let him in. His persistence has only
stoked the flames of my anger. I shake with it, but I'm also afraid. I'm home
alone—John is out with friends and my mother is working—and I feel the
weight of having to deal with my dad on my own.

After thirty interminable minutes of the buzzer going off incessantly, a
sudden silence descends on the apartment. I am relieved. I've successfully
kept the enemy away and protected my mother.

When I go to sleep, I think about how my father's absence doesn't
bother me. I am suddenly grateful for the years of preparation I've had
to help me get used to him not being around. Still, when I close my eyes,
I imagine I'm back in my bedroom on Pearl Street and my parents are just
a staircase away, busy cooking up orders in the restaurant. It's a soothing
thought that comforts me to sleep. In the morning, I squeeze my eyelids
tight, not wanting the mirage to end.

But of course, it does.

My dad keeps trying to win my mother back.

Every time he presses the buzzer, my fury grows.

"Why didn't you try this hard before you sold the restaurant and ruined
everything? Leave us alone!"

Dad starts to write Mum letters. He begs her to take him back. He must realize that letters are a more effective way to plead his case because his insolent, angry daughter isn't there to block his attempts.

Mum doesn't tell me any of this, of course. I find out years later from my sister, who at the time seemed a planet away in Australia. My sister, who was always the most responsible child—or at least, the child whom my parents expected to be the most responsible—left home for university and never looked back. She's in Australia on a working holiday visa. To unshackle herself from the stress of the restaurant and the burden of being whatever our parents needed her to be, Linh makes herself scarce. She never calls home. She and I talk about everything except what's happening at home when we chat on ICQ. She escapes, relishes her freedom. Her original plan to stay in Australia for only four months quickly changes. She extends it to a full year.

Linh doesn't know what's happening at home. For her, it's easier that way. It's easier to not be there and to not have to witness the carnage and implosion of our lives. I envy her and wish I could be anywhere else but here, in this unhappy, musty apartment with my dad's pitiful buzzing ringing in my ears and my mother's sadness cloaking everything.

In the year Linh's in Australia, she calls twice. On Christmas Day, she calls and gets an earful from my mother about what's happening. Mum tells Linh about Dad's letters and how he's pleading and crying to be taken back. How he's been told by everyone what a big fuck-up it was to separate from her and sell the May May Inn.

"I don't know what to do," Mum says to her eldest child. "Should I take him back?"

I understand completely why my sister doesn't call again. I wish I could join her on the other side of the world.

—⁓—

When I meet new people and make new friends in high school, I still tell them my parents own the Chinese restaurant on Pearl Street. I don't know how to let that part of my identity go. I'm still hoping this is temporary.

I don't think about how there were certainly contracts and legalese involved. I don't know that my parents have signed paperwork giving my uncle and his family everything they had worked so hard to build from scratch. I don't know that they've agreed not to open up another restaurant—not just another May May Inn, nothing—to prevent competition between the businesses.

I feel like a new adult in my first year of high school, but it's never been more apparent just how little I know. How much of a naive child I am.

The next time I see my dad is when I visit my cousins. My dad has been staying with my uncle, one of his younger brothers, and his family. When I get there, my cousins tell me how annoying it's been to share a house with my dad, who's particular and moves things around to suit his preferences. I nod and feel grateful that he's no longer the thorn in my side. He can be an intrusion on someone else.

I'm so fucking angry and hoping I won't see him, but he's there. Of course he's there. Where else would he be? The restaurant is no longer his. He's been barred from its doors, from our lives.

When Dad sees me, the hope that flickers across his face thaws me out, just a little. A spoonful of resentment dislodges itself from my chest, and I let it go without a fight.

"How are you? How are you doing? How is your mum?" he asks me. He searches my face for answers, like he's a fortune teller reading the stars. When I answer with a shrug and a simple, "Good," he deflates a little but invites me to see how he's been living since the separation.

He shows me his room. It's spartan, with barely anything in it. I feel a pang in my heart that my dad, who has worked so hard for twenty years in this country, is here. He has almost nothing. The empire he built has collapsed around him. He is, in his eyes, a parasite living off his younger brother. As the eldest in his family, he is expected to be the one who takes care of everyone else. He has fallen so far.

He sits on the bed, a broken shell of a man. He looks up at me, gestures to the window, points to the blinds. There are specks of black around the window frame.

"Look at this," he says. "This is my life now. I worked so hard only to end up here, living in a room in your uncle's house with mould on the windows."

He repeats it. "This is my life now."

The tears come unbidden to my eyes, and I turn away. I've convinced myself that I hate my dad without really knowing why. Feeling sorrow and sympathy for him doesn't fit into my narrow teenage worldview of anger and angst. As a fourteen-year-old, I feel sorry for him, but I can't yet fully grasp how desperately sad this is. What it must have felt like for him to have everything he had worked so hard to build slip through his fingers. And now, his child—his youngest and the one he shamelessly calls his favourite—is seeing him in his sorry state.

I turn from him. "I'm going to go." When I turn back to catch a look at him, he is in shadow. A sad, sunken silhouette slumped on the bed. I shake my head and try to relight the rage I've been cultivating all these months. It refuses to light.

Mum takes Dad back a few months later. Of course she does. The two of them don't know how to exist without each other.

Dad moves into the musty, cramped apartment with us. Though the rage I feel towards him has settled down to a simmer, I still don't really talk to him. When he's in the room, I'm practically mute. I give him one-word answers if I have to engage and focus on my mother and brother instead. It's frosty.

He doesn't give up. He gives me money. When he makes elaborate dishes, he's the first to serve me generous spoonfuls of the lobster or crab or whole fish. I eat silently. He fills my bowl.

When I'm not listening or in the room, my parents talk about what's next. What else can they do? Mum can't go back to the mushroom farm. She hates working in the kitchen with her brother. Dad doesn't want to be a grunt working in someone else's kitchen either.

They decide the only course of action is to open a new restaurant. Start over again. They've done it so many times before—what's once more?

Except there's one huge obstacle standing in their way: the pesky contract they signed when they sold the restaurant to my mother's brother. The contract included a non-compete clause preventing them from opening a restaurant within ten kilometres of the May May Inn.

What were they going to do?

My parents are plucky. They're resilient. If there's one thing they know how to do, it's adapt and survive. They find a much smaller location in nearby Leamington, about fifteen minutes away. To bypass the non-compete, they create a sneaky loophole for themselves. They find a way, no matter what.

In 2003, not even a year after Dad's reckless decision to sell the May May Inn, my parents open a new Chinese restaurant in Leamington. They call it China Village. To circumvent the contract, they open it under my brother's name, despite the fact he's only twenty-two. With Linh gone, they turn to their second-oldest child to shoulder this new responsibility, forever saddling my brother with the family business.

My parents aren't thinking about that, though. They're officially back in business.

The new restaurant is my parents' way of taping together the many shattered pieces of our lives. They saved our family and their own livelihoods. But the cost is severe.

My mother's side of the family shuns her from that moment on. Her brother, who now owns the May May Inn, and her other brother, who owns a long-standing, beloved restaurant just a five-minute drive from our new one, are livid. One of my aunts goes to town hall in a futile attempt to fight the opening of our restaurant.

We don't talk to them for twelve years. We go from spending Christmases and other holidays with them to nothing but a bitter, resentful silence. The shunning is total, complete. My mother has saved her own family but lost her relationships with her siblings. The loss, yet another on the long list she's already faced, is great.

A few months later, when most of Ontario plunges into darkness during the great blackout of 2003, my friend Susan and I are at the apartment gorging on garlic breadsticks from a nearby pizza joint.

"What the fuck?" we yell, our mouths full of cheese and carbs.

When my brother comes home and tells us there's a blackout across the province, I think nothing of it. "It'll be back soon," I say with all the confidence of someone who has never lived through a blackout before. By the time Susan leaves an hour later, the power still has not returned.

As the hours pass, my anxiety grows. "Okay, so it's not back yet?" My stomach grumbles as I worry about food and what we'll eat. The garlic sticks are long gone.

My parents swoop in to pick me and my brother up. They drive us to the restaurant in eerie darkness. There are no traffic lights, no lights at all, to guide our path. The lights of our Buick Rendezvous cut through the heavy sheet of blackness.

"What are we doing?" I ask. "Why are we going?" I'm fully starving at this point and prone to catastrophizing. I'm certain I'm going to perish before I hear that reassuring hum of power all around me once again.

When we get to the restaurant, Mum, John, and I sit outside on the curb. It's cooler outside than it is inside, where there's no air conditioning to blast away our beads of sweat.

Not long after we arrive, my dad comes outside, carrying a giant bowl of hot, steaming noodles. In a massive blackout, my dad made beef *lo mein*. I have no idea how he made it, but in that moment, I look at him with so much admiration and child-like wonder. Suddenly, my dad is my hero again. He will find a way to pull off miracles to make sure none of us starves.

I hug him tightly, forgetting all the animosity I still have for him.

"Thank you, Dad."

He looks at me with an unreadable expression on his face. He nods and pushes the bowl over to me. We quietly eat in the stillness of the cloaking darkness. It feels like respite. It feels like an olive branch. A thawing.

6

"IS IT TRUE YOU HAVE A SLANTED VAGINA?"

In high school, something shifts in the way boys see and treat me.

In elementary school, boys were sweet and gentle. I even had a few boys tell me they liked me and ask me to be their girlfriend. None of these relationships lasted more than a few days, but still, they counted! Someone liked me enough to publicly be mine, even fleetingly. There were flashes of what was to come, but for the most part, there was innocence.

Once high school starts, the boys get meaner. They get sneakier. Boys tease me and tell me to get deported in class, but behind a computer screen, they sing a different tune.

"Hey, would you ever want to hook up?"
"Hey, have you ever given a BJ?"
"Hey, is it true that Asian girls have the tightest pussies?"

I am distressed and confused by these boys who shame and belittle me in public but try to get with me in secret. Over time, their actions teach me that I am a shameful thing, a disgusting thing, someone not worthy of love. I make the obvious assumption that I am not lovable. I am not the kind of girl you bring home and claim as your high school sweetheart. I am something to be hidden. I am exotic and forbidden. I am the girl you use and abuse in private, in darkened cars parked on shadowy side streets, while, during the day, you hold your girlfriend's hand, put her name in hearts in your MSN name, and reassure her that you're okay with taking things slow.

———

I am fourteen years old the first time I find myself on my knees in front of a boy.

I've internalized what boys want, so naturally, I'm wearing a schoolgirl uniform borrowed from a friend who goes to a nearby Catholic school. My skirt is hiked sky-high to show off my smooth thighs.

I'd shaved my, admittedly minimal, pubic hair earlier that day in anticipation of this moment. I feel fresh. New. Desirable. I told myself that morning I was going to make my new crush like me, no matter what. And if he didn't, at least I could say I got high from the chase.

The boy is a drummer in a punk rock band with a truly horrible name. He is not handsome—his nose and teeth are both way too big for his face—but there's something about him that makes me feel raw inside. He looks at me like he wants to devour me. He shows no love or affection for me at all, but I can still tell he wants me.

He asks me to steal a twenty-sixer of vodka from the restaurant, so I do. I put the skirt on and make myself bare for him.

When I sit on his lap in my friend's backyard and feel his roving hand trail the length of my thigh, it feels like I'm on the edge of a rollercoaster about to go down. He works his fingers over to the place where only my own fingers have been before. It feels like the big drop.

This is it! The moment I've been anticipating for so long. All I've ever wanted was to be known and touched by someone who wants me back. *It's finally happening.* We're smoking hash and I think I'm being slick with the way I'm wriggling on his lap. I can feel how much he wants me through his shorts. He can feel with his exploring fingers how much I want him.

"Do you want to go over there?" he whispers in my ear. He's looking at the shed. I nod. My heart is a thunderous hammer in my chest.

The smirks and knowing looks on our friends' faces when they watch us get up and walk to that tiny woodshed make me stand taller. I feel proud for some reason. I feel like I'm finally living up to my potential. I feel the heady high of being chosen for once. The smoke from the hash curls and swirls around us and leads us down the path to the shed.

When I take him in my mouth, I think, *Yes, I can do this. This is where I will excel. This will make him love me.* He squeezes my ass and gives me a tight hug when we part. His slow grin tells me he's happy. He's pleased with me. He sends me off with a promising, "I'll see you around, yeah?"

Afterwards, I wait for him to call me, email me, send me some kind of signal, but I never hear from him again. He takes the bottle of booze I stole for him—my brother gives me hell for it later—and tells his friend to give me one parting message.

"You're very talented."

It hurts for a time, but I move forward. I get back to chasing the high.

I am fifteen years old the first time I am with another girl.

We are in a sparsely decorated living room in the home of some guy whose name and face I can no longer remember. The party's cleared out and we are the stragglers—just me, the friend from elementary school who so kindly told me I had "good dick-sucking lips," the forgettable boy whose house it is, and a girl my age from school.

She and I are friendly, but we aren't exactly friends. We spent much of ninth grade avoiding each other after she called me a bitch because she didn't like the way I looked at her. In reality, any glares I cast her way were because I was heinously nearsighted and hadn't discovered contact lenses yet. I squinted not out of hate but out of necessity.

Needless to say, we weren't close.

That night, the four of us are sprawled out in a circle with cheap beers purchased using fake IDs, meticulously rolled joints, and a heavy cloud of teenage hormones. We talk about whether a young, conventionally attractive teacher at our high school is getting too close to girls in our grade.

Forgettable Boy says, "Imagine being surrounded by hot young girls every day? It's what any guy would want." The other boy nods seriously, as if this fact is the secret key to the universe. Fuck a young girl and reach nirvana!

The girl rolls her eyes. "Who fucking cares what guys want? You're all fucked in the head and think only with your dicks."

Forgettable Boy laughs a mirthless laugh. "You all say that, but you all care about what guys want. If I told you," he gestures in her direction, joint gripped tightly between his index and middle fingers, "and you," he turns his attention to me, "to make out because we'll think it's hot, you would do it. Guaran-fucking-teed." He puffs deeply on the joint for emphasis. When he blows the smoke out in our faces, he's wearing a sleazy, smug grin on his face.

My mouth goes dry, and a heaviness settles in between my legs at his mere suggestion. I am at once flooded with feelings of confusion, annoyance, and want.

The girl puts her beer bottle down. "That's where you're wrong, dick. If me and Rach are going to make out, it's not going to be because of you dumbasses." She fixes me with a look, her head tilted to the side, like a dog that just heard its favourite word. "If we're going to make out, it's because I think she's cute and I want to."

The heaviness grows. Heavy, heavy, heavy. *Me? Cute? Kissing her? I've barely even kissed boys. Why would I kiss a girl?*

The boys watch us. One's mouth is slightly ajar, while the other's Adam's apple is bobbing as he swallows in anticipation. My head is cloudy and fuzzy from drink and weed and nerves. I don't make a move or a sound. I won't break first. If she doesn't mean what I think she means, I'm certainly not going to embarrass myself by leaning in.

It turns out she means what I thought she meant because she leans in first. Her lips are parted slightly and curled up at the corners with a gently teasing smile. I am struck dumb but not so stupid that I'm willing to miss my chance. I meet her halfway, and my head swims with all the women of wrestling I've imagined late at night.

When her lips touch mine, she is gentle and tentative. The boys are hooting and hollering and spilling their beers all over their fingers while they watch us with their mouths gaping open. We wrap our arms around one another and laugh. We ignore them and their boners. She takes off her shirt and I swell with pure, unfiltered need when I take in her body. She looks so much better than the two-dimensional images on my pixelated computer screen.

Afterwards, Forgettable Boy tips his beer bottle in our direction and says smugly, "I told you. Bitches always care what guys want."

—␣␣—

There's a boy who lives fifteen minutes away from me that I'm crazy about. He has these warm brown eyes that are so sad I mistake them for being soulful. Plus, he's in a band, so you know he's emotionally mature.

He always messages me the second I sign into MSN Messenger.

"hey"

I am blown away by the power of his attention.

"Hey! How's it going?" I'm so cool and aloof. He can't know how widely I'm beaming or how hard my chest is beating.

We make small talk like this for a few minutes before he drops the bomb on me. "I have a new gf." My face does that annoying thing it always does when my heart is hurting. I flush beet red and thank God we're not having one of our video calls. It would be just my luck to have my shitty webcam freeze on my face while I'm flushing violently. He must notice that I've taken more than a minute to respond because he's saying something about how this doesn't have to change anything between us. We can still be friends. We can still talk about anything.

I say, "of course!" and am immediately hit with a "so, u ever try anal?"

I'm not proud of it, but I let it go on and on. I pretend I love butt play even though I'm a big-time virgin. He makes a comment about how he "knew it" because I'm Asian, and don't I know that Asian girls are the wildest and most sexually adventurous of all girls? I wonder what the ranking is and how lucky we are that we rank so highly.

Over the next few weeks, I see photo after photo of him and his girlfriend all over Myspace. She's famous on the platform for being one of those scene queens with dramatic side bangs. Meanwhile, in private, we're having racy conversations on MSN, and later over the phone. I don't let myself think about his girlfriend. When you're so deprived of something for so long, you settle for scraps. You find a way to live with your choices if it means you can feel the high of being loved even for a little while. When you're a teen girl who barely knows herself, though so many others seem to know who you are, you start listening to what they have to say. And this is what they've told me: I'm only good for this one thing. I'm destined to be the filthy little side piece.

He comes over one time—I'm home alone because my parents are working—and keeps his distance, until he can't. He's sitting on my bed, hands curled tightly into fists. It's not long before his fingers are on me, pulling off my jeans, giving me pleasure. He doesn't kiss me. He doesn't even take off his pants. When I'm on the come down, he suddenly remembers himself. "I have to stop. I can't do this. I have to go," he says.

They date for a long time after that. He messages me for a long time, too.

After that, I surround myself with guys. They become my best friends. I'm the cool girl who will smoke joint after joint with you. I'm the smart girl who will study with you for the big biology test. I'm the girl no one wants to date but everyone wants to fuck.

A few years later, I turn eighteen and still believe that virginity is real. It's taking forever for me to lose it even though I am uncomfortably and infuriatingly horned up. I am so impatient for it to happen that when it does, I wonder why I made such a big deal of it.

No one knows that I lose my virginity on the floor of my parents' abandoned bedroom, surrounded by things left unpacked, discarded. We're now living in Leamington, where the new restaurant is, but I still have the keys to the dinky two-bedroom apartment in Kingsville. While my parents settle and sleep in our new house fifteen minutes away, I am here, on my back. It's one of those many nights when I don't tell them I'm not coming home. I don't think they care where I am anyway.

Gigantic stuffed animals my brother won for me at a town fair litter the carpeted floor along with everything else that remains of our largely unhappy life in this apartment building. This era of my angsty teenage years is mercifully coming to a close.

I am with a friend whom I've flirted with for months. We talk on the phone for hours and have earned a cozy place in each other's Myspace Top 8. We are seriously into each other. We get high together all the time, and when he blows smoke into my wide-open mouth, our friends whistle and make a gesture with their hands like a knife.

"The sexual tension!" they mouth.

It's all led up to this moment.

Tonight, in my empty, chaotic apartment, is the first time we've had privacy overnight. Our friends are passed out in the living room, where my brother's bed used to be. It's two or three in the morning when he slides the condom on.

As my legs spread open, I think, *I can't believe this is finally happening. Am I seriously getting fucked on the floor of this shitty apartment right now?*

It feels good. My years of exploring my own body come in handy as I tell him where to touch and how much pressure to use. We don't kiss—I'm self-conscious about my lack of kissing experience—but we hold each other close. It's an intimacy I've never experienced before. A part of me wishes I were sober to enjoy it more.

When he finishes, he throws the condom over the balcony. We laugh and fall asleep on the floor of garbage and discarded things.

No one knows I am a virgin up until this moment, certainly not him. Throughout all of high school, I am full of bluster and lies about my sexual experience. Everyone thinks I've hooked up with men on my visits to my sister in Toronto. They think I've been fucked in the back of a truck, on a balcony, at a party. They think that because that's what I tell them. I joke about how I am Asian and how that makes me the best fuck of their lives. I am a virgin in slut's clothing.

They believe me. They high-five me. They tell me they watch girls like me in porn, so they know that what I tell them is true. One by one, they tell me in private that they want a turn.

I don't say yes until this moment. I hold my friend close and relish the newfound soreness and ache I feel in my body. I think, *Things must be different now.*

They're not.

My friend and I continue to have sex whenever we can. We're shameless about it. We don't care who else is in the room with us or even who's in the same bed. We are groping and slipping and sliding and keeping our mouths clamped shut to lessen the noise that escapes during those fantastic drops of ecstasy.

But everything is done under the influence in complete darkness. We are too high. We are too drunk. We are too scared to let anyone know about us. We would disrupt the dynamics of our friend group if anyone found out.

Not for the first time, I bury the secret longing I nurture in my chest, the one that yearns to not be someone's dirty little secret. I want my name to be in between two hearts in someone's MSN Messenger name. I want to take up that coveted first slot in someone's Myspace Top 8. I want to know, just once, what it's like to have someone say with their full chest, "This is *my* girl."

It doesn't happen. My friend gets a new girlfriend. He tells me when he takes her virginity. He still flirts with me.

When they break up, he finds me at a party and tells me how much he misses me. "You give the best blow jobs," he says. I smile and feel proud. I knew I'd be great.

—∞—

Back then, I spend almost all my time at my friends' houses. I go days without telling my parents where I am. I never ask for permission. I don't even have a cell phone where they can reach me. I have endless sleepovers in cold basements with four, five, six of us packed onto one pull-out bed.

My parents and I dance around each other's lives like orbiting planets. They don't ask me where I've been or what I've done. I don't even bother to make polite small talk. I don't ask them how their days are. I don't ask about the restaurant or the customers or which waitresses are driving my mother mad. We are strangers to each other.

My brother, on the other hand, is shockingly perceptive when he wants to be. He never has any issues when I have friends over, but he hates the guy I lose my virginity to. I don't know how he knows—I'm certain teenagers are quite subtle—but he does.

Whenever my brother sees him sitting on the couch, sandwiched between our other friends, he goes into a red-hot rage. He throws his keys at the wall. He kicks everyone out. He says things like, "I hate that fucking prick!"

I curse him under my breath. *Why does he care so much if our own parents don't? Why is he the one being so protective over me?* He must not have gotten the memo. *No one else in this house cares about me, so why does he?*

———

There is a guy in my friend group who is truly the worst. I loathe him for being pretentious and smug and for saying things like, "When I go to university, I'm going to go by my middle name because my first name is too 'working class.'"

I really, really hate him.

We hardly ever talk even though we have many mutual friends. I avoid him in hallways. I refuse to laugh at any of his awful jokes. He doesn't laugh at mine, which are subjectively much funnier.

Except there's one night when we're both sleeping over in our friend's basement. It's a terrible idea. We're both at risk of smothering the other in their sleep. The silence is awkward but so is any stilted conversation we might have. I close my eyes tight and pretend I'm already sleeping.

He starts to talk in a sleepy drawl. About nothing. About inane high school things. About his hopes for his first year in university. About how he can't wait to move out of this small town and into the big city.

I listen and start to respond in kind. We're not talking about anything deep. There are no sparks flying. I don't feel any heat in my loins or my heart. But we're also unsupervised teenagers in a pitch-black basement with no windows and no hope of even a sliver of moonlight streaming in. I could be talking to anyone. I could be talking to someone I actually like.

It's not long before our hands are on each other and I'm saying things like "I'm just finishing my period," and he's telling me he doesn't care. He's on top of me and my eyes are still closed tight and I am so full of self-loathing because it feels shockingly and unbearably good even though I fucking hate this guy.

We tell each other that it can't—it won't—happen again. But it does, again and again and again. We have sex in his car in darkened subdivisions, behind shuttered restaurants, in apple orchards, on my friend's front lawn while the mosquitoes swarm over my bare exposed legs. I tell him we can't kiss because I hate him and he tells me he hates me too, while he's driving himself into me.

With him, I learn what it's like to be desired and hated in equal measure. The wanting is so strong in the heat of the moment, but as soon as it's done, you might look up and catch it. That vacant stare that tells you you're not even human to them.

Of course, I'm still a big secret. The lengths he goes to hide me—to hide us—are the stuff of comedies.

One night, we are at a party. He whispers in my ear, "Do you want to slip away?" I nod and watch him take his leave. Two minutes later, I follow. We meet beside my friend's dad's car. We are rude, horny teenagers, so we think nothing of jumping into the back seat of a car that belongs to neither of us and getting naked. While we're having sex, we hear the loud voices of our inebriated friends getting closer and closer. "Shit!" he says. "Are they coming?" I nod. "Fuck!" he exclaims. He jumps out of the car, buck-ass naked, and leaps inelegantly into the bushes.

"Who was that?" I can hear my friends say. They are shocked. They are confused. "Did someone just jump out of the car naked?"

I am desperately trying to put my clothes on with clumsy, clammy fingers when the door opens and our friends peer in. When they see me, their faces dance with a dozen different emotions. More surprise. More confusion. Processing. Questioning. Suspicious.

"Rachel? Were you in here with someone?" they ask sternly as if they're my older brothers. They look disappointed. They look like they're dying for gossip. They look like they want to hunt my lover down and flay the skin off his naked body.

I play it cool and shrug. "No one important."

They needle me for the rest of the night. "Who were you with? We saw him! He was naked! Who was that?"

I say nothing, not even when he comes back to the party, his cheeks flushed and his button-up shirt slightly askew. "Where were you?" our friends ask. Their voices drip with suspicion.

He plays it cool and shrugs. "Nowhere important."

The next day, we discover he jumped right into poison ivy. He is covered in red, itchy splotches. I laugh because I hate him. Our friends start to figure it out. But he never once admits to anything. A secret, I remain. I tell myself it's a good thing.

One night, we are at a party, and I'm hoping we'll be able to sneak away again. But he's flirting openly with someone else. She's white and pretty with glossy brown hair and an earnest girl-next-door smile. He doesn't talk to me. He doesn't even make eye contact.

My disappointment isn't just disappointment. It's disgust. *Why do I even care about him? I don't! He's the worst!*

When someone offers me shrooms, I take it. I need a distraction from these weird, conflicted feelings. *This is just because I'm horny, right? I'm not actually jealous?* I shovel an extra piece of magic fungi in my mouth, just to be sure.

When I'm tripping on mushrooms, I tend to laugh while simultaneously crying. "This looks weird," my best friend tells me. I am weeping and cackling and feeling like all of space is pressed right up against my chest. I can't breathe. I see a gnome come to life in the corner of the room. A blinding burst of light escapes from a friend's chest, her eyes, her lips.

Everyone's teeth are far too sharp. And the dude I hate but love to fuck is nowhere to be found.

"What . . . the fuck?" I breathe. People crowd around me and ask if I'm okay, but their questions and presence feel extra oppressive. I need air. I need to get out of these clothes. I need to get out of this skin.

"She's tripping balls, man," someone says.

I find this hilarious. I find it tragic. I beg someone to call me a cab so I can go home. When the cab arrives, I drag myself into the back seat and squeeze my eyes shut, afraid of what I might see. Everything is all swirly colours and dripping neon. Everything is both too much and not enough. I am both too much and not enough.

When I get home, Mum is already there. She's gotten out of the shower after her long workday. She looks at me with open concern.

"Mum, I'm sick," I manage to say even though my throat feels like it's been scraped raw by sandpaper.

"Go upstairs. I'll make you tea," she says gently.

After I've thrown on whatever clean clothes I could find, my mother comes to my room with a cup of her expensive premium loose leaf Chinese tea and two pills.

She does something I can't remember her ever doing. She tucks me into bed. She rubs my back while I swallow the medication for a sickness I definitely don't have but I can't tell her that. She does that "shhh" noise that everyone does when they're soothing someone. My tears well up, not from psilocybin, but because her affection and care for me feel overwhelming and new. I missed this. I missed her.

She caresses my hair and tells me to sleep. She says she'll make me congee with century eggs in the morning.

When she turns out the lights, I feel wired. Too awake. Still tripping. I am plunged into darkness and despair. I think about the boy I definitely still hate and how I shouldn't have left the party just in case he came around looking for me. I think about how I'm glad I did because I need my mother, and how on earth had I ever convinced myself that I didn't? I cry silently until the shrooms wear off.

In the morning, my mother makes me congee and asks me how I'm feeling.

"Fine," I say. I've already forgotten how much I need her. I no longer remember to miss her.

This is the extent of my dating life in high school: two secret affairs with boys who make me swear I won't tell anyone about us. They both tell me how good I am, how I'm the best at this and that. It's a weighty thing to be a teenage girl and feeling so proud of your sexual expertise. I start believing this is the best I have to offer. I think, *of course, I'm good. I'm Asian!* I don't know when it happens, but at some point along the way, the expectations of what an Asian girl *should* be shape who I become.

Over time, I learn that to be an Asian woman is to be metaphorically cut up and reduced to your body parts—and to just roll over and accept it.

It's minding your own business at a beach party and having a guy walk up to you to ask what colour and shape your nipples are before asking if you want to touch his penis.

It's me, shocked, with a shitty vodka cooler in my hand, digging my toes into the sand and saying, "What colour do you think they are?" I'm trying to play cute and coy while my insides are screaming shame and embarrassment. I respond this way because I don't want him to call me a prude. I don't want him to get mad.

He doesn't get angry. He just smiles and responds, free of any self-consciousness and shame, "They're either puffy and round. Or small and hard, like this." He curls his pointer finger into the cradle of his thumb to make an imperfect circle. "And pink."

I cringe inwardly because I know from flipping through my brother's dirty mags that pink nipples are often the pretty, delicate gems that sit atop the chests of white women. And I am no white woman.

It's also having a conversation with a friend who's home for Christmas after his first semester at university and him telling me, proudly, that he slept with his "first Asian" and that the rumours about the tightness of our vaginas are true. "I bet yours is just like that," he says, adding a new twist to the racist stereotype that "all Asians look alike."

I learn to repress how ashamed and small these comments make me feel. *What's your problem, Rachel?* I think to myself. *This is what it feels like to be wanted.* In my mind, I had been given the choice of continuing to hide and being invisible or being wanted and desired. I chose the latter, every single time.

After years of fetishization and objectification, I internalize the belief that this is what it means to be an Asian woman. Although others may have stopped believing the lie we hear as young children—"he hurts you because he likes you"—I let myself see racial abuse as the price to pay to be granted attention and affection, especially from white men.

Of course, I'm not only attracted to white men. I'm not only attracted to men! But the precedent was set for me to see white men as my best option. All my older cousins have white partners. If it was rare for me to see a woman who looked like me on the TV screen, it was even rarer for me to see one who was considered a viable romantic partner. When I did, her partner was more often than not a white man. During my summer visits to see my sister in Toronto, I'd see a factory line of beautiful Asian women, each holding the hand of some white man who was usually so plainly average compared to her that trying to understand their pairing often broke my brain. I see it all and I learn.

Before I know any better, I am swept up in this feeling I get whenever a white man shows an interest in me. I feel like the best, most prized, most beautiful show-winning pony when a white man, who could have anyone, chooses me even for one night, even for two minutes at a bar. If a white man chooses me, I am the lucky winner who has been selected to enter his privileged world. I am no longer doomed to being on the outside looking in. I am not like those poor Asian women whoring themselves out for a little "sucky sucky." I am not the Fu Manchu villain twirling my cartoony moustache. I am chosen. I am protected. I am good.

But what happens when the white man only wants you for a secret late-night phone sex session while his girlfriend sleeps cozily in her bed on the other side of town? What happens when your body is all they seem to want from you? They don't care how funny you are or the inner workings of your mind. They just want to know if you're into anal. If you'll gag on their cock.

I become all too familiar with the pick-up lines that men somehow think will win them the key to my heart. Or at least, a coveted notch on their bedpost.

"I have yellow fever," they say, as if I should feel proud that desire for me could be compared to a disease.

"I'd love to get my yellow belt," they say, as if I am some kind of prey to be shot so they can turn my pelt into a cozy rug to step on.

"Is it true?" they ask, a sinister twinkle in their eyes. When I naively ask them the follow-up question they so desperately want me to ask, they say with a smirk, "Is it true you have a slanted vagina?"

I hate how their shameful comments never seem to cause them shame, whereas I am choking on it. I am overflowing with the type of shame that feels sticky on the fingers, the kind of shame that demands long minutes under steaming hot water and aggressive sudsy scrubbing. The kind of shame that stays on you, reeking and rotting.

As the years pass, my self-worth craters. I convince myself that it is enough—*of course it's enough*—to be wanted solely for my body. To be wanted solely because I represent a fleeting, exotic experience to be crossed off someone's bucket list. I tell myself that who I am as a person doesn't really matter. It's not like I know who I am anyway.

7

"I FEEL SAD ALL THE TIME."

I have my first introduction to the black pit in the summer before tenth grade.

I've just returned from my annual two-week stay in Toronto with my sister, who came back from Australia and settled four hours away from home. Although I always love my time in the big city with her, I'm excited to go home and enjoy the last few weeks of glorious, slow summer with my best friends. On the VIA train home, I excitedly think about what's ahead of me: summer pool parties, baby-oil-slicked skin in the sun, sleepovers and all-nighters with contraband Smirnoff Ice, and sneaky after-midnight walks to my crush's house.

But when I get home, something feels off. Something feels wrong. My phone calls to my friends go unanswered and unreturned. There are no lazy days by the pool, no late-night confessions or peals of laughter in our pajamas, no rush of adrenaline when I meet my crush in the small hours. There's nothing but me waiting by the phone for a sign that I'm missed.

It's not long before I discover the painful truth. My group of friends has replaced short, dark-haired, non-white me with a girl who is my exact opposite: tall, blonde, blue-eyed. My usurper fits in so naturally with them that I almost can't fault them for the substitution. Now, their friend group makes sense. Now, they are a uniform set. There is no one amongst them who sticks out like a sore thumb the way I did. Everyone belongs and looks the part. Even my crush becomes obsessed with her.

My feelings of belonging have always felt tenuous and fragile, as if one wrong move on my part could be enough to destroy everything. I am lucky to be liked and I always have a group of friends, but I also have the tendency to lose friends. I lie awake at night and wonder if there is something wrong with me to explain the high turnover rate. On the nights I let myself think deeply about it, my treacherous mind takes me to an awful, painful place.

I think about my parents, who were always too busy to spend time with me. I think about how much of my life I've spent feeling like a burden, a nuisance, an obligation. How could I expect my friends, who don't have the same familial obligations, to make time for me?

I consider what it is about me that makes it so easy to cast me aside. *Is there something wrong with me?* To my parents, I must be defective in several ways. I am a girl. I am too lazy to help them out on a daily basis. I am too disobedient because when I do help out, it's with a scowl and a nasty stink-eye on my face.

But my parents' absence in my life is an old bruise. My sudden erasure from my treasured friend group on the other hand—that one's new. That one *hurts*. I was gone for only two weeks. That was all it took to be left behind and forgotten.

My mind spins. The pit swallows me up inch by inch. Like the last time I was cast out of a friend group, I wonder if it's because I'm different. So Chinese. Too Chinese. *Is it because boys don't flock to me the way they do to my replacement? Am I ugly? Do I talk too much? Is being funny worse than being hot?* I'm a teenage girl, so of course I know that being hot is way better than being the funny girl. No one's first romantic choice is the funny girl. Now, apparently no one wants to be friends with the funny girl either.

These thoughts are my only company for the rest of summer. I nurture them and let them run wild and free until they become cruel, dangerous, and consuming. Combine this with my overwhelming loneliness and teenage angst, and this toxic mixture—this thick, tarry soup of emotions—washes over me like a suffocating tidal wave. The pain is unbearable, and I struggle to understand the enormity of my feelings. Even though I have other, likely more steadfast friends I could call, my ejection from this particular group of friends makes me feel so worthless and unlovable that I don't bother trying. *Better to be alone than rejected.*

It all just plain *hurts*. But I can't explain exactly why I hurt or where I hurt. All I know is that while my old friends are out laughing and drinking and enjoying life, I am at home, alone and crying and wanting to end mine. While they fantasize about each other, I am fantasizing about ending my pain in the most permanent way possible.

I become a casual observer of my own life. The black pit of despair is infectious. It's spreading. There is no joy anywhere now that it's come for me.

I start listening to angry, screaming music and drawing pictures of guns, knives, and blood. I learn to numb myself to my overwhelming emotions. When I can no longer feel anything, I turn to self-harm. Physical pain, I learn, is preferable to feeling nothing. At least this way, I'm in control of the pain. On the outside, I am emotionless like a robot, but on the inside, a war is being waged, and the only way I can find release from it is to feel the sting and trickle of blood down my arm.

The first time I cut myself, I feel pain, but it is a pain that makes sense. I can point to it and say, "My arm hurts," and pinpoint the exact source of the ache. I can clean it up, put a bandage on, and do something tangible to fix and soothe myself.

I did this. I did this. I did this.

My spirit-crushing sadness and loneliness is different. I can't point to it. There is nothing tangible to show. No warm running water or bandages can make it all feel better.

But, I think, the root cause is all the same. I have clearly done something. I have been too much or not enough of something to cause grave offense. There is a reason why my friends no longer want to hang out with me. *I did this. I did this. I did this.*

I start seeing a therapist at the hospital in Leamington. He's an older white man who's prone to closing his eyes and resting his chin on his chest while I answer his questions.

"Hmm?" he says. His chin wobbles and tilts downwards.

"Yes," I answer. I roll my eyes, but he doesn't see me.

"I'll see you next week then?"

"Yes."

———

To make matters worse, it feels like I'm being tormented at school.

When a girl in one of my classes overhears me saying I'm hungry, she cracks a joke for everyone to hear.

"Rachel's hungry! Hide your pet cats and dogs!"

There's a stunned silence. I'm grateful no one laughs.

For the first time, I stand up for myself. I say the words so many people hate to hear. The phrase that gets people so riled up and defensive. The one that causes so many white tears.

"You're racist."

She cries and says she didn't mean anything by it. She denies having a racist bone in her body. She says anyone who knows her heart would know she was just joking, and God, how was she supposed to know that I wouldn't be able to take a joke?

My blood is boiling. I count down the days until I am free from this small town. From this small life. I'm tired of always being on edge and having to be hypervigilant in every single social interaction. I hate that I'm never allowed to forget I am Chinese, no matter how hard I try to distance myself from it. I am never allowed to forget that I am different. I am never allowed to relax. I can never just exist.

When did I stop being a human and become the joke? And how do I make it all stop?

———

After tenth grade passes by in a lonely blur, I eventually find a new group of friends—people who also listen to screamy music and wear clothes from West49 and have dramatic emo side bangs like I do. They're as sad and emotional as I am. We bond during shows at the town arena, where we pay a couple bucks on the weekend to have local bands scream in our faces.

I become best friends with a boy. He is one of the smartest people I've ever met. He futilely tries to show me how to properly wrap presents based on math and angles, and we spend hours holed up in my room watching movies, and listening to AFI and Gogol Bordello in his car.

There is a girl at school who has a crush on him. She and I were best friends in the eighth grade, but we didn't survive my friendship turnover rate. We had a falling out because I was "too demanding." I was.

Ravaged by jealousy, she begins to harass me at school, too. It starts with snide remarks in the back of a science classroom. She tells me she hates me. She says I am a bitch. She tells me he's too good for me and that he'll know soon enough how awful I am. She tells me she won't let me treat him the way I treated her. She calls me worse things.

I switch to a different science class, but our high school of four hundred students is small and she always finds me in the hallway. I get used to the sound of her cruel laughter and cutting remarks trailing me.

Her tormenting reaches its peak at a Halloween party. I am dressed as a saloon girl in a flimsy red dress and chatting with friends when she walks over to me. Before I can say a word or move away from her, she's pouring her full bottle of lukewarm beer over my head. The liquid seeps through my hair and drips down my neck and back.

Embarrassment and shame course through me and heat my face red. I can hear her laughing in the face of my public humiliation. A hyena laughing as it eats its prey alive.

The black pit swallows me whole then. I despair. There's no standing up for myself now. *How many people saw her do it? Who was laughing with her? Will I ever be able to show my face in school again? God, why does this hurt so much?*

The night's horrors are just beginning.

—⁓—

Some boys from a different high school flock to me because they are friends with my cousin. One of them—a short boy with a weak chin and gigantic teeth—doesn't ask for my name or make an effort to engage in actual conversation with me. He just smiles a slimy, lazy smile and says, "So, what's it like to be a rice [n-word]?" His eyes are glazed from the potent combination of weed and booze, but they're trained on me. Focused. Expecting an answer.

My hand grips tightly around my bottle of green apple Sour Puss. I lean in, certain I'm not hearing correctly. "What?"

That slimy smile again.

"You're a rice [n-word]. What's that like?" He gives no additional explanation. I am expected to know what this slur means. I am expected to claim it as my identity. It is meant to be who I am.

My mouth goes paper dry. But before I can respond, one of my friends is grabbing me by the elbow and dragging me away. "Ew, don't talk to him. He's a loser."

I am alarmed and taken aback by this stranger's audacity. I think about how he is my cousin's friend. I wonder whether they call my cousin these names and tease him for being Chinese. I remember this same cousin telling me how it would be easier if he weren't Chinese, and I just know in my gut that, yes, they do.

Another boy at the party takes to calling me "bird flu" because, back then, avian influenza was widely referred to as "Asian bird flu."

"Is 'bird flu' still here after getting that beer dumped all over her? Is it safe to have 'bird flu' here?"

Bird flu. Bird flu. Bird flu.

I try to avoid him whenever I can at school—he's annoying and quite dumb, clearly—but his words trail me wherever I go. Of course they'd follow me here, to one of the worst nights of my life. I am not human to him. I am a disease. I am someone to avoid at all costs. Better yet, I am someone to eradicate entirely. I feel with certainty that everyone at the party feels the same way.

I go home and cry and hurt myself, but there's no relief this time. I am numb and tired of living. I think the only way to get out of school—out of seeing these people ever again—is to remove myself entirely. My joy of finding a new friend group where I belong and feel accepted is fleeting. Already gone. I'll never belong. I am dumb to have thought so. Dying is better. It's easier than always feeling like I'm on the outs.

The next day, I bluntly tell my parents that I want to kill myself.

I choose the moment carefully. We're in the kitchen of the restaurant and my parents both have their backs turned to me. Their focus is on the woks in front of them—always looking down and never directly at me. I don't remember the words I say or what happens. I've become used to feeling like I'm outside of myself and watching my life happen as an invisible bystander.

But what happens next defies the churn of painful memories. My parents—maybe my brother, too—stop what they're doing and rush me to the hospital. The people working in the ER at the Leamington hospital don't know how to handle a suicidal teenage girl, so I am sent via ambulance forty-five minutes away to Hôtel-Dieu Grace Hospital in Windsor.

I am diagnosed with severe clinical depression. I become a psych ward patient.

My parents are at their wits' end. Why is their youngest daughter always crying? Why does she want to die? Does she not have everything she could ever want? Does she not have more than they could have ever dreamed of while they were growing up, hiding in the mountains of Vietnam? And what is this "depression" the doctors keep talking about?

As in so many other Chinese families, the stigma of mental illness—although existing everywhere and transcending all cultures—is especially prominent within mine. My parents grew up in a culture where the mentally ill were not seen as suffering from a medical condition, but rather from a character flaw. The pervasive ignorance and misconceptions regarding

mental illness in Chinese diasporas meant my inexplicable sadness terrified my parents.

In my family, the emphasis in healthcare is on the physical—things you
can feel and touch and see. Because I can't easily point to a body part and
say, "Hey, I have a broken so-and-so," my parents don't understand what
the hell is wrong with me.

"Chinese people, we don't talk about things like depression," Dad says
to me, much later. "We don't know there's that kind of disease. We never
hear about it. If you get depression over there, they don't say anything. We
don't even have a name for it over there."

My family members aren't the most delicate when it comes to speaking
their minds, and culturally, it wouldn't be seen as cruel or insensitive to call
someone a "crazy lunatic" to their face. Because my parents don't actually
have the terminology to discuss mental illness, many of the words used to
describe mental health conditions are, regrettably, variations of the word
"crazy," or *chi sin*.

A Chinese psychiatrist once tells me, "The Chinese, even though we have
such rich languages, have no names for feelings. If you have no words for
it, then it doesn't exist." Teenage me would have loved nothing more than
for the bad feelings to not exist.

This refusal to give such illnesses a name feeds into several cultures'
complicated histories with and treatment of mental disorders. A complex
interplay of factors influences the attitudes of the affected, their families
and friends, and Chinese communities across the globe.

During the Cultural Revolution, which took place in China from 1966
to 1976, Chairman Mao Zedong had mental illness declared a bourgeois
self-delusion and enforced that the ill be treated with his readings. The
stigma of mental illness then percolated from mainland China and other
regions with historically Chinese populations, like Hong Kong and Taiwan,
into various Chinese communities throughout the world, including Canada,
where China is consistently one of the top source countries for immigration. In the People's Republic of China, mental illness was often treated
as a government problem rather than a medical problem, and throughout

history, people considered to be mentally ill—whether they actually were or not—were thrown in prison-like asylums. It was not uncommon for ill individuals to be shackled, ignored, and left to languish in the basements of family homes by relatives who were either too poor, too ashamed, or too ignorant to seek help. Between 2007 and 2010, mental health workers rescued 339 people from such a fate.

It was also not unheard of for the mentally ill to be murdered, either by relatives who could no longer deal with the burden and shame of caring for an individual with an illness they didn't understand, or by perfect strangers who feared the ill. These deaths were often not mourned or treated as criminal cases because many saw the mentally ill as being less than human.

In recent years, China has worked to reform its mental healthcare system to improve standards of care and combat stigma. The way people perceive and view mental illness has gradually shifted over the years thanks to increased public awareness campaigns and education efforts by mental health advocates and government agencies.

Because of these shifting attitudes, a recent phenomenon indicates that new immigrants are often more progressive in their ways of thinking, whereas immigrants who came decades ago, like my parents, are still living with the cultural beliefs that were prominent when they left their home countries. Whatever advances in mental healthcare have happened in their home countries haven't been translated to them in their new countries. Their beliefs and misconceptions are essentially frozen in time.

These beliefs include the notion that mental illness is contagious and capable of making you "crazy" just by association. It's a scourge that prevents you from being a productive member of society—that is, employed and married with a family. It infects and shames entire families. These persistent attitudes directly affect an individual's ability to seek and obtain proper treatment. Statistics show that when people do seek help and are properly diagnosed, many harbour the diagnosis like a dirty secret, afraid that the shame will make them lose face.

The concept of "having face" is deeply rooted in several cultures across Asia, particularly in East Asian and Southeast Asian communities. It doesn't mean one's literal face, but rather their social standing. Face is a metaphor for a person's reputation and prestige within the workplace, their family, their friends, and society at large. One's position and status in the eyes of others dictates how much respect they can expect to receive. The better one's reputation is and the more prestige they appear to have, the more secure their face is. In the eyes of many—including my family—a mental health condition is enough to ruin a person's reputation, as well as the reputation of their family.

According to a 2010 study in the *Asian Journal of Social Psychology*, only about 25 percent of Asian Americans who had been diagnosed with psychological problems actually sought treatment, compared to more than 50 percent of the general population of the United States. In 2022, another study found that only 2.2 percent of first-generation Asian Americans, 3.5 percent of second-generation Asian Americans, and 10.1 percent of third-generation or later Asian Americans sought out specialty mental health services. Overall, Asian Americans are 50 percent less likely than other racial groups to seek help for mental health conditions. The fear of discrimination, rejection, and social repercussions prevents many people from seeking help or being open about what they are experiencing.

Interestingly, different studies show that second-generation Chinese Canadians actually have more mental illness than their immigrant parents. One hypothesized reason is that the children of immigrants don't have a root culture to hold onto—that third-culture kid phenomenon—while another suggests that the second generation is simply more open to admitting a problem and seeking help.

I can't speak to the studies and the academic numbers. But I can understand not fully belonging anywhere. I understand feeling untethered and unmoored, with no roots anywhere to anchor you down. I understand how this makes you feel like you're on an island, alone and without the hope of rescue.

Beyond the perceived social impacts of mental illness, cultural beliefs also contribute to the stigma. Chinese collectivism versus Western individualism means there's more at risk when a Chinese person becomes mentally ill. In traditional Chinese culture, a heavy emphasis is placed on family honour, harmony, and saving face. Instead of it being an individual problem, the entire family is responsible for the sickness. A person who is mentally ill may be perceived as disrupting the family harmony and bringing dishonour to the family. Individuals then become reluctant to acknowledge an illness and seek treatment for something that will make the entire family look bad.

This means it's not uncommon for families to keep mental illness a secret. The family lies about it to save the family's face or to increase the marriageability of its members. It's a sense of shame that the family protects and keeps close to home.

I have an aunt whom family members talk about in whispers and half-statements.

"She went a little crazy."

"Your uncle woke up and she was throwing everything into the garbage, screaming and yelling like a crazy person."

Sometimes I ask about her. It's been years since I've seen her.

From what I can gather from the dribs and drabs, she hardly ever leaves the house. She's usually left all alone. She can't drive or speak English and is almost entirely isolated while her husband works long hours.

I think, *if that were me, I would go "a little crazy" too*, but I don't dare say that out loud.

I know the Western stereotypes of Chinese parents.

You have your Asian tiger moms and dads who only accept A grades from their children—"We're A-sians, not B-sians!"—whom they push to study and to work exceptionally hard so they can become successful doctors, lawyers, or engineers. But excelling in school and at work is only part of the deal. On the side, children must also be able to play violin or piano. They must be well-rounded and deeply attractive prospects for future partners. They must marry equally successful partners and add successful grandchildren to the family. They honour their parents' hard work and sacrifices by extending the ancestral line and taking care of their elders as they age. There's no time for mental health breaks and no room for character flaws and familial stains like mental illness.

Although these stereotypes and generalizations are fundamentally damaging, there's no denying that the pressure to succeed is often too much for the children whose reality this is.

My parents hardly ever follow the blueprint for stereotypical Chinese parents. They never once utter the words "engineer," "doctor," or "lawyer" to us. They never look at our report cards. And I am never forced into piano or violin lessons. Yet, although my parents don't explicitly pressure me to succeed, their actions are enough to put the burden on my shoulders all the same. I watch the way they work long-hour days, every single day, to build a stable life in their new country. I tell myself their sacrifices have to be worth it in the long run. I have to succeed, do better, make it all worthwhile.

The pressure intensifies with other words spoken.

My dad is always quick to regale us with stories about growing up during the Vietnam War. If one of us complains about the cold morning walk to school, we are met with a scoff. "When I was nine years old, I had to walk two hours to get to school—two hours! You can't walk five minutes?" Or if one of us leaves some food behind on the plate: "When I was young, your grandpa only made enough money to buy one *bánh mì* a week—we all had to share!" My siblings and I groan, "Here he goes again," but we always stop complaining and quickly eat the offending leftover food.

Although it's true my parents were never tiger parents to us, I still feel the pressure to succeed at all costs. My parents crossed an ocean, started from scratch in a completely new land, and worked their bodies to the bone to give us everything we could ever ask for.

When I am in the hospital, I feel so much self-loathing and shame for the way I've paid them back for their sacrifice.

How soft and weak am I that I have turned out this way? What kind of ungrateful daughter am I?

On top of this self-imposed pressure, we become familiar with the feeling of never being good enough. There is always something about us to critique.

I always say my parents are so laid-back, they're horizontal. I get away with so much more than my friends do. But for all their bucking of the stereotypes, my parents regrettably continue one time-honoured Chinese tradition: offering cruel, ruthless, unsolicited commentary about their children's bodies.

I grow up hearing the adults in my family—our endless aunts and uncles on both sides—calling my brother, "*fei jai*," or "fat boy," or commenting on my sister's "thunder thighs." My poor sister also struggles with acne, perplexing my parents, both of whom are blessed with clear, seemingly pore-free skin.

"You must be eating too much fried foods or pizza. Too much *yeet hay*," Dad tells her, his voice chiding, his tongue clicking.

In Cantonese, *yeet hay* literally translates to "hot air" and often refers to foods that are spicy, fried, or greasy, like chips, fries, and pizza. *Yeet hay* is also used to describe the symptoms a person may experience after eating these types of food, including sore throat, fatigue, and yes, acne. It's rooted in the traditional Chinese belief that there is *yin* (cold) and *yang* (hot) energy in food. When your body has elevated levels of *yang*, an imbalance occurs and you may suffer the symptoms above, or "too much *yeet hay*."

It's also a classic way for my parents—and many Chinese parents around the world—to manipulate and shame their children into eating cooling (read: appropriate) foods while providing easy solutions to save us, their hapless kids. "Linh, *wah*, look at your pimple," Mum says, pointing, peering closely at the offending pimple as if my sister has ceased to exist and all that remains is one angry red spot. "Drink this tea. Help with *yeet hay*."

The fun doesn't stop with just my parents. Our whole extended family joins in whenever the moment is right, which for them is whenever the thought floats into their heads. To them, such comments are meant to be helpful, as if we need them to call attention to it, as if we aren't already aware.

For Christmas one year, our aunt brings each of us presents. Linh's is heavy, and we wonder at the promise and treasure that could be held within. When she rips open the wrapping paper and sees the contents, her shining eyes turn sad. Her excitement shifts to confusion.

In her hands lies a gigantic hardcover textbook with what must be hundreds upon hundreds of pages. Emblazoned on the front cover is a mouthful of a title: *The Doctor's Book of Home Remedies: Thousands of Tips and Techniques Anyone Can Use to Heal Everyday Health Problems*. Needless to say, this book was not on my sister's Christmas wish list. When my sister looks at my aunt with questioning eyes, my aunt looks puzzled by her response.

She grabs the book from my sister's hands and turns to the table of contents, her fingers trailing over the page until she finds what she is looking for. She turns it to face my sister.

"See? There's a chapter in there on skin conditions and acne," she says, her smile huge. Her eyes are earnest and well-meaning. As if she needs to provide more exposition—as if my sister might not be following her train of thinking—my aunt says in a voice she must have thought was her kindest, most gentle, most helpful one: "It can help you with your pimples." Her eyes rove over my sister's face and stay there, as if she is counting, taking stock.

My sister's excitement shifts from confusion to anger to shame to embarrassment. The jolly merriment of the holidays evaporates from the room. I don't know what to say, so I say nothing. We always say nothing. You don't talk back to your elders. You smile and say "thank you" and save the tears for later, when you are alone in your bedroom and there is no one but yourself to judge.

I don't know if that's what my sister does because I never bother to ask how the gift made her feel. I am still of the age when I trust that the adults in my life know best. I still believe that their good intentions are there to protect and guide us, and if something makes me sad or feel an inexplicable pain in my chest, it is because there is something wrong with me. It is simply a sign that I need more protection, more guidance, more cruel words. We are lucky to be corrected by so many smiling, well-meaning

people. We are lucky to have so many people in our lives who are so free
with their advice.

—⁓—

At my lowest, it was not uncommon for people to have reservations about
whether I was actually sick. From my parents to my friends to my own
psychiatrist, people were confused by the smiling, high achieving girl who,
when she was alone, wanted nothing more than to feel the sharp edge of
a safety pin against her skin.

I remember sitting in my psychiatrist's office a few weeks before
my hospitalization, feeling defeated and hating every second of being
alive. My psychiatrist, who is not Chinese, walks in and tells me that
I "look good."

Taken aback, I respond, "I tried to kill myself last week."

He blinks, processing this vital piece of information, before dismissing
my revelation with a quick flick of his wrist.

"No, you look good."

Then he stands up and walks out of the room, leaving behind an emotionally destroyed teenager. Our session lasted five whole minutes.

When he does listen to me, which is very rare, my psychiatrist's only solution is to either prescribe more medication or increase my dose. By the time I
am seventeen years old, I am on four different pills: two types of Wellbutrin,
Celexa, and an antipsychotic called Risperdal that helps me focus and sleep.

This same psychiatrist also works at the hospital where I am staying.
He comes to see me a few days after I am admitted. I squirm under his
gaze as he assesses me. It is the most he's looked at me since I became
his patient.

"What happened, Rachel? I saw you not that long ago and you
seemed good."

I wasn't. But I'd learned that he wouldn't listen to me even if I corrected him.

I shrug and say, "I feel sad all the time. I want to die."

He nods and jots something down in his notebook.

"We can up the Wellbutrin then," is all he says.

———

At first, I don't mind the hospital. The people in my wing are nice and happy to leave me alone with my books. I do hate the early wake-up calls and the hospital gowns that gape in all the places I want privacy. The food is flavourless mush and my roommate often stands over me in the middle of the night while I'm sleeping, but I prefer it a thousand times over mean girls and high school.

When I talk on the phone to my high school guidance counselor about how I've been tormented by that girl and what she did at the Halloween party, she reassures me in a deeply apologetic voice that she'll speak to her. "This is unacceptable and will not happen again. But don't you worry about that right now. You just focus on getting better."

I'm so happy to be away from that awful place that I don't even shoo my roommate away the next time I catch her watching me sleep.

Visiting hours at the hospital are from six to seven every evening. I don't think anyone will come to see me. The restaurant will be busy with the dinner rush, and even if that weren't the case, driving from Leamington to Windsor at the same time everyone else is leaving work for the day sounds like a tremendous inconvenience.

When six o'clock rolls around and Mum and Dad show up, I am moved to tears.

"But . . . the restaurant?" I say in between sobs. Mum hugs me and rubs my back and waves me off like she's saying, "Oh, shut up, you silly girl." Dad looks at me with so much care and concern that I have to look away because it's so unfamiliar. I feel too seen, too held. *This is what I've been missing my whole life.*

We sit together and make small talk—they ask about the food, how I'm feeling, whether I've been sleeping. I ask about the drive and the restaurant. We dance around the topic of my depression and the confession that landed me here. When they leave, I hug them both with so much ferocity that my mother winces. They squeeze me back.

For the rest of my time in the hospital, one—if not both—of them comes every single day during visiting hours. It's the first time I've felt like a real priority. It's the first time I've believed I come first, even before the restaurant.

A few days into my hospital stay, I am moved to another wing.

"You should be with girls your own age," the nurse tells me.

I share my new room with three other girls. They look at me and sneer before turning to each other and laughing. I deflate and feel like I'm back in the hallways of my high school all over again.

They talk about me in the middle of the night while I squeeze my eyes shut. I try to force myself to fall asleep, but I am hanging on their every word.

"Stuck-up chink bitch," one of them says. "You can tell she thinks she's better than us. Well, surprise, bitch, you're in here just like us. Fucking psycho."

I bury my face in the scratchy hospital bed-sheets and let myself cry. In the morning, I tell myself I need to be gone.

"The doctor says you cannot leave yet," the nurse says the next day. Her voice is firm, but her eyes are soft. The girls in my room have teased her, too. ("Ay Miss Piggy, why are you such a dumb bitch?")

I can't bear the thought of spending another night in that room. My tenuous control over my own emotions is too fragile. Their taunts might send me over the cliff's edge entirely.

"Well, can I be moved?"

She shakes her head and tells me there's no space anywhere. "It's Saturday. We had a lot of people admitted yesterday," she explains. "But how's this? Your doctor said you could go home for one night, but your parents have to bring you right back tomorrow, alright?"

Relief floods through me. I'm so happy that when I call my mother, my hands shake.

I pack all my things carefully, making sure nothing is left behind. It's not like I brought much anyway.

When I sign out for my overnight visit, I hustle out of the hospital like I'm a criminal. I wait for someone to guess my true intentions and call me back. I expect to be put in a straitjacket and thrown into solitary for being a wicked, lying, misbehaving girl.

I jump into my mother's car and urge her to go fast.

"Go, go, go," I say.

I already know I'm never coming back.

When I don't return the next day, no one calls or comes to pick me up. No one says or does anything.

It's only when I call my psychiatrist a few weeks later that his receptionist tells me on the phone, "I'm sorry, Rachel. The doctor says he refuses to see you because you didn't listen to his order to stay in the hospital. You are no longer his patient."

I am seventeen years old, and I am left completely on my own.

The first thing I do is take myself off all the pills. I get drunk for the first time in almost a year. It turns out my emo music–loving friends still like me and want to hang out with me. I wonder, not for the last time, whether my depression was lying to me when it convinced me I was all alone and had nobody.

"Something's different. You're human again," one of my friends says at the party, after I drink a single shot of Absolut vodka.

I tell him I took myself off my heavy cocktail of antidepressants and antipsychotics.

"I can tell. You were like a robot before. Just blank," he says, clinking his bottle against mine. "Welcome back!"

Even though I throw up all over his bedroom floor not even an hour later, I feel happier than I've felt in a long time. I'm not a heavily medicated automaton anymore. I nurse my headache and nausea while Death Cab for Cutie's "I Will Follow You Into the Dark" plays and my friends talk and laugh on the other side of the door—and I feel everything.

A few months later, a girl in my high school hangs herself outside of the school. A gym class finds her body in the morning.

I am in math class when my school therapist pokes his head into the classroom. He spots me and his body sags with relief. When he pulls me out of the class, he simply says, "Oh, thank God. I heard the news and worried it was you."

My drama teacher finds me in the hallway later and says the same.

I don't know what to say. I'm just glad it wasn't me.

———

A Canadian-born Chinese friend once tells me that we tend to rationalize anything that can be a symptom of mental illness. Instead of receiving medical care and attention, the sick are often treated with insensitivity for not being able to deal with their issues.

"They're always like, 'Oh, you're not hurting. You're just being sensitive. Why are you being so emotional? Why can't you just suck it up and think about something else to make it go away?'" she says.

I think about how my mother would comfort me when I was at my lowest.

"Just don't think too much, okay? Don't think too much."

I hated that she didn't get it and that she didn't get me. I hated that she thought the solution to my depression was as easy as turning my brain off. I hated that she laid the blame for my sickness at my feet. It was *my* fault for thinking too much.

I'm more sympathetic to her now. I think about how helpless and lost she must have felt. What else could she say?

For my parents, it must have been difficult to grasp the fact that I was so ill. After all, I was still getting As, and I could still occasionally joke around. I've also always been a headstrong, stubborn girl. Someone of my strength couldn't possibly be "weak."

"Our parents felt helpless and didn't understand why you were like that," my sister says. "They wanted you to be happy, so they would agree to all your requests, whatever they were, in order for you not to be sadder. Mum and Dad were just overcompensating to make sure you would be happy."

Sometime after my stay at Hôtel Dieu Grace Hospital, my parents allow me to rescue a senior, diabetic cat from near euthanasia to serve as my constant companion. A year later, my dad adopts a dog to make me happy. Family members come out of the woodwork to offer their support, including an uncle who buys a very expensive Fender guitar for me to barely play.

Even before my hospital stay, my parents supported me in the ways they knew how. Since I was on so many different types of medication, my treatment was very expensive, costing upwards of $300 per month. My parents paid without question because they wanted to make sure I was getting better. But still, their understanding of mental illness remained naturally, insultingly primitive.

When Seung-Hui Cho shoots and kills thirty-two people at Virginia Tech in 2007, my mother has a conversation with one of our waitresses about the shooter. She says completely nonchalantly, with zero malice and self-awareness: "Oh, he had what Rachel had."

My mother doesn't understand that mental health is a spectrum. Symptoms can range from just feeling a little tired and lethargic to the more severe that can lead to school shootings. To her, if you're mentally ill, you're all the same. Sadly, this is how many people think.

At my most sick, I remember feeling so low and worthless because my parents had always given so much, beginning with their journey to Canada, to give their children a better life. It was a vicious cycle: the depression made me feel worthless, and those feelings made me feel guilty, which in turn, made me feel even more worthless. I wished more than anything that my condition could easily be explained away with a little *yeet hay*.

When I think about my past and that terrible time in my life, the bright light that grounds me is remembering my parents' visits every day, restaurant be damned. They didn't understand my illness—it scared and confused them—but they still drove forty-five minutes every day to see me.

"I feel sad and I cried. I didn't understand. I don't know what happened and I can't do nothing," my mother would later say to me, before I quickly changed the subject, not wanting to reopen the wound that took so long to heal.

Fast-forward almost a decade, and I am in my mid-twenties. I live alone for the first time in Toronto.

I am having a breakdown on my bathroom floor. The kind of breakdown in which you hyperventilate and your body convulses with deep, wracking sobs. The kind of breakdown in which you call your parents and start bawling and they say, "We're coming."

It's a Saturday, the busiest day of the week for the restaurant. When I resist and tell them they have to work, they make a sound like "Oh, shut up, you silly girl." It's like déjà vu.

They drive for four hours—three and a half, probably, knowing my dad's driving—and arrive in the city. My hands grasp for them and I cry in their chests, their shoulders. They hold me and look at each other, not sure what to say or do. We turn to food, like we always do. Our shared love language.

"Are you hungry?" Dad asks. "Let's go to Chinatown and get dinner."

My parents order three times the amount of food we'd normally order. "For later, so you have food to eat," Mum says. She tells Dad to order extra *siu mai* because it's my favourite.

We don't talk about my sadness or why they dropped everything they were doing and closed the restaurant so they could come be with me. We sit together and eat, and it feels like a healing ointment for my battered spirit.

When they drop me off at home a few hours later, they give me another round of hugs and say goodbye. They drive the four hours back and get home around midnight, just in time to sleep before a new day at the restaurant.

Another decade later, and I am in my mid-thirties. My dog, Ivy, is dying from hemangiosarcoma, one of the deadliest, most aggressive canine cancers.

For more than ten years, Ivy was my anchor. My source of comfort during periodic bouts of depression. My constant through life's major events: the first decade of my career, living on my own for the first time, being single, being slutty, falling in love, getting engaged, getting married.

She is dying, suddenly, and I am a wreck.

It's a Friday and my parents are still working at the restaurant. But they leave right when it closes, around ten o'clock. They drive the four hours and get to the house I share with my husband at one-thirty in the morning. They are here to say goodbye to Ivy and to comfort us. They come bringing a box of food.

We fall into a fitful sleep at two in the morning and wake up six hours later. My parents say their goodbyes, shake one final paw, and caress Ivy's velvety soft ears one last time. By 10 A.M. they are already on the road back to Leamington.

I am thirty-four, and I am finally realizing that my parents do put me first, even at great inconvenience to them—*especially* at great inconvenience to them. I couldn't put their perceived abandonment of me in perspective when I was a lonely child or angsty teenager. But I'm starting to understand now.

Their love for me may not have looked the way I wanted it to look when I was growing up, but I can see how they always did the best they could with the puzzle pieces they were given. They show up where and when it counts. My struggle with depression is the backdrop upon which their deep love for me is thrown into sharp relief. It has also allowed me to recognize and appreciate my innate ability to survive—a gift I inherited from my parents.

This is what I know now: their love and care mean everything to me. It might have been the difference between choosing life or death.

8

"HAVE YOU EATEN YET?"

Unlike my sister and brother, who are forced to work weekends and weeknights at the restaurant while growing up, I make my own hours, which is to say, I barely work at all.

As a child, I sometimes hear my mother and aunt talking about me. "*Hou laan*," they'll say. *Very lazy*.

It's not that I'm lazy. I still make trays and trays of wontons faster than everybody but Mum. I blast dirty plates with the high-pressure hose so they're already sparkling clean before I run them through the restaurant's commercial dishwasher. I fold crisp white napkins into the shape of a crown that will make a customer beam with joy when they jokingly place it on their head. I help out when asked. The difference is that I have the privilege and luxury of being asked. It is not a weighty expectation placed on my shoulders the way it is for Linh and John.

Because of that, I am soft. My hands don't know the grind of hard work the way the bodies of my family do. They coddle me and spoil me and do everything for me whenever they have a moment to spare.

"You're my baby. I take care of you," Mum says when she peels my grapes, debones my fish, makes me congee.

By the time I am nineteen and about to leave home for the first time, I am certifiably clueless. I don't know how to do laundry. I've never had to cook. I am a hunched-over mess with a broom and a mop. Despite spending most of my childhood in my own company, tending to my own needs, I'm not in the least prepared to be independent and self-sufficient. For the first time, I start to understand and appreciate just how much my parents have done for me, out there on the fringes of my life.

Before the realization comes, I finish my final year of high school, where the pressure mounts to know what I want to be when I grow up. I decide on journalism. It's a natural fit. It makes sense.

Never once do I remember my mum and dad asking me what I want to be. I don't even remember telling them I'd made the decision. When I get my acceptance letters to various universities across southern Ontario, all I tell them is that, like Linh, I'll also be going to university. They beam at me.

"Good girl!" they say. "Smart girl!" They look at me for a beat before they're back to wiping the sweat off their brows and working the wok. I know they're happy I'm going to school. My parents, having been robbed of an education by the Vietnam War, see this as evidence we're surpassing them.

"It's my biggest regret in life, not going to school," Dad often says. "You're lucky you can get an education. You can do anything."

But I don't feel like I can do anything.

It's 2007 and I'm crammed in my dad's SUV with my parents, my sister, and all the things I've decided I can't possibly live without. There are pens and binders, an absolute brick of a Toshiba laptop, and a set of three pairs of too-long pajama pants from Costco. My legs are covered in mosquito bites from a tryst I had on the grass of my friend's front lawn.

I am clearly not an adult.

When I get to my residence, I am relieved to see there is a queue to get inside. I'm milking as much time as I can get with my family while I still have them here. For a teenager who found family time an inconvenient nuisance, I am suddenly clingy and needy.

My sister takes pictures of me—proof that the baby is finally flying the coop. I am a mess of nerves. *What if no one likes me? What if no one looks like me? Will I be all alone?*

As a young girl, I was prone to homesickness. Whenever I spent a week in Toronto with my cousins, I would inevitably call the restaurant crying on the first night, then the third night, and so on, until I started actually having fun and decided I didn't want to go home after all.

"Mum, I want to come home," I'd cry, hearing the clattering of plates and the ring of the bell in the background telling the waitress a hot plate was ready to be served. I'd long to be there in the thick of the action. How strange. When I was at the restaurant, I hated it, but when I was away, I didn't feel free. I felt untethered and unmoored. I was lost.

Mum would sigh and tell me I'd be home soon. "Don't cry," she'd say, more of a reprimand than words of comfort. "Why you crying? You're a big girl."

The thing is, I didn't feel like a big girl then—I was seven—and I certainly don't feel like a big girl now at the age of nineteen.

It all happens so fast. My parents and Linh help me move my giant Rubbermaid containers into my apartment-style dorm. We say hello and awkwardly introduce ourselves to an exceeding number of smiling strangers. I notice, fleetingly, that most people are white. My parents and sister hug me tightly. When Mum squeezes me like one of the lemons in her sugary-sweet lemonade, she reminds me not to cry. "You're a big girl," she says. This time her tone has no jagged edge. This time, she is all care and comfort.

It makes me miss her all the more when they leave me. I feel the weight of their absence press in from every direction. I am well and truly alone. I don't feel free at all.

It helps that I become fast friends with the four other girls in my apartment. We stay up late talking, harbour crushes on the boys on our floor, and drink most days of the week. They are all white, but it doesn't bother me. I am already used to being the only Asian.

The girl I share a room with becomes my best friend. We make each other howl with laughter each night with delirious, sleep-deprived jokes made at four in the morning. We dance and sing along to Britney's latest album release, *Blackout*, on repeat. I tell her about the pressure I feel to be perfect and why I want so badly to succeed as a journalist. She tells me that all she wants to be is a mom. Her maternal instincts enable me and make it so I don't have to grow up just yet. She cooks for me so I'm not surviving only off roast beef sandwiches, instant noodles, and Sidekicks. We strike a deal in our first week after I confess that I've never done laundry in my life. "I'll pay for laundry," I say, holding up the bulging burgundy bag of coins my mother gave me before I moved, "if you actually do the laundry." She, recognizing an excellent deal, agrees all too happily.

Another girl in our apartment shows me the most effective way to wash dishes. I am paying for my own schooling, but really, it's all student loans, so others show me how to eat economically—one roommate swears by canned sardines, another favours frozen tortellini. My preference is for the containers of fried rice and curry chicken my parents made for me before I moved away. They sit in our freezer, slowly accumulating freezer burn. I relish these tastes of home and try my best to space out when I eat them. I reach for the containers when I feel sad, stressed, lonely. I reach for them when I miss home.

Even though I miss my family, I don't always call home because I am nineteen and inconsiderate and unavailable.

When I do call, Mum asks the first question Chinese parents ask their kids: "*Sik fan mei*?" or "Have you eaten yet?" For us, it's a common greeting that serves the same function as asking "How are you?" In my family, like so many other Chinese families, eating well and eating properly is critical, so asking someone whether they've eaten yet is a way of expressing care and concern for their wellbeing.

"Takeout again?" Mum asks after I tell her what I've eaten. She always asks if I still have leftover frozen food from her and Dad.

Our phone calls are brief, if I even remember to call her at all.

—~~—

When the last of the food from my parents runs out in the freezer, it hits me harder than expected. I call my mother and whine. She laughs and says, "Well, come home then!" I ask her how much they'd charge to deliver three hours away. We laugh and joke, but I feel a gnawing ache in the pit of my belly.

I don't know how to cook, let alone how to cook Chinese food. I'm the only one in my family who never learned how—and I certainly wasn't going to try, in a dorm kitchen, to cook the mouth-watering dishes my parents make. Anything I do would be a sad bastardization of the magic they pull together, so why try?

But now, all I want is the warm comfort of Mum's *gon choy tong* or Dad's *zheng shui dan*. I am keenly aware of how far away from home I am. I am surprised by the intensity of the pain I feel because of that.

Hours away from home, I settle for what I can. I find out there's a Chinese restaurant within walking distance of school called Oriental Restaurant. I am still too young to flinch at the name.

When I go, I get a cozy feeling when I am greeted by the Asian waitstaff. When I see their faces, I smile wider than usual. Everything about the experience feels familiar and comforting. When the waitress tells us to "Sit wherever you like" and brings me a giant, sweating glass of ice water, I think of Mum, running around with her black apron tied around her waist.

The food isn't great. The fried rice is pale and bland, and the honey garlic spareribs are dry. But I am so happy to be eating food that bears even the smallest passing resemblance to the food from home. Growing up, Mum would always tell me to eat everything—"Every grain of rice you leave behind is a pockmark on your future husband's face!"—and I honour her at the Oriental Restaurant by eating every dry morsel.

When I'm at home, I hardly ever crave the food that our customers eat. As a teenager, I don't see Canadian Chinese food as "real" or "authentic." But living on my own for the first time in a town where there are no other Chinese options slowly trains me to be grateful for what I do have. In a neighbourhood rife with poutine, gyros, wraps, and wings, the Oriental Restaurant feels like an offering. It feels like a gift. I don't care that it's "bad"

Chinese food. It's still Chinese—and I am surprised to learn that that's more than enough for me. It's a drop of water gladly received in a desert.

"How's the food? Good food?" Mum asks when I tell her about it.

"Not as good as yours. The chicken balls have almost no chicken, and the wonton soup is so salty!"

"Ah, Mummy cook better food. When you come home, I make you more fried rice. When you coming home?"

She asks and sounds like she misses me. It's unexpected. I spent my whole life feeling like my parents and I were ships passing through the night, so I am surprised that we miss each other now. As a teenager, I would have said, "What is there to miss?" But now that I am away from home, I am suddenly aware of how much it means to know that I can always go home at the end of the day. No matter how much I stood out at school during the day, my family was always there in the evening. They were my refuge. They gave me the space to recharge, so I could go back to school the next day and face whatever cruel taunts and jokes came my way.

But when I'm at university, I am constantly a fish out of water. There are fewer than ten racialized people on our entire floor. I always feel like I'm performing in some way at every given moment.

So when Mum asks when I'm coming home, I tell her honestly, "Soon. Very soon. I miss you."

When she tells me she misses me too, it feels like we're navigating new terrain. I start calling home more often.

———

While I'm missing my mother and the familiarity of home, I'm learning to embrace my time away at school.

In that first year of university, we are obnoxious like all teenagers are when they strike out on their own for the first time. Our newfound freedom is wild and intoxicating. We're driven by hormones and the adrenaline that comes with having no grown-ups to monitor our every move. That kind of freedom is nothing new to me, but I'm charmed by everyone else's introduction to it.

I meet Ethan on the very first day, right after my parents and sister say their goodbyes. When he and his roommates in the apartment two doors down from ours stop by to say hello, we shyly introduce ourselves to each other in the kitchen. I am taken by the size of his teeth.

Falling in love with Ethan is not seamless or easy or all that enjoyable. It requires hard work and effort on my part. Like all the other boys who came before him, I have to chase and manipulate to earn his love. I wonder if I deserve to be more than someone's dirty little secret for once. My mind fills with lofty daydreams of what it might be like to have someone want me enough to tell the whole world. To make it official on a silly little site like Facebook.

What I know for sure is that I can't be loved just as I am. I must prove myself and my worth first. I must cut off bits and pieces of myself—my dignity, mostly—to fit inside a little box that contains everything I believe makes me A Girl Worth Loving.

I am sexually free but not slutty. I am ambitious but not cold. I am funny and I know how to take a joke. I blow smoke up Ethan's ass so he sees me as agreeable, complimentary, submissive. I make him feel good about himself all the damn time. I force myself to chug bottles of Miller Genuine Draft to keep up with my peers. I watch sports with the boys. I'm an excellent student without being an uptight stick in the mud.

I am perfect. I wonder if it'll be enough.

Ethan and I slowly fall into a natural intimacy. We become close friends and make each other laugh. He tells me things like, "Unlike other girls, you're actually funny." We sleep in the same bed, but never fool around. He drinks to excess and tells dumb, childish jokes, and because I am a dumb, childish nineteen-year-old, I laugh. I lean in too close at a bar selling dollar beers that taste like piss just so I can feel his warm, boozy breath on my face. I betray my country and switch my allegiance from the Toronto Maple Leafs to his favourite team, the San Jose Sharks. I'm so used to moulding myself to cater to the needs and tastes of the people around me that it now feels rote.

Blend in. Don't ask questions. Make people feel comfortable. It's what I do. There's urgency this time because I'm not the only one circling him. I'm not the only one who has his attention.

Dia is a quiet girl on our floor, who I hate to admit I like because she's smart and fun and, unlike most people in our year, she's never once made a joke about me being Asian. Her not being irritating or racist makes her stand out for all the right reasons. She's genuinely a cool girl, whereas I'm just play-acting as one.

"I've been hanging out with Dia a lot," Ethan says to me one day while we're watching TV in his dorm. My heart starts to thunder so loudly in my chest that my ears feel like they're being boxed on both sides.

"Oh?" My face is a placid river. My insides are a roiling sea.

"Yeah, she's really cool."

Even though I like Dia, I want nothing more than to strike her down. I feel the heat of jealousy and a bone-deep frustration that's festered after years of never being anyone's first choice.

I make a plan. I scheme. I start to hang out in Dia's suite, even though it's not a place I really frequented before. I worm my way into her life, and because she's a legitimately kind person, she welcomes me warmly. I ask her how things are going with Ethan ("Good, we're hanging out") and try to plant seeds of doubt in her head. ("Didn't he just break up with a girl?") I become an outwardly innocuous, but deeply insidious, cancer in their fledgling relationship. By befriending Dia, I eat up the minutes in her day, cutting off whatever limited time she can devote to Ethan.

I am always, always there, and because of that, their relationship sputters and dies before it can even start.

I suppose, as the relentless chaser, it only makes sense that I have to carry my exhausted body over the finish line myself.

It happens on one of those nights that make the very beginnings of relationships so intoxicating. We've stayed up until the early morning hours, luxuriating in the sounds of each other's voices. To go to sleep would be a cruel separation, so we don't dare give in. Our eyelids aren't yet heavy. We're wide awake and wrapped around each other.

While the sun makes its slow, lazy ascent, I blurt, "Why haven't you asked me to be your girlfriend yet?" I'm officially tired of waiting. I feel safe enough to admit I have needs, too.

"I was waiting," he says. I'm relieved he doesn't seem put off by my speaking out, but I still hold in a tiny breath just in case. "I wanted to take you out for a nice dinner this weekend and ask you there."

I curse myself for my impatience. *Why didn't I just wait?* But everything feels deliciously worth it when he says, "I don't want to wait anymore. Do you want to be my girlfriend?"

I see stars. I hear church choirs and angels singing. I feel like a candle has been lit in my belly and the light and warmth is pulsating through my entire body.

It's the first time since elementary school that someone's asked me that question. The ensuing high I feel is potent. I can see myself becoming addicted to it.

"Yes, yes, of course!" I whisper, not wanting to wake my roommates up. When our lips meet, I feel like it's a promise. It's a warm welcome. I've finally made it. The gruelling marathon has finally ended, and I hope I never have to race it again. I'll do anything to make it so.

We celebrate with a nice dinner at the place people our age consider fancy high-end dining: Red Lobster. I feel lightheaded and buoyant the entire time, like I could die the next day and be happy that shrimp linguine alfredo was my last supper. I could die knowing I was finally worthy of someone's love.

I'm so excited to tell my mother that I call her the next day.

In Cantonese, I say, "Mum, I have a boyfriend!" I expect her to squeal with excitement. I am the first of her three children to have a real tell-my-parents-about-you boyfriend or girlfriend.

"Is he Chinese?" she asks.

"No."

"Is he white?" She says *baak gwai*. White person. White ghost. White devil.

"Yes."

"Is he nice to you?"

"Yes, Mum, very, very nice."

"Good. That's cool. You have someone to take care of you now."

———

"This is Rachel, my Asian girlfriend."

This is how Ethan takes to introducing me.

I smile, shake hands, try to ignore how weird it is that he needs to say what's already written plainly on my face. It's strange how so many of our jokes revolve around race.

For Halloween one year, I dress up as a sexy Chinese takeout container and let him parade me around. I laugh it off like it's natural and hilarious for me to wear a giant fortune cookie on my head with "Thank you" emblazoned over my crotch and "Enjoy" over my tits.

"I'm ravaged by yellow fever," he jokes. "And you have Lyme disease." He says this because he's British and "we're called limeys." It's a derogatory nickname given to the British navy by American sailors who thought it odd that the Brits used limes to ward off scurvy. I swoon and think he's so clever.

Once, when he's about to orgasm, he yells out, "The British are coming!" We laugh and laugh.

I'm so young and in love that I don't get the ick the way I would now. I don't think about colonialism and the way Asian countries have been the victims of Western conquests for several centuries. I don't think about how the bodies of Asian women have been and continue to be stolen, raped, and conquered by GIs, sex tourists, and random men on the street. I don't think about the correlations between rape and war and the commodification and exploitation of Asian bodies. I don't think about how the sexual violence that's so often perpetrated by white men against Asian women is the direct result of the legacy of Western imperialism in Asian countries. I don't think about the long history of Western political, economic, and military domination of developing countries—and how the Western conquests of Asia have shaped the way Asian women are seen and treated the world over. I don't think about how the ripple effects of these conquests—and the stereotypes and ideas they created—continue to force those of us in Asia and across the diaspora into sexual submission to men.

Instead, I think, *this is just a joke. I can take a joke.* I laugh and bear it. I force my thoughts into submission.

When I bring Ethan to my parents' place for the first time, it's a big deal. My brother texts me non-stop to ask what he likes to eat, what he likes to watch, whether he likes games. My mother echoes his questions about food. "Does he eat shrimp? Does he eat fish? Does he like Chinese food?"

I tell them not to worry. "He's easy. We're easy. Don't stress!" I tell my mum that Ethan loves Chinese food because I've seen him inhale a dinner combo at the Oriental Restaurant.

Although I'm telling my mother not to stress and to take it easy, I am very much stressed and not taking it easy. I know this is different from all the times I brought guy friends to the restaurant. The stakes are so much higher because my family is about to meet the guy I fully expect to marry one day. *What if they don't like him? What if he doesn't like them? What if he can't understand their accents?* I think about the restaurant then. I think about its cheesy name, China Village, and find I'm still not over the loss of the May May Inn. I think about the kitchen with its signature Phan chaos. Will Ethan—a clean freak and germaphobe who won't even let me touch him after I eat—be repulsed when he sees the oily fingerprints on the fridge doors, the scuff marks on the floor, the wayward onion peels that have fallen to the ground and are awaiting the evening sweeping? Will he take one look around the kitchen and shudder?

I ignore the feeling in the pit of my belly when I think about his reaction. How will I feel if he reacts badly? I will take it personally, of course. The restaurant is an extension of my family. It is the life's work of my parents. The restaurant has made us.

If he rejects the restaurant, is he not also rejecting me and my family?

I push these thoughts aside and repeat to myself that Ethan loves me. He won't reject me. He won't reject my family.

I try to rationalize what he might see and say. Yes, the restaurant can get a little dirty—but that's just normal wear and tear! It's impossible to keep a deep fryer and its environs completely clean of lard residue.

It'll be okay. It'll be great. He'll love the restaurant. The restaurant made me, so he'll love it because he loves me.

When we arrive, Ethan is shy but not rude. He smiles widely and is polite. He talks about hockey with my brother and my dad.

"He's a nice guy," Mum says before she lowers her voice to a whisper. "Lots of pimples though." I sigh. I know it's futile to tell her not to comment on someone's body.

I try to see the restaurant through his eyes. I see the boxes and bags of unopened snacks that are strewn haphazardly beside the fridge. I see that the waitress is making wontons out front and raining white flour all over the table and the floor, her fingers gunky with the residue of wet flour and egg yolks. I see that some customers are covered in grime, their jeans ripped at the hem and spotted with mysterious brown stains because they came here right after work. A couple is sharing a smoke in front of the restaurant. There's a group of four rowdy teenagers in the corner eating egg rolls and chugging cans of pop. A woman wearing bright red lipstick leaves marks on her cup of water as she watches her elderly father shakily slurp his wonton soup.

I'm not embarrassed, but I try to imagine how this cast of characters must look to Ethan, who is wide-eyed and taking it all in. I don't tell him that this is more or less how I grew up—an equally wide-eyed child observing our revolving door of customers. These folks are harmless and help pay our bills. They're nothing compared to some of the sleepy drunks, awful dine-and-dashers, and nasty, mean-spirited people who have berated us because they had a minor complaint.

Still, I imagine what he's thinking. *Townies. Dirty, smelly small-town folk.* In my rational mind, I know he probably isn't thinking this since he grew up in a small town, too. But I'm suddenly hyper aware and self-conscious about the restaurant and the people who dine here. It's like I'm thirteen years old again and feeling embarrassed that my parents aren't fancy lawyers in their clean, fancy offices.

Ethan doesn't say anything. He just looks and nods and smiles. I'm relieved. I squeeze his hand and kiss his cheek.

But it turns out he's not easy. He doesn't eat shrimp. He doesn't love Chinese food, at least not the dishes my parents make just for us. When Dad makes spareribs that melt off the bone in a savoury sauce with potatoes and carrots, Ethan wrinkles his nose and says it's "too cow-y." When Mum makes juicy braised chicken wings with mushrooms in a flavourful soy sauce, he shakes his head. "What about chicken balls? Or *soo guy*? Can I have that instead?"

This becomes our dance for the entirety of our relationship whenever we visit my family. While we eat the food of our people, he's eating deep-fried meats. When my parents wrap up their long workday, they have to make two separate dinners: one for us and one for Ethan.

I'm embarrassed that he gives them something else to do after they've already worked so hard. I dip my head apologetically and tell my parents I'm sorry for the extra work.

Mum waves me off. "He's a white guy. White people love deep-fried." Dad cackles and parrots her. "Yeah, white boy!"

Ethan grits his teeth and whispers in my ear. "And you think my dad's bad?"

I think about his dad, and what he's implying, and my insides start to simmer.

Ethan's dad is a character. When allowing me into their home, he somehow manages to be simultaneously welcoming and hatefully offensive. He hates Catholics. He makes disparaging comments about Black people,

Muslims, Asians. He wonders why Black people are always dancing or eating fried chicken or bothering to get tattoos. He questions the hygiene of Muslims. He calls Chinese people "panfaces" because we apparently have flat faces. He tells me that White Anglo-Saxon Protestants (WASPs) are the most superior people on the planet.

The apple has not fallen far from the tree.

His son tells me things like:

"When we have kids, I wouldn't feel comfortable with them eating the food that your parents make."

"My dad will definitely tease our kids about being half-Chinese."

"White privilege doesn't exist. How can it exist when affirmative action is a thing?"

"Being called a 'cracker' is just as offensive as any other racial slur."

I don't know how to explain to him that my parents calling him a "white boy" and saying he loves deep-fried foods when he does is not "just as bad" as these statements. I don't yet have the vocabulary to describe how these sentiments make me feel bad, less-than, unseen. I don't know if anything I can say will make him hear me. For a time, I stop saying anything at all. What's the point?

I turn to him and smile, placating. In private, I tell my parents to stop teasing him.

***

The holidays are the busiest time of year for our restaurant, with New Year's Eve being the most chaotic and stress-inducing day.

As kids, we know we can never miss it.

It's a tense time in the kitchen. Someone is usually yelling, another person is giving someone else the cold shoulder, and we're each busy with our specific tasks. John's on the deep fryer and soup station, Mum's making fried rice and running around doing one-off tasks, Linh's packing takeout orders with Dad, who's busy with the wok and all the stir-fries. Waitresses are yelling, "Can we squeeze another order in?" Phones are ringing. And someone, somewhere, is complaining about not getting the extra sweet and sour sauce they asked for. I'm washing dishes, making wontons, and chopping vegetables with my headphones in to drown out all the yelling.

It's functional dysfunction in that kitchen, and as much as I hate having to be there every December 31, I don't dare refuse to go. Not helping out at the restaurant would feel like betraying my family and my duties.

The three of us kids long to be like "normal people," who go to parties and see the ending of the year as a time for celebration instead of yet another trial to endure. But the restaurant comes first. Helping Mum and Dad comes first.

Except there's a year when Ethan asks me not to help out at the restaurant. "My buddy's having a party. Please come," he asks, fixing his green eyes on me and looking so earnest. I nod.

"That should be okay. I'm the most disposable person in the kitchen anyway," I say.

When I tell my family, I can feel the resentment radiating off my brother. "Wow, I can't believe Rachel is skipping New Year's," he says. It's like our childhood all over again, when they're chained to the restaurant on the weekends, working hard, while I get to float around, hang out with friends, shirk my responsibilities.

I feel terrible. I come up with a compromise where I'll help out for an hour and then catch a train in the middle of dinner service so I can be with Ethan before midnight.

When I leave, it's the busiest time of the night. I wave and say bye, but everyone's so focused, I'm not sure they can even hear me over the din of the kitchen. I'm full of guilt and self-loathing. I feel like I'm failing my family. I feel like the worst daughter.

I go to my first New Year's Eve party that night and find it boring. Overrated. I am shocked to find myself filled with FOMO for the restaurant and wondering what my family is doing. Are they cleaning up? Tallying the bills and determining it a successful New Year's Eve? How much did they make? Are they showering the day's oil and grime off their bodies and feeling proud of a job well done? Are they watching the ball drop or have they already fallen asleep after such a gruelling day of work? Are they all together and missing me?

I'm drinking at an underwhelming party somewhere in the suburbs with my boyfriend and his friends and longing for the chaos of the holiday at the restaurant. I feel useless, like I have no purpose. I look at who I'm with. Everyone is white. Girls wearing Uggs are rapping to Jay-Z and dropping the n-word like it doesn't carry any meaningful weight. I hate it here.

It's the first and only time I skip New Year's Eve at the restaurant.

—⁓—

Mum continues to ask if Ethan is good to me. "Is he nice to you? Does he yell at you or hit you?"

At first, her line of questioning makes me laugh. "Yes, Mum, of course he's nice to me."

But as the years go by, I notice I no longer laugh. My eyes shift downward instead of into the back of my skull. When this happens, I start repeating a mantra in my head: *He's good to you. He won't cheat on you or hit you. He's good, he's good, he's good. I won't find anyone better.*

Even when he says things that make me feel like he hates parts of me, I stay. I think of the nineteen-year-old girl who desperately wanted his love and worked hard to get it, vowing to never let him slip away. I think of how much she wanted to be loved and desired and how grateful she was to be granted the privilege of being someone's girlfriend. I tell myself we have to be together forever, no matter how shitty I feel. This is what I worked so hard for.

Meanwhile, I start taking classes about gender and race and come to understand the feeling I've always had of being uncomfortable in my own skin, that constant physical feeling of wrongness in my body. Sometimes my skin feels too tight, like it's constraining me and keeping me stuck and small. Other times, it feels like I'm drowning in how much skin of mine there is. I learn words and concepts like "Othering" and "assimilation" and "fetishization." I learn about how marginalized people often cope by shrinking themselves. I learn about how common it is for racialized women to be told they're too loud, too aggressive, too sexy, too challenging. We're made to feel small and told it's still too much.

I see myself in the course material. I learn. My discomfort grows with my understanding. I acknowledge that I actually really hate the racist jokes that have dogged me since high school and followed me to undergrad. I start to speak up against it. I can tell my sudden outspokenness rankles Ethan. He asks me, "What happened to that fun and chill girl I fell in love with? Why do you have to make everything about race? It makes me uncomfortable."

Instead of staying silent, I start asking questions of my own. How come you're allowed to bring up race whenever it's convenient for you, but I can't? And why does your discomfort matter more than mine?

As the years pass—three, then four, then five—my attempts to force these questions out of my brain and into his are unsuccessful. It's becoming harder to ignore the feeling that something isn't quite right. My relationship feels the way my skin sometimes does. Too tight, there's an uncomfortable squeeze, I don't fit.

But he won't cheat on me or hit me. He's good, he's good, he's good. I can't get anyone better. The mantra plays on loop in my head, but the conviction behind the words lessens by the day.

And it's not just my relationship I'm outgrowing. I'm outgrowing my university and the town we're in, too.

The people who are supposed to be my friends make me cry on a regular basis when they rip on me for being Chinese, for probably eating dogs, for bleeding MSG. A guy in my friend group jokes that, "unless you're white, you aren't a real person." There's another who loves saying my name in a cartoony "Chinese" accent. And these are people who know better! They're my fellow editors at the school newspaper. They're prominent figures behind our school's diversity initiatives and inclusion groups. They're allies in public but my tormentors when the stage lights are off.

As a young reporter for my campus newspaper, I write a piece about my experience with racism. I call out how commonplace racist jokes are on campus. I write about how proud I am to be Chinese. How, if given the chance to choose my ethnicity, I'd always choose to be Chinese. How I simply can't bear to hear anyone making a mockery of my ethnicity.

I naively think my friends will read the piece and take my message to heart. I anticipate feeling validated and heard and cared about.

Instead, when I walk into the campus newspaper office, I am greeted with the all-too-familiar sounds of my friends and colleagues saying my name in their signature offensive Chinese accents. Their belly-deep laughter echoes in the air. It's a punch to the gut.

Ethan and I are going to a party in his small hometown. "It's going to be fun," he says.

The moment we get there, I know we're not going to have fun.

"Hey Chun-Li!" a man yells at me. Chun-Li is a fictional Chinese martial arts practitioner in the game *Street Fighter*. The man's lips are wet with beer, and his smile is leering, grotesque. I don't know him. He doesn't know me. I give him a close-mouthed smile, and he tells me I'd be pretty if I showed some teeth. I want to bare mine and take a bite out of his throat so he'll stop speaking. Stop breathing. I know nothing good will come out of this conversation.

He proceeds to show me the Chinese characters tattooed on his bicep. "Come on, what does it say? Read it to me." I shrug.

"I can't read that."

He's like a battering ram with his comments. He asks me how to say this and that in Cantonese. He tells me I'm so uptight. "You chinks need to learn how to loosen up."

I look him square in the eyes, my blood boiling and my face flushed, and tell him he's a fucking racist. He acts like he's been shot even though I'm the one who's been on the receiving end of his "jokes" and comments for well over an hour.

"Are you fucking dumb? I'm not racist. How can I be racist when my cousin is married to someone Black?" He goes off and I tune him out. I'm used to the spiel.

Suddenly, Ethan comes out of nowhere and tells the guy to fuck off. He actually says the words. "You're a racist."

I look at him with new eyes. I look at him with love and appreciation. Is he defending me and validating my experience as a racialized woman? Is he recognizing that racism exists?

When Ethan immediately takes me home after the exchange, I cover his face with kisses. I squeeze him tight. I think this is the turning point for us. *He's seeing me!*

The next morning, he tells me his buddy was there for the entire awful encounter.

"Ryan said it wasn't that bad. Are you sure you didn't overreact?"

It's a bitter pill to swallow but I do, right then and there. I know he isn't coming to my defense. I know for sure now that he hasn't seen me. The veil has covered his eyes again. I'm invisible.

In 2011, when I start grad school in Toronto, I'm amazed by how many shades of Brown and Black and tan I see on the street and in my classes. Still, I spend the first few weeks clenched, heart hammering, waiting for the barbed words and racist jokes.

No one in my class makes one.

I am so shocked and relieved that I cry with joy. I hadn't realized just how much tension I'd been holding in my body for years.

It's the first time in my whole entire life that I feel like I belong. My culture and family aren't a source of derision or mockery but something people are genuinely interested in.

I grow and thrive in the city and at school. For the most part, I don't feel Othered. I don't feel different. I feel comfortable in my skin—it feels like it fits me perfectly now. The compulsion and desire to shed all that holds me back grows stronger.

I feel like I am constantly evolving and becoming a smarter, better version of myself, but it's clear that Ethan has stagnated. He's nearly identical to the boy I fell in love with at nineteen. I can't overlook the fact that his racist beliefs are tearing away at my spirit in a way I no longer find funny or excusable. Once, after a hangout with my classmates, I mention that one of my friends, who is ethnically Indian, is beautiful.

"She's beautiful because she has white features," Ethan says.

The comment pierces my heart. *I don't have any white features. Does that make me less beautiful? Why does someone need white features to be considered beautiful to you anyway?* But I keep those thoughts to myself because Ethan hates when I bring up race. I know that if I want him to listen to me again in the future, I need to pick my battles carefully, no matter how much the silence feels like a rope squeezing around my neck.

This painful, clunky dance goes on for years. Until it suddenly stops.

Some romantic relationships end amicably and with minimal ripples after two people mutually agree that—although the love they share is still there—the relationship itself has reached its natural end. They may hug and wish each other the best, vowing to stay in touch. The most enlightened and evolved may even successfully remain friends after they've stopped sharing a bed and bodily fluids.

That's very much not what happens with me and Ethan.

Our relationship ends in a dramatic and hateful fashion. The kind of total annihilation that sees two people try to inflict the deepest wounds on each other by weaponizing intimate details learned throughout the relationship. These details—their biggest insecurities, your private fears—were once held securely in the palms of your hands to protect the person you loved, but are now grenades you can use to destroy them. This type of break-up is brutal and ugly and renders both parties losers.

It's 11 P.M. on November 14, 2013, and I'm being kicked out of the apartment I share with Ethan. We'd been together for almost six years.

Earlier that night, we got into an all-too-familiar fight in his car. For what felt like the thousandth time in our relationship, he expressed his discomfort with me making a passing comment about how I was the only person of colour at his friend's wedding. It's a thing I do out of habit when I enter a room. I scan and take stock of who's there. This dictates the way I speak, how much of myself I share, how comfortable I feel in the space.

But Ethan doesn't get that. He doesn't know what it's like to walk into a room and not feel like he immediately belongs. He doesn't understand why this is my impulse, my lifeline.

He especially hates when I "pull the race card" in response to his friends cracking jokes about the darkness of someone's skin or the slant of a person's eyes. To express my discomfort with these jokes is to invite his scorn, or worse, to watch him tune me out in real time.

"You make everything into such a big deal," he says, his eyes trained on the road. The rational part of my brain knows our very lives depend on him staring straight ahead. But the irrational side of me wants to accuse him of failing to really see me yet again. "Why do you have to make everything about race?" The comment confirms what I already know: the painful reality that this person with whom I had made love, forged a home, and planned a future was digging in his heels and refusing to see me and all the raw scars I laid bare for him.

We're rounding a particularly bendy corner not far from home when I turn to him and say, "I think we should end things."

The statement hangs in the air between us, so quietly said that it almost feels like I can reach out and stuff the words back in my mouth. If I want to, I can pretend it was a badly timed joke. I can face his disbelieving anger and favourite command for me ("Apologize!"). I can roll over and put on my most timid, submissive, pleading voice, "I didn't mean it, baby."

Instead, I let the uncomfortable, suffocating silence cover us. I can dig my heels in, too. I realize, a second too late, how it was not my best decision to stick a knife in a relationship with the person currently controlling the dangerous hunk of metal and rubber we find ourselves trapped in.

The silence drags on, heavy and oppressive. Inwardly, I contemplate how I might break the silence. Outwardly, I open and close my mouth like a slack-jawed fish. I almost want to ask if he heard me, but I know he did. The redness of his face is enough of an answer for me.

We stay angry and shell-shocked in that stifling car all the way home before we finally do away with the speechlessness. "Tell me why," he demands as soon as the door to our third-floor apartment closes. The question takes me by surprise. Has he somehow forgotten how he just accused me, again, of not knowing how to "take a joke" and of being "racist to white people"? I almost laugh.

"Because we are no longer compatible." It's the truth, albeit maybe not the full truth.

"I disagree. I think we're perfectly compatible," he says. His green eyes are almost manic under the warm light of the living room in our first and only apartment together. The intense emotion he wears openly on his face is poetically complemented by the accent wall we spent a whole afternoon painting red. I am calling it quits after only five months of living under the same roof.

I bite my tongue, unsure of what to say and angry that, yet again, he is disagreeing with me and making me question my own thoughts. I add this to a list already overflowing with reasons why we no longer fit.

You don't excite me.

I wish you were capable of meaningful conversation.

Your sense of humour and overreliance on racist jokes are appalling.

I'm not attracted to you anymore.

I look at him and feel like I'm seeing him for the first time in a while, or maybe ever. His perpetual defensiveness, which has always rankled, now makes me pity him.

I am flooded, then, with six years of memories. Six years of him making me feel small and ashamed for being Chinese. Six years of him invalidating my feelings and making me feel too sensitive and overly hysterical. Six years of comments like, "White privilege doesn't exist, Rachel."

I'm not proud of it, but those memories make me want to plunge the knife in deep and twist. I want to tear at the very fabric of his soul the way I feel mine has been ripped apart, slowly and methodically, over the years. But I don't have years. I have minutes, and I know exactly how to get him to bleed out, fast. So I say, blankly and without remorse: "I slept with someone last night."

An interminable beat—and then the breaking of the dam.

"You fucking whore. You slut."

It's cruel and it stings, but I almost feel a bizarre relief upon hearing it. This is confirmation of my worst fears and the realization that my most private thoughts about myself are shared by someone else. *I was right.*

After all, there is nothing quite like finding out with certainty that the person you love is just like everyone else. He can think as little of you as all the men before him. It just took him six years to finally say it.

***

When my family finds out I broke up with Ethan, they are in disbelief.

"Is this a joke?"

"But he's so nice!"

"Who will take care of you now?"

It's only when I tell them about what life was really like with him that their sadness turns to rage.

"Fuck him!"

"It was so annoying, how he always made us make him separate meals."

"He never ate anything!"

In the midst of heartbreak, my family makes me laugh, commiserates with me, supports me financially because I'm a single woman living in Toronto. They welcome me home and I go running back whenever I can. The restaurant transforms from being something to run away from and resent to the one place where I feel safe and held.

***

After the breakup, I go on a series of bad dates with people who somehow make me feel as small and ashamed as Ethan did.

I'm tucked away in an intimate corner of a crowded rooftop patio the first time I'm walloped over the head by the force of my own self-loathing.

It's a Friday night at Hemingway's, an iconic Toronto institution in the city's bougiest neighbourhood. To the naked eye, everything appears normal: hollering men in untucked dress shirts clink glasses of beer while couples on first dates self-consciously nibble on their first bites of a shared pizza.

In that quiet, dimly lit corner, I am on my own first date with a loud, charmless man I matched with on Tinder. When I try to remember his face now, I can't. He's nothing but a shapeless blob in my memory, just another man dripping with overconfidence, telling tasteless jokes over warm beer and mediocre wings.

He leans in close suddenly, like he's about to tell me a secret. Immediately, my shoulders stiffen, and I already know violence is going to slip out of his mouth. You don't grow up in predominantly white towns without developing a keen hypervigilance that alerts you to impending danger.

His breath is warm on my face, and I wish desperately I were anywhere but here. His face cracks apart into a smile—it's sinister and I hate it—and he says the words I know I'll remember for the rest of my life, long after I've forgotten his face.

"I bet your pussy tastes just like General Tso's chicken."

He says it like it's the funniest statement that's ever been spoken, like he's a comedic genius and I'm so lucky to be in the presence of his greatness. He says it like it's normal and decent. He says it without shame. *Shame.* I fill with it.

Still, I sit there and smile politely. I eventually force a laugh and teasingly slap his arm. "Oh you," I probably say, although I can't really remember since my spirit has disconnected and checked out, as if saying to my body, "Hey, you can deal with this on your own." Later, I let him take my dis-associated body to his cold, industrial-style condo, where I let him fuck me like a jackhammer, doggy style. He doesn't come because he "can't with a condom on," and I tell him he has until 1 A.M. to finish—in the condom—before I leave him.

At 1:02 A.M., I'm on the sidewalk outside of his building, marinating in my own self-hate. *Why didn't I speak up and tell him his joke was terrible and offensive? Why didn't I end the date? Why did I let him touch me? Why did I let him fuck me?*

I don't have any answers then. I'm too cold and tired and I just want to get the hell out of there. But later, I'll look back on this evening as the moment I realized there was something broken within me.

I don't hear from him again for almost a week, when he texts me out of the blue with his signature charm. "Shallow vag, care for a follow up?"

I ignore the text.

When I talk to my sister about the experience, she tells me how common it is to be wanted so badly by men who treat us just as badly. Men who act like they hate us. Men who probably actually do.

She tells me how one of her exes only dated Asian women and how he would rank each one by putting stars next to her name. Chinese, Japanese, and Korean girls got five stars. Single stars went to Filipino women.

This is what we have to deal with. There are so many ways to dehumanize us. But when you grow up the way we have—never having healthy relationships modelled for us or seeing Asian girls as desirable romantic partners in the media—it's easy to see how we start believing that dehumanization is real, genuine desire.

Imagine now what it does to a person—a young woman—to date people who continuously abuse and traumatize you. How painful it is to believe that these men are your only viable romantic option. How much abuse you allow yourself to accept because you think you don't deserve anything better. How little you start to think of yourself. How impossible it can seem to ever break the cycle.

9

"HE'S LIKE A UNICORN."

It takes years of therapy with a Chinese therapist to unlearn everything I spent my whole life believing about myself.

In my sessions, I dig and discover how deeply it impacted me to never feel like my parents "saw" me. No matter what I did or how many A-pluses I got, I never felt like they paid attention to me in any meaningful way. Their ways of spoiling and coddling me were relatively superficial without any attempts to really get to know me. Therapy helps me see how hard I tried my whole childhood to earn their love, and how in doing so, I learned that this is what love is: the chasing, the begging, the never feeling good enough. I see how this ended up bleeding into all my relationships. If someone pursued me and was interested in me before I had the chance to "earn" their attention, I was turned off. They were clearly desperate. If someone was interested in me too early, I wouldn't trust their motives. I only became interested in someone if I had to work for their affection.

Love, I thought, should be a battle. It should never come easy, if it even comes at all.

I swear off dating for a year and a half after that horrible man compares my genitalia to crispy, deep-fried chicken coated in sweet, tangy sauce. I practice voluntary celibacy and delete all dating apps off my phone. I learn how to live on my own and end up falling in love with it. "This is our vag pad, Ivy!" I squeal happily to my dog. "Who even needs a man?"

I stay in therapy to work on improving my self-worth and feel with certainty that I never want to feel as small and diminished as I did in my previous relationships. I want to live life as a proud and confident Chinese Canadian woman. I want to move through the world with my head lifted, eyes looking forward, shoulders pushed back. I never want to shrink and cut pieces of myself off for anyone ever again. I want to stop cozying up to racial abuse and seeing it as love, as all I deserve.

In 2016, my friend Ishani tells me about a silly dating app she's just downloaded called Coffee Meets Bagel. She explains that you only get a certain number of matches a day, and if you want more, you have to buy virtual coffee beans. I think it sounds ridiculous, so naturally, I download it as a joke. I don't even bother setting up any parameters because I'm not looking to date seriously.

On my twenty-eighth birthday, just one day after I download the app, I'm matched with a man named Michael. At first, I'm uncertain about swiping right because he's younger than me and white, and after my disastrous track record with white men, I'm not keen to repeat those experiences. In the photos he chose, his smile is so wide and warm that his eyes crinkle in the corners. It makes me think he's the type of person to share his joy freely. I swipe because of that, not thinking anything of it. I'll know soon enough whether he's a walking red flag if he messages me something heinous about my body.

He doesn't. He asks me about food, specifically the strangest thing I've ever eaten. I smile and message him back.

After a few days of lively back and forth, Michael asks me out and I agree, even though I'm still not really on the market. On the day of our date, I take Ivy to the dog park and find myself running late. I'll have no time to shower, but since my expectations are so low, I'm not fussed about it.

When I finally show up at the patio in Kensington Market for sangria, I am unshowered, sweating profusely, and thirty minutes late. (In my defense, it was Pride weekend and there was no streetcar service.) When Michael sees me, he is not repulsed or angry. He gives me the biggest smile, and I'm thrilled to see his eyes crinkle in the corners in real time.

Surprisingly, there's no awkwardness at all even though I'm rusty when it comes to dating. The conversation flows easily. He's as warm as he looks in his photos, and he asks thoughtful questions about me, my childhood, and my family. He doesn't make any racist jokes or unsolicited comments about my body. He doesn't bring up my being Asian at all, except when I mention it first. He seems genuinely curious about me. I hate how novel it is.

Before I know it, five hours have passed, and we still haven't run out of things to say. When I go to the washroom, I text my sister and close friends and tell them I'm on the best date of my life.

Michael and I text each other as soon as we get home. There are no bullshit games about waiting three days before texting, and it's so damn refreshing. I don't know it yet, but when Michael gets home, he deletes Coffee Meets Bagel from his phone.

I am pleased that we continue to text every day. Unlike all my previous relationships, I'm never left waiting by the phone or wondering whether he's thinking about me. He is, and he lets me know.

In the past, this behaviour would have turned me off. I'd have gotten itchy feet about the relationship. I'd have wondered why the guy was trying so hard and not making me work for his time and attention. But after continuous therapy, I've slowly come to accept that I am worthy of love and inherently lovable, or at least, I'm wanting to believe it.

I'm also *tired*. I don't want to chase after anyone anymore. After a year and a half of blissful singledom, I have no interest in adding needless stress and anxiety to my life by playing "he loves me, he loves me not." He either does or he doesn't. I'm not desperate for a relationship to work because I'm no longer afraid of being alone.

After our first date, I go back to Leamington for a pre-planned visit home. While I'm there, Mum makes *gai jai dan*, also commonly known as *balut*, which are fertilized duck embryos eaten directly from the shell. My ex-boyfriend would have wrinkled his nose and called us inhumane savages.

I take a picture and tell my mum I'm going to send it to a boy I went on a date with.

"Don't do it!" she shrieks. The panic is written all over her face. "You're going to scare him away!" She remembers my ex-boyfriend, too.

I shrug and hit send. This is a litmus test. I want to see how Michael will respond. I want to see if he's respectful of my culture and open to trying new things.

To my relief, he responds with questions about how it tastes, what the texture's like, and how one eats the egg. I tell Mum, "It's okay. He's not afraid," and she breathes out a long, drawn-out sigh.

As the weeks pass, I take notice of how Michael never once makes me feel like he only wants me for sex or my body.

On our second date, I'm the one who impatiently looks up at him and says, "Are you going to kiss me or what?"

He gives me his crinkly-eyed smile and dips his head low, obliging. We kiss in the rain, and I feel my stomach do that annoying little flip that everyone's always talking about in romcoms.

Before he can meet my family and friends, Michael has to meet my dog, Ivy, who wasn't a big fan of a lot of the people I brought home after dates. She would run to my bedroom, dodging their attempted pets on her way there, and wait for them to leave.

When she meets Michael, her tail wags high and she brushes her face against his thigh. She lets him hold her leash while we're walking and doesn't pull once. She's on her best behaviour. "Huh, I think my dog likes you," I say to Michael. When he beams at me and gently caresses Ivy's head, which she allows, a little voice pipes up inside me: *This might be something. This one's special.*

In those early days, we see each other only on weekends. I find myself so impatient to see him that my leg starts bouncing whenever I'm on the subway to go on our dates. I hear my mother's voice in my head—"Stop!

You're going to shake out all your good luck!"—but I don't care. This subway needs to hurry the fuck up so I can see him. I can't even wait the five minutes to get there.

He makes me dinner and bakes me cakes. We stay up all night talking and laughing and kissing. He listens to what I say and writes notes on his phone so he doesn't forget. When I mention I want to try a restaurant, he surprises me with reservations. When I say in passing I need something around the house, he buys it for me. The way he anticipates my needs and cares for me is unlike anything I've ever experienced in my life. It's the first time a romantic partner hasn't made me feel like our relationship was transactional, like their actions entitle them to more from me. Michael does it all without expectation. He does it because he just wants me to be happy.

We do the *New York Times*'s "36 Questions on the Way to Love," which was created by psychologists for a study exploring whether intimacy between two people can be accelerated by having them ask each other a specific series of personal questions. We spend hours going back and forth answering questions like, "What roles do love and affection play in your life?" and "Of all the people in your family, whose death would you find most disturbing? Why?" He's all-in and open, never making me feel silly or "girly" for the exercise. He listens so intently and is so thoughtful with his responses that I actually do feel myself falling in love with him.

Two months into our relationship, I ask him if he wants to go on an impromptu trip together that very weekend. Without hesitation, he says, "Yes, where do you want to go?" I nearly weep. Spontaneity was anathema to my ex-boyfriend, but here Michael is, ready and willing to go on a weekend trip away to Boston just because his girlfriend suggested it on a whim.

On the trip, we discover we travel beautifully together. Like me, Michael is comfortable with planning a few things, but also leaving time to walk around aimlessly and explore. Being with him feels as easy as breathing. I don't have to pretend or put on airs or edit myself before I speak. He holds my hand wherever we go, even when we're sleeping. We're unguarded with each other. We let ourselves intertwine completely.

Sometime between eating squid ink linguine *aglio e olio* and Boston cream pie, I know it for real. I am in love with him.

Once I know I love Michael and want to be with him, I feel pressure to tell him about my history with depression, that I still fall into the black pit sometimes. I want him to know what he's getting himself into. I want to give him a chance to leave if he can't handle it. With Ethan, my depressive episodes were always treated as a personal attack on him. He would get defensive and make me feel guilty for making *him* feel like shit.

I'm so nervous about telling Michael that I delay it. I can't bear for him to decide it's too much. I don't want him to be like the others, not when I'm already in love with him. But it spills out of my mouth when we're lying in bed on a lazy weekend morning. We're holding each other and studying each other's faces like besotted teens when I blurt, "I have something to tell you."

I let myself cry in front of him for the first time when I tell him. He kisses my cheeks and doesn't care that my tears are salty on his lips. He tells me it's okay, that I have nothing to be embarrassed about. He tells me he wants to be there for me. He tells me he's not afraid. He's so supportive and kind that I cry even harder. It doesn't scare him away. He's still there the next morning, holding me close.

When it's time to bring Michael home, my parents are wary.

"Another white boy?"

"This one's different," I swear. "He eats everything."

And he does.

I beam with pride when Michael eats traditional Chinese herbal soups, *gai jai dan*, and my mother's to-die-for Vietnamese *bún riêu*, a traditional crab tomato noodle soup.

"Wow, this one does eat everything!" My mother says it with so much admiration and awe in her voice that it makes my heart squeeze.

Michael doesn't just eat it all—he falls in love with it. He views everything with a childlike wonder that's reminiscent of how my friends in elementary school always thought unlimited chicken balls was the coolest thing ever. He wants to go to the restaurant all the time to help out. He does the dishes without complaint and helps my dad tenderize meat when he's asked. He carefully cleans the grime from the commercial dishwasher without being asked. He says the words every restaurateur parent wants to hear: "How can I help?" He sacrifices every New Year's Eve to come down to work. He grabs and squeezes my hand when the yelling in the kitchen reaches its roaring crescendo.

He treats the restaurant the way he treats me: with care, respect, and lavish attention. In an odd way, he reminds me of the restaurant itself: a provider, a path filled with promise, a stalwart and reliable presence, seemingly always open.

Through him, I see the restaurant not as something shameful or dirty or embarrassing the way I always thought Ethan did, but as something worth bragging about. The restaurant is cool. It's the manifestation of my family's dreams coming true.

"It must be so nice," my friend Ishani says to me once. "To have someone who loves the restaurant as much as you do."

It is, and it's not just the way he loves the restaurant or me. It's the way he cares about my parents, too. He vacuums my parents' house when they're at work and changes their light bulbs. He buys new dishwashing sponges and cleans the vent in their bathroom. He does it all because he doesn't want them to have to worry about these little things when they already work so hard.

"I love him, man. I love him very much," Mum says. Dad nods and says Michael is "very smart." He's a good man, they agree. They even start to call him "son."

It's not long before Michael and I are seeing each other every day. We can't get enough. When my sister, who has since moved to Germany, comes back to Canada for the holidays and stays with me, I let her have my bed while I sleep on the couch with Michael. We push my sectional together because we can't bear to not sleep curled up around each other. This is how inseparable we've become.

"He's like a unicorn," my sister says. She tells me she sees how he loves and cares for me. It's like nothing either of us has ever seen, and certainly, nothing we've ever experienced ourselves. "He's so good to you."

When we move in together nine months into our relationship, every day brings me fresh reminders of just how good he is. He runs out and buys me ginger ale if I even mention I have a stomach-ache. When I find myself bedridden with a concussion for three months, he adjusts to living in semi-darkness because lights give me a headache. He looks up and consumes TV shows, movies, and books by racialized creators because he knows it's important to me. He always makes sure to ask me how my day is, and the sun never sets without us making time to talk, bear witness to each other, laugh. He tells me I'm the "wittiest and the prettiest." I never question or doubt that it's me he wants, because he never looks at anyone else. He has eyes only for me.

We agree that neither of us wants kids and start to build the life of our dreams. We're always trying new food and restaurants. In our quest to eat our way around the world, we go on at least two international trips a year, where we enjoy Michelin-starred restaurants, street food tours, and endless museums. Our love is uncomplicated and pure, the kind of love where no one takes more than they give. The kind of love where you feel like you're having a never-ending sleepover with your best friend. The kind of love you thought only existed in the made-up stories you once wrote in your spare time to escape the sadness that permeated all your real-life romantic relationships.

After I meet Michael, I stop having to write these little fictions. I no longer need to escape, because my reality is better than anything I ever wrote on the page.

But the black pit of depression sometimes opens up again, of course, as so many who have ever struggled with it will know. The self-doubt comes periodically. So does the temptation to self-sabotage. The Rachel of Yore, whose voice sounds a lot like Gollum's in my head, says things like:

You don't deserve him.

You don't deserve this love.

You're going to fuck this up like you always do.

He'll end up seeing who you really are and leaving. They always do.

In those first few months, I find myself picking fights and trying to push him away. But Michael—even-keeled, reliable Michael—stands his ground. He wraps his arms around me, confirms he heard what I had to say, and vows to work through whatever distressed me, together. No matter what I do, he stays true. His consistency proves me wrong, shows me I am lovable and worth staying for. After a while, I stop fighting and pushing. I wrap my arms around him, squeeze, and accept his love. He's never once made me question it.

When Michael asks me to marry him, he does so with a ring he designed with a local Vietnamese jeweler. The ring has a pink sapphire at the centre surrounded by two diamonds on one side to represent my parents and three diamonds on the other to represent me and my siblings. The band is designed to look like stylized water waves on one side before transitioning to a single band on the other. It symbolizes my family's journey from Vietnam to Canada. It's unconventional. It's full of meaning. It's him asking for my hand and making sure my heart and the people and history who have made me are part of our story, too.

It's the easiest "yes" of my life.

The truth is, before Michael, I didn't think I would end up marrying a white man. I didn't want to be a walking cliché—just another white man, Asian woman couple on the street. I didn't want someone to look at me and assume I only date white men. I didn't know if I wanted to be in a relationship with someone who will never know what it's like to walk through life feeling like they don't belong. I didn't know if I wanted to be put in a situation where time spent with prospective in-laws would require me to be in a room with only white people. I didn't know if I'd feel safe in those situations. I didn't know if I could be myself.

But that changes with Michael. My love for him renders anyone else's opinions about me and our relationship meaningless. Although it's true he'll never know what it's like to be a racialized person, he tries to understand. He works on educating himself. He listens to my stories and experiences without interjecting or getting defensive. And when we're in a room full of white people, his steady hand in mine makes me feel safe. I can always be myself with him.

We elope in 2019 because we don't want to wait, and we want a day just for ourselves without the pressure and price tag of a full-on wedding. It's a good thing because COVID-19 hits just a few months later. Our planned reception gets pushed, then pushed again. It finally happens in November 2021.

In the planning, we agree that both of our cultures should be on display. From our wedding invitations with the double happiness symbol to our wedding favours of personalized chopsticks, there are little touches of my family's culture everywhere. We serve *dim sum*, barbecued duck, soy sauce chicken, and *bánh xèo* because Michael wants his family and friends to experience the flavours I love most. I fall more in love with him when he says it. I change into a red *cheongsam* with a traditional headpiece. We play Chinese songs that are beloved to my family during my dance with my father and our Chinese tea ceremony.

Throughout it all, I am looking up at this man and his eyes that crinkle in the corners, and he's looking at me with the biggest smile on his face. I had no idea one could be this lucky.

10

"RACHEL, DOES YOUR DAD HAVE A PERM?"

As we grew up, my siblings would tell me that our parents fought about money at least once a week, but I was oblivious. I was clueless about when times were lean or when too much had been lost at the casino tables. For me, money was plentiful and abundant. It was always placed in the palm of my hand whenever I asked. I wanted for nothing. In my childish eyes, we all had exactly what we wanted, whenever we wanted it. I saw money as an infinite resource and couldn't understand why my parents' voices rang out in harsh tones over something we had in such rich supply.

As an adult, I book appointments with financial advisors and planners to help me acquire the financial literacy I never learned in school or from my parents. After the childhood I had, my relationship with money isn't complicated. I have it, I spend it. Simple. The older I get, the more I realize this approach causes unnecessary anxiety in my life. I decide I need to learn what this "saving money" concept is all about. I need to unlearn what I learned as a child.

—᙮᙮᙮—

When I revisit old memories, I remember unexpected markers of my parents' complicated relationship with money and status. In one specific memory, I remember the exact sound of my best friend's gasp when she caught sight of my dad. A sudden inhalation of breath. A sharp nudge of her elbow.

"Rachel," she said, slowly, as I clutched my ribs. "Does your dad have a perm?"

I looked up and saw Dad in his usual place—his head turned down toward the sizzling wok, the steam greeting his face. There were tight, merlot-red curls adorning the top of his head where coarse, straight black hair usually lay flat. It was jarring, like a bright red stain on carpet.

I winced and died on the inside. "God yes," I said through gritted teeth. *Please don't ask for more information. Please don't ask. Please don't ask*, I silently begged, my eyes pleading with her.

Instead, she laughed and said, "But why?"

"I don't know!" I wailed. Embarrassment flooded through my body. *Why are my parents so embarrassing?* It was the early 2000s and Dad was single-handedly keeping the '80s alive with his hairstyle of choice. My friend snickered under her breath and called out to Dad, "Love your hair, Mr. Phan!"

I remember how his face split in half with a huge, toothy grin. He looked at me like, "See? My hair is awesome!"

I just shook my head and grabbed my friend's elbow, dragging her away from the kitchen and this man I couldn't believe was my father.

More than a decade later, in 2015, the groundbreaking sitcom *Fresh Off the Boat* aired its first season. It wasn't until I watched its fourth episode, aptly titled "Success Perm," that I realized just what "the perm" must have symbolized to Dad.

In the episode, Constance Wu's Jessica and Randall Park's Louis prepare for a visit from Jessica's sister, Connie, and her family. Jessica and Louis are worried Connie will realize they're not as successful in America as they've been letting on. Their family business—a restaurant!—isn't doing well, but they, of course, don't want anyone to know that. In their family, like so many others, a remarkably high premium is placed on appearances and social standing, with immense cultural pressure to be successful and high achieving. To be anything less is often considered shameful and embarrassing.

Ahead of Connie's visit, Jessica and Louis do everything they can to make themselves look more impressive. They set up fake lemon trees, buy fancy toiletries, and hide coins under couch cushions. "Basically, everything they could to look like ballers," says Eddie, Jessica and Louis's son. Their ace in the hole, however, comes when Jessica and Louis agree they need "a new look that instantly says 'success.'" The scene cuts to Jessica and Louis looking proud and smug. Both are curled and coiffed to the gods with what they call their "success perms."

"Another thing Chinese people did to show prosperity was get a perm. I don't know why, but to my people, curls were like dollar signs," narrator Eddie explains. Jessica remarks that the perm was a great idea, while Louis, chest lifted with pride, says, "I feel like a curly-headed lion surveying my kingdom."

When I watched this for the first time, my mouth dropped open and hung there for a second before I let out a deep belly laugh. I had no clue perms were a symbol of prosperity and success. This whole time I thought Dad was just high-key embarrassing for no reason.

There are a few theories why perms became a beloved status symbol for so many Chinese people. One is obvious: perms can be expensive! Dad remembers how perms used to cost him $40 to $50—not an insignificant amount back in the day. For those who could afford it, it was a sign of their success. They could throw dollar bills at something as frivolous as a hairstyle.

In total, Dad permed his hair "four, five times." The first time was when he was in Vietnam after some good ol' fashioned peer pressure. "A couple of my friends did it, so I did it too," he says. "It was a status thing, a high-class thing. Everyone back home has straight hair, not curly. When you have curly hair, you look like a businessman."

In families like ours where the concept of face is deeply embedded, significant emphasis is placed on symbolic materialism and the social hierarchy. That means a perm is never just a perm. Each perfectly unnatural curl is a sign of success and wealth. It is a sign Dad and his family are living the Canadian Dream.

Ironically, in Canada, the response is less warm. "People said I look funny," Dad laughs. He stops getting perms.

My parents grew up in Hải Phòng, Vietnam, during a time of extreme poverty and starvation. My paternal grandpa, my *ah yeh*, worked in the harbour carrying imported goods—rice, sugar, MSG, fertilizer—from the boats to the warehouses, where he made the equivalent of just $60 a month. Sometimes during the war, he would be sent to different harbours for two to three months at a time. For every twelve-hour shift, *ah yeh* would get one *bánh mì*, which he'd save in a bag to bring back for his children. Upon his return months later, the bread would be hard as a rock, but his kids didn't care. My dad would watch his younger siblings fight for the dried-up bread, ignoring the rumbling in his own stomach. As the eldest of seven, Dad knew it was his responsibility to take care of his brothers and sisters first.

As a child, Dad saw horrific scenes. Starving people eating lice off each other's heads. People throwing up off the sides of boats and others fighting to eat the vomit. People eating their own belts because the leather could be considered meat. For Dad, the most luxurious thing was his birthday gift every year: a single soft-boiled egg.

When the city started getting peppered by bombs, my father's parents sent him and his siblings to live in the mountains, where food was even more scarce. "No one was thinking about dreams," he tells me. "We weren't thinking about going to school or becoming doctors and lawyers. We just worried about our stomachs. If you were full, which we never were, you were successful. We had no choice, no dreams at all."

This is a kind of extreme poverty that I could never imagine. When I think of my own "poor days," I think of living paycheque to paycheque. I think of cutting my takeout down to once or twice a week. I can't imagine having absolutely nothing—no home, no hopes, no sense of security or place. I can't imagine how dehumanizing and demoralizing it must have been for the soundtrack of your childhood to be screams in the dark, your growling stomach, and your crying, starving siblings. I can't imagine wasting away to mere flesh and bone and thinking it won't ever get better.

Growing up with absolutely nothing and zero prospects, my family saw the West as overflowing with opportunity—a place where their children could be raised with abundance and full stomachs and where one could get a good night's sleep without the fear of dying from malnutrition or Americans flying overhead.

I'd wager that this extreme poverty is the reason why no one in my family is good with money and why the fast life of gambling and acquiring extravagant status symbols appeals so much across three generations. It's a safe bet.

It's only upon reflection that I see the signs of my family's frivolous, reckless spending. When I started losing my baby teeth, I was delighted to find that the very generous Tooth Fairy had left me $50 to $100 for each tooth I placed under my pillow. I didn't understand why my friends at school gasped when I told them about my haul after each Tooth Fairy visit. I didn't know that the average going rate for one of their teeth was a paltry $2. I chalked up my fortune to being well-behaved and obedient. The mythical, magical Tooth Fairy rewarded me for staying quiet when asked, being a good student despite never being asked, and never bothering Mum and Dad when the restaurant swarmed with hungry customers. I thought: *My classmates must be horrible children outside of the classroom!*

When my belly groaned from hunger, my parents went over the top. Once, mum made me a plate of three hamburgers, stacked high with bacon and oozing with mayonnaise and ketchup, and I ate every single one. What a difference time and displacement make that I could gorge on meat and bread instead of splitting a single meatless *bánh mì* amongst seven people. "We wanted to make sure you guys were okay, not hungry, like me when I was a little kid," Dad says later.

When I was in the fifth grade, I asked Dad for money for a new pair of shoes. He reached into his pocket and handed me a $1,000 bill, unblinking, dead serious. "Dad!" I howled in shocked exasperation. "That's too much! Give me $100 instead." He shrugged, reluctantly took the $1,000 bill back—I haven't seen another one since—and put $100 in my hands. I dashed off, the crisp bill shoved in my back pocket.

We were able to buy whatever trendy thing we wanted, from Tommy Hilfiger jeans to the most coveted pop albums on their buzzy release days. When fashion trends took me and my classmates by force, like the staggeringly tall platform shoes popularized by the Spice Girls in my fourth-grade year, my parents handed over bills without question so I could secure my seat on the bandwagon. We had the latest computers and high-speed internet when few others did. My brother always had the coolest Air Jordans in various colourways and kept himself basted in expensive colognes. My parents traded in the old red Chevrolet Lumina for a Buick Rendezvous—shiny, new, but still practical for our family of five.

These affordable symbols of upward mobility—easy, obvious ways to flex one's newly attained status and success—are not uncommon amongst aspirational middle-class families like mine. My parents were no longer starving kids living in abject poverty. Mum was no longer working seven days a week at the mushroom farm, making meagre coins for every mushroom she cut. Dad was not digging in the dirt at night for critters after an already long day working at the Happy In. They wanted to show off.

For them, the lure of the casino wasn't just about the potential jackpots. Gambling transcends language barriers. People can gather in one spot where their motivations and interests are not critiqued or judged. At the most basic level, everyone at a casino understands each other. No one pushes for answers or explanations. You can be left alone if you want to be. For immigrants in a new country where belonging is more often a pipe dream than a reality, the allure must be that much stronger. Why wouldn't you flock to a place where no one questions your existence—a place where you're safe to be in community with others who have the same hopes and dreams you do?

Although gambling is a popular pastime within all cultures, and gambling addiction is as much a problem in North America and Europe as it is across Asia, I can't deny that gambling has always been spellbindingly alluring to my family. Gambling isn't seen as taboo or shameful the way it is in Judeo-Christian cultures, where it is—though not outright condemned—evidence of two activities that *are* condemned: loving money and seeking get-rich-quick schemes.

In my family, gambling isn't done under the shroud of secrecy or shame. Instead, it is often seen as a social event. As a child, I spent many a night falling asleep to the sounds of my extended family gambling over spirited games of mahjong.

Studies even show that gamblers of Asian descent are much more likely to visit a casino as a large group rather than as lone wolves. I didn't realize just how true this was until I moved away to university. In Brantford, I seldomly saw other people like me, yet when I walked into the city's casino for the first time, I was stunned momentarily silent by all the East Asian faces I saw sitting around tables or in front of slot machines.

"Where did all these Asians come from?" I asked in wonder. I saw with my own two bewildered eyes how this garish place was like a community centre of sorts. I saw how casinos in all their neon-lit glory masquerade as a place akin to a holy land, where odds are fair and your path to unimaginable wealth and power is tantalizingly within reach if you're ballsy enough to grab for it. We're all susceptible to its gaudy allure. We're especially vulnerable to it when we come from nothing.

Although no one is immune to the appeal of striking it rich fast, it's also true that people of East Asian descent are one of the most targeted populations for casinos. Every day, casino buses roll through Chinatowns and Koreatowns across North America as part of a strategic—and predatory—effort to exploit cultural attitudes around gambling.

These casino bus programs started decades ago to reach gamblers who didn't have their own cars. It's now become the norm. Many of these gamblers are vulnerable older immigrants from China, Vietnam, or Korea who are low income and live in isolation. My paternal grandmother, my *ah mah*, is one of these targets, having spent many of her days chasing luck and fortune at casinos in Niagara Falls well into her eighties.

My *ah mah* treats the casino as a form of entertainment and a way to combat the crushing loneliness that comes with living in a country where she's an outsider in almost every way. Since many senior gamblers like *ah mah* aren't English speakers, they often struggle to find employment, community, and a place where they feel safe and seen. In other words: What the hell else are they going to do?

My parents settled in a town with few other Asians. Of course they were drawn to the casino, where people who spoke their language congregated. It also happened to be a place where, if they didn't want to, they didn't have to speak at all. My mother, who's self-conscious about her English, could perch herself in front of a slot machine and pull the lever. No language barriers. No scrunched up, confused faces. No "Excuse me?" You don't have to speak English to gamble.

In 2021, the Massachusetts Gaming Commission funded a report examining the root causes of problem gambling in the Asian community. The findings showed that working-class Asian immigrants often experienced a double whammy of stress and social isolation, which made them easy prey for casinos.

The writers of the report interviewed forty people from Asian communities in the Boston region and found that a quarter went to casinos because there were no other entertainment options accessible and available to them. In America, it seems, there is "no [other] place for Asians," one respondent said. When one cannot speak the language of the country they're living in, it is much harder to go out to a bar where the waiters and menus are all inaccessible to you or to catch a show at an often all-English theatre.

Many immigrants, like my parents, also work at restaurants, where the hours and days are long. There is a dearth of nighttime activities late in the evening when most get off work. "Lots of time, we go there to see the people," Dad explains. "Lots of friends working at different restaurants would be there because it was the only thing still open. Friends working at other restaurants would call us up and ask if we wanted to go." The answer was almost always "yes."

"When we had a hard day at the restaurant, we'd go to the casino," Dad says. "You forget about it all at the casino. It's like new oxygen. It feels like a different day, a new day."

I get the appeal now. But as a kid, it was harder for me to understand why my parents went away to the casino so often. All I knew was that I got so little of them during the day. It was hard to comprehend why they'd rush off to spend their free time and evenings someplace else—somewhere so far from where I slept, wishing they were home to tuck me in. If I had a nightmare and needed comforting in the middle of the night, I'd run to their room and find only a cold, empty bed. I'd look out their window, at the midnight black sky stretched wide above me, and feel awfully, tremendously alone.

When they came home, it was usually around the same time I was heading off for school. Mum would offer me a massive peanut butter cookie from the casino to eat for breakfast. They'd bring home king crab legs and prime rib smuggled in napkins from the casino's smorgasbord buffet for us to eat as an after-school snack.

With the cookie crumbling soft and delicious in my hands and mouth, I'd forget how upset I'd been in the night. I'd say thanks to the gods of wealth, fortune, and longevity that watched over us from our shrine for bringing my parents back home to me again.

The limited studies out there on problem gambling and race tell us that Asian Americans are at greater risk of becoming problem gamblers than the rest of the population, leading to greater rates of addiction, debt, and painful consequences for loved ones.

Will my parents—who already have a rich history of gambling—be among those bored, lonely elderly folks who see the casino as their only source of entertainment? How do I stop that from happening?

I think about how so many of my most vivid memories of my parents from my childhood are of me asking for money and them pulling wads of cash out of their pockets, no questions asked.

I think about how our roles will reverse one day. Will I give them an allowance? When they ask me for money, what will I say? I already know I won't give freely, no questions asked. I can already see how those interactions are going to go.

"How are you spending your money? What will you do? No, no, no."

It makes me feel like absolute shit, like I'm not holding up my end of an unspoken deal.

—⁓—

"Saving" and "investing" weren't words in my parents' vocabulary. Neither of them takes a salary, so everything they make goes right back into the restaurant and our family, which, growing up, meant food and clothes and all the other basic and not-so-basic necessities each of us wanted. A Columbia House CD subscription for my sister, basketball jerseys for my brother, an over-the-top sequined dress I saw in a store window.

Their winnings from the casino though, that was pure, full-fat gravy on top of all the other blessings. They could do whatever they wanted with that. First, Dad bought a boat for $9,000 even though he's the only one of us who can swim. He bought it because he likes fishing and, I found out later, he saw it as an activity we could enjoy together. "I got it for you guys," he says. Sadly, he learned too late that Mum, John, and I are all prone to seasickness and that Mum was still too traumatized from her time as a boat person to go out on the choppy waters of Lake Erie. After a few years, Dad sold it for $7,000.

Then, there was the time Dad bought a racehorse named All Win Vicky. He was told by a family friend, Sam, that a horse was like playing the lottery. If the horse was good, you could win a lot of money. All you had to do was take a chance. Having beaten the odds all his life, Dad couldn't help but be an idealistic dreamer. He went with Sam to check out the yearling.

One look at the foal, full of promise, and he was sold. He and Sam each put in $15,000 to buy her. "We had big hopes," he says. Her name was All Win Vicky—how could she ever lose? The truth was that she did lose, often. The return on Dad's investment was remarkably poor. To cover her training and health and dental care, and all the other necessities that horses require, Dad estimates he lost about $30,000 on the investment. She won just one race with a purse of about $8,000 before she fell, broke a bone, and couldn't race anymore.

Before tragedy befell her on the racetrack, Dad took me to meet All Win Vicky at her stable. He encouraged me to hop on her back and go for a ride even though I'd never once ridden a horse. He lifted me up by the armpits to look her in the eye, and I shivered at her immense size. She was so tall and broad! Her brown coat shone like she caught moonlight on her flank. She was beautiful, imposing. Her hooves were the size of the plates we serve egg rolls on. Next to her, I felt so small and breakable.

I wiggled out of Dad's grasp and refused to even touch her, so afraid I was of this majestic, expensive beast. When her trainer let her out of her stable, I scurried off to stand as far away as possible. While Dad watched her trot around, I watched him. He looked so proud and happy. His face was aglow with something that looked like expectation, as if the key to endless possibilities and wealth could be found on those four remarkably fast legs. It's a shame she was never fast enough.

You might read this and think we lived extravagantly. In some ways, we did. We never wanted for anything and I rarely, if ever, heard the word "no."

It wasn't until I was much older that I came to the realization that my family could have been considered "poor" compared to my classmates, whose parents were teachers, doctors, and suits in offices. Looking back now, I see the little things that may have seemed like indicators of our socioeconomic class to outsiders looking in. We had no extended health insurance. We rented our apartment above the restaurant. We enrolled in zero paid extracurricular activities. And my parents' hard labour and long hours put them solidly in the working class—the social class marked by jobs with reduced educational requirements that typically require physical labour. I can't deny that my parents fall into this category when I see the impacts of their work written so plainly across their bodies.

Once, I let it slip to Dad that I am feeling a tingling sensation in my wrists from too much work and far too much tech. He laughs and I can't blame him. He doesn't have to say anything. His unrestrained laughter says it all. "*Your* wrists? *Your* pain?"

I blush a furious shade of red. Sheepish. Full of shame. What is my wrist pain compared to his? To Mum's?

In their sixties, my parents remain the hardest working people I know. Their bodies, once strong, indestructible, have been worn down by three decades of back-breaking work at the restaurant. For my mother, day after endless day of flicking her wrists over a wok to fry rice, along with never-ending wonton making, vegetable chopping, and meticulous shrimp peeling, has left her with carpal tunnel in both wrists and arthritis pretty much everywhere. Recently Dad, in a show of great love for my mother, agreed to switch to buying pre-peeled shrimp, damn the expense. Gone are the days of their reckless youth when extravagant expenses were equine in nature. Now, they just want life to be a little bit easier for their aging bodies.

Mum isn't the only one who's hurting because of her job. Dad, so close to retirement and yet so far, holds physical trauma in his body, too. At sixty-six, he still lifts the heavy soup pots and overflowing garbage bags, but with half the speed and triple the wincing. He says words I've never heard him say before: "I'm tired."

My parents could never imagine a life where they get to sit for most of the day and stare at a screen. They're in awe when I tell them I get to work entirely from home. When I tell them I'm pursuing three different post-secondary degrees, they never ask "Why?" They just encourage me—seeing opportunities for me to avoid their fate. They see possibilities for me that could lift me out of the hole they found themselves in, of working entirely too hard just to have their minimal profits poured right back into the job that's killing them. They want me to be free, to have more than they ever dreamed.

"I just wish we could help you," Dad says one night. He's just picked me up from the train station in Chatham, and we're driving in near total darkness. The moonlight shines into our car, and I can see his face in shadowed profile.

"Hmm?" I say, half-asleep.

"With your school. Your mum and me. We wish we could help you pay for things so you don't have debt," he responds.

I think about the $50,000 I've accumulated in student loans. Because my dad and I have a relationship marked by few words, all I say is, "Me too."

—⁓—

By some miracle, it takes me only five years to pay off my student debt. When I excitedly tell my parents, I can see their pride swelling in their chests, emblazoned on their faces.

"Good girl," they say. "So good. So smart."

I glow from the inside.

11

"I THINK I WANT TO
GO BACK HOME."

I spend years getting my house in order. After years of weepy therapy and begrudging conversations with my inner child, I finally feel like I know who I am. I extricate myself from toxic people and relationships. I find belonging and peace in Toronto. I meet and marry the man of my dreams.

With so much inner and individual healing done, I start looking for new projects. I turn outward to explore what else needs mending. I fix my gaze on my parents and come to the unsurprising realization that I'm tired of the restaurant getting in the way of me connecting with them. As I get older, I find myself desperately wanting to know who they are as people, outside of being my parents and busy restaurateurs. I want to know where we come from. I'm finally at an age when their stories aren't met with a groan and an eye roll.

I want to know about what life in Vietnam was like and if they're happy with where their lives took them. I want to know how they keep the demons of their pasts—the sounds of bombs overhead and the memories of their bloodied feet from so much walking, running, fleeing—from haunting them today. I want to know if coming to Canada and spending decades doing this body-destroying work was worth it in the end.

For a long time, I'm too afraid to ask. I keep pushing it off to another day when I might feel emotionally ready, stronger. It's a constant string of "not yets" that turn into months, then years.

My parents must sense my desire for connection because they seem to want to connect with me, too. In contrast to when we were younger, they start saying the words "I love you" over and over again—that's true assimilation!—and begin to show me glimpses of their secret dreams. "Dad wants to move back to Vietnam when we retire," Mum tells me. "We can live like kings and queens over there!" Dad hollers in the background. When I call, I usually talk to my mother for an hour. If I'm lucky, I'll get Dad on the line for two minutes tops. It's progress. I used to never catch him on the phone at all.

For the longest time, my mother rejects the idea of going back to Vietnam. She hasn't returned since 1978. For one, she couldn't travel without a passport, and she didn't get her Canadian citizenship until after she turned fifty-five and was no longer required to take the citizenship test. Second, she's in no rush to go back to a land still soaked in blood and mired in misery for her. "Why I want to go back?" she'll say, her voice dripping with scorn. "There's no one left for me there." She dismisses the idea so quickly that I can't help but think about the many ghosts she must be keeping at bay with her refusal.

"But you haven't been back in so long," I'll reply, not wanting to dig too deeply. These types of surface-level conversations are part of the well-worn texture of my relationship with my mother.

She'll usually respond with a scoff, "I don't want to go back. It will look so different. Nothing will be the same." But she surprises me one day, when the conversation doesn't go down its usual, expected path. "I think I want to go back home," she admits.

"You do?"

"Yes, your dad showed me on YouTube."

"But I thought you said it'll look too different?"

"Yes, everything change now. But I think I want to go back home."

When she repeats it, I'm suddenly struck by her use of the word "home." It sends a shockwave through me. *When did my mother stop seeing Canada as her home? Or did she ever feel at home here?* I don't ask her, of course. Instead, I just say, "When do you want to go?"

Michael and I plan and book the trip. We're going to travel across Vietnam with my parents and sister for four weeks. John decides against going because he's already booked a cruise with his girlfriend and he's worried about surviving the long flight and Vietnam's heat.

The trip will be the most time I've ever spent with my parents.

I expect total chaos. A disaster. Surely, we'll be at each other's throats the entire time. The Black Blood of the Phans will rain down on us all.

I think about the worst that could happen. *What if the trip ends and I realize I love my parents, but I don't particularly like them? What if they realize the same about me?*

After a two-day layover in Seoul, where my parents pick apart the cold, snowy weather and the unfamiliar food, we land in warm, vibrant Hà Nội.

Suddenly, my parents come to life. Although they're lost and mostly silent in Seoul, they're animated in Vietnam. All around them, people speak a language they understand. I'm not prepared for my mum to speak up in the car in crisp, loud Vietnamese. The driver says something, and both my parents laugh. They talk the entire car ride to the hotel.

My parents are in their element. They are home. *This* is where they belong. Everywhere there are people who look like us and stalls selling familiar foods like *bánh cuốn* and *bún riêu* and *xôi khúc*. Unlike in Seoul, where people with flawless faces and skin are dressed immaculately in designer clothes, there are no airs in Vietnam. We look around and see people with their bare feet out—food stall be damned—and people excavating their mouths with the ubiquitous toothpick.

About twenty minutes into the car ride, Dad says, "I think me and your mum are going to live here."

I observe my parents obsessively on the trip. I'm eager to take in every morsel of information I can about these people who have given me everything but themselves.

I want to know who they are individually and what the dynamics of their relationship are when the restaurant isn't wreaking havoc and dysfunction on it. I want to know everything and anything that will give me a better understanding of myself and how I came from these two people and what of them I carry with me. What traumas of theirs and our ancestors lie deep and dormant in the spongy, brown marrow of my bones?

Everywhere we go, my parents throw themselves into new experiences. After decades spent inside the four walls of the restaurant, this is one of the first times in their lives they can play and explore. All they have to do is show up and be themselves.

My dad amazes me with his ability to make friends everywhere he goes. Whether he's chatting with the concierge and doorman at our hotel in Hà Nội for hours or giving out Canadian cigarettes to our tour guides ("This one cigarette costs $1!"), we get used to hearing the sound of his voice. People are so naturally drawn to him and his stories and his free-flowing laughter that I'm awed by how willing they are to impress him. There are the two separate tour guides who sing songs for him when he asks and the young guide who tells Dad he'll get him weed next time Dad's in town and the many people who readily share personal details about their lives just because he asks. There are no secrets among friends, and Dad has collected them in each of the corners of Vietnam we visit.

His childlike curiosity is infuriatingly delightful to behold. While kayaking on the less than pristine waters of Ha Long Bay, Dad dips his hand into the murky waters and brings his fingers to his lips. We gasp and admonish him for drinking such dirty water, but Dad just shrugs, unbothered by our concern and disgust. "I didn't know if it was salt or fresh. I just wanted to taste it!"

Mum, who is usually more reserved, comes to life in unexpected ways. Before the trip, she is so afraid. She's worried about getting sick, going on the back of a motorbike, walking too much, being on a boat. "Do we have to? I'm not going to," is her common refrain. But every time she pushes herself to try, she falls in love with the adventure, the thrill of trying something new. She walks for hours at a time without complaint or pain. She climbs up rocky steps like a champion and travels through caves like she does this type of adventuring as a hobby. When we ride on the backs of motorbikes in lively Sài Gòn for a food tour, she tells the drivers how frightened she is, but by the end, she's the only one of us who doesn't grip the back of the bike for dear life. Even now, she talks about how much she misses riding a motorbike and the freedom and fun it gave her: "I love it, man. I love it so much." It's a blessing to watch them slip out of the collars leashing them to the restaurant and actually enjoy life. Their tentative first steps are like watching a child learning how to walk and then becoming emboldened. Denied a childhood and a chance to really live, this is their time. They thrive.

"I don't want to go back home," Dad says as we near the end of the trip. "This is a good life, just thinking about what we're going to eat the next day. Not thinking about how many chicken balls we need to make."

Mum echoes his sentiment. "Aw Rachel, Mummy have fun. I don't want to go home. I don't want to go back to work. Back home, I feel so heavy, but here, I feel so light." This is who my mother and father are outside of the restaurant, when they're free to just be themselves. They're happy.

They're finally learning who they are when they're not fighting for survival. It feels like a revelation. It feels like getting to know strangers, as much for me as it is for themselves. I am awed by how inquisitive and friendly and compassionate and adventurous and caring they are. I didn't know there were so many adjectives I could use to describe the parents who have always just been "hard-working" to me. I feel like I'm being introduced to them anew each day. It's pure joy.

I witness firsthand my parents' great love and compassion for the people in their home country. Dad hands out Vietnamese *đồng* to anyone he finds in need, which in his eyes, is most people we encounter. When one of his new friends tells him that the average monthly salary for a Vietnamese person living in the city is 6.4 million *đồng*, or 350 Canadian dollars, Dad is deeply affected. He wants to help.

Once, we're walking through a small market in a village near Huế when we stumble upon an old woman selling *balut* eggs for 7,000 *đồng* each, or thirty-eight cents Canadian. Her smile lights up the space and pulls my dad, who has a headache, out of his foul mood. We buy five *balut* eggs and hand her 50,000 *đồng*. She beams, grabs for my parents' outstretched hands. The woman tells us that she didn't sell any eggs in the morning and that we made her day by supporting her. Dad later tells us that he wanted to give her more money but held back because he was afraid we'd be mad. It saddens me to think we were a chain holding back his open heart.

It's understandable why Dad is so free with his money. Here, they are not seen as low-class labourers. No one judges them for not working in an office or not having enough. In Vietnam, they are the ultimate success stories. They beat the staggering odds against them and their survival and succeeded in starting over and excelling in a prosperous land. Dad brags about me writing a book, their successful business, his son-in-law. The respect and admiration he garners from the people we meet must feel so good. "It makes me feel proud," he says.

In our second week in Vietnam, we board a train that takes us to Hải Phòng, my parents' hometown. They're jittery with nerves. "You're going to see your house in three hours," Dad says to Mum as the train rolls away from Hà Nội. "I hope so!" she replies. Neither of them has any idea whether their old houses are even standing. They don't remember street numbers or names. They're relying on muscle memory to guide them home.

When the train pulls into Hải Phòng Station, Dad says, "Forty-five years ago, I left here with my mum. Now, I come back with my wife, two daughters, and son-in-law." He says it with his chest lifted and a reflective look on his face.

I wonder what they'll find here, if it'll live up to their expectations, if the ghosts they left behind will come out to haunt us all.

—◆—

"Holy moly macaroni. This used to be nothing, nothing at all. It used to all be rice paddies. Now, look! Everything's different."

My parents are amazed by what Hải Phòng has become. No longer shell-shocked and barren from the Vietnam War, no longer rife with abject poverty and starvation. It is a flourishing city with paved sidewalks, a flower-lined promenade by the river, and flushing toilets. When my parents last lived here, Tam Bac Lake was framed only by its own muddy banks. The dirt streets were covered in piss and shit. Dad mimics how he used to walk to avoid stepping in excrement, as if dodging mines.

Their eyes widen with how much has changed in forty-five years. No, this is certainly not the homeland painted in their memories. It's grown, matured, gotten better. It's moved on without them. "I really, really, really like it," Mum says. For the first time, she echoes what my Dad's been saying for years. "I think I want to live here."

We catch a cab from our hotel to the Hải Phòng Opera House, a landmark opened in 1912 that features a giant portrait of Hồ Chí Minh. From here, my parents retrace their steps from four decades ago to find the homes of their childhoods. I'm amazed that their muscle memory actually does get them to where they want to go. They never seem lost. They just keep walking forward and turn when they need to turn.

In Vietnam, shophouses are everywhere. In these houses, the ground floor operates as a storefront and the floors above are where families reside. As a child, Mum lived in a shophouse with her family, which consisted of her dad, his two wives, her five full siblings, and eight half siblings. Mum's mum, my *ah po*, sold beer out of the storefront, and her second mum sold *phở*. It's only on this trip that I learn that Mum didn't grow up impoverished the way I always thought. Since she rarely talked about her childhood, I let my dad's stories about how he grew up shape what I assumed about hers.

When we see a parkette with a gigantic golden statue of the female warrior Lê Chân, Dad points excitedly. "Me and my friend, we used to sit in the garden there and look at your mum and her half-sister." My parents didn't meet in Hải Phòng—they met in a refugee encampment in China—but as fate would have it, Dad took notice of Mum from afar long before they met. He watched her while she sold beer, oblivious to the fact that her future husband was across the street.

We're walking up a street with a row of shophouses when Mum sees one that strikes a chord in her memory. What used to be her family's *phở* and beer business is now a baby formula store, but it's closed. To pass the time, Mum and Dad make conversation with the ladies who run the store next door. They in turn introduce us to another man who runs a store selling elaborate gift baskets for the upcoming Lunar New Year. Although none of them remember my *ah gong*, Phuc Hoang, and his family, they will be the first of many to gather around my family that day.

After spending time taking family pictures and lighting incense in the parkette where Dad used to watch Mum, we notice that the baby formula store is opening. Linh and I urge Mum to go inside and talk to the store owners, but she is suddenly hesitant, uncertain.

"No, it's okay! They're busy and I don't want to bug them." She and Dad are already walking away. They know better than anyone the value of having people stay out of their way when they're working. But my sister and I are persistent, pulling Mum in the direction of the store. The friendly woman working in the store next door sees us and smiles. She has no qualms about bugging anyone and leads Mum and Dad to a middle-aged man who's setting up an ice cream freezer outside. (The baby formula store also sells snacks for adults.) She facilitates the conversation between him and my parents.

Suddenly, my parents are shouting excitedly and Dad is shaking the man's hand. Mum is beaming.

"This man, he remembers your grandpa!" Dad says to us. The man was just a little boy when my mother's family lived there, but he remembers my *ah gong*, who was famous in town for having two wives and working at a company similar to a taxi service. He vividly remembers grandpa picking people up and driving them around town since having a car back then was such a rarity. *Ah gong* was a big deal. He tells us that we are not the first of my mother's family to come by over the decades. My uncles and cousins have returned, poked around, looked for this same connection to the past.

He graciously lets us go to the back of the shop, where the residential part of the shophouse begins. Mum lets out a gasp. "This looks the same," she says, eyes wide with awe. They rove around the store, desperate to recall every crack, every tile, every link to her family and childhood.

Mum points to a kitchen in the corner. "We make soup in there." She gestures to the stairs. "And that one, we go upstairs, and at nighttime, we sleeping upstairs." When she turns to look at me, her eyes are glassy with emotion. There's a gigantic smile on her face. Even though so much of Hải Phòng has become strange and unfamiliar to her, this has stayed the same all these years. It's a small comfort. She can hardly believe it. She tells me she feels better after seeing her house.

"It's a good one, Rachel, you help Mummy," she says. "You told me to come back. Thank you."

After Mum's house, it's Dad's turn to show us where he grew up. We set out in the direction of Dad's house, which was in a workers' residential area called Hạ Lý. The Tam Bac Lake separates the area where Mum lived with her middle-class merchant family from my dad's, whose family was poor. "They used to say you shouldn't date a boy from Hạ Lý," Dad says. "They had a reputation for being bums."

On our way there, Dad shows us the river, where he'd come every day to bathe. It's where he learned to swim. What used to be nothing but mud has become a quaint riverfront. The rickety suspension bridge is gone and has been replaced with a proper concrete bridge. Buildings line both sides of the water. "None of this existed before," Dad says.

We cross the bridge and enter Dad's old neighbourhood. He shows us the tiny yellow temple where he met with a fortune teller as a young man. When we're there, a man comes out of his home, intrigued by the four Asian strangers and one white man outside his door. He becomes another new friend to point us in the direction of Dad's old street.

We follow his advice and make it to Hạ Lý, which is now dotted with houses. It wasn't this densely populated when Dad lived here decades ago. Dad shows us the house on the corner, where the man who used to cut his hair lived. "If I see anyone I know, I'm going to give them money," he tells us. He says it like a warning and a challenge. *Try to stop me.* We wouldn't dare.

While Dad is showing us where his barber used to live, a woman running a stall out of her home calls out to him. They talk in Vietnamese and Dad tells her he grew up here. "Poon," he says, giving her our Chinese name. As luck would have it, she was Dad's neighbour when they were children. He knew her brother. He had watched her dad struggle with and succumb to lung cancer.

We walk down the narrow street, and Dad is stunned by how different everything looks. There weren't this many houses before. It confuses him, makes him think he's found his house. He takes us down a darkened alley, but it's not the right place.

Everywhere we go, there are people willing to help us. They are eager to welcome this prodigal son of Hạ Lý back home. They offer to help with a pointed finger or by approaching a neighbour who might know where the Poon family lived. My dad's old neighbour leaves her stall in the hands of her friends to meet us down the street. She, too, wants to see my Dad's home.

As we're chatting with an elderly woman through her window, one of the women points to a small man in a khaki jumpsuit walking towards us. He is thin, and his skin and face reveal he's worked hard in life, probably months on end in the sun. The woman tells the man who we are, and a flicker of remembrance flashes across his face. He remembers them. He miraculously starts naming my dad's brothers. Then, Dad is shaking his hand, speaking exuberantly and corroborating the man's incredible memory.

The man recalls stories about my uncles, including the harrowing tale of my Uncle Hac falling off the bridge and being saved when a hook caught him through the armpit. Dad nods, excited. "Yes, that was my brother!" Dad remembers the man too, telling me later, "We used to beat him up for being Vietnamese!"

The man, hopefully forgetting that my dad and his brothers used to torment him, leads us down the correct darkened alley, and the rush of memories comes to my father immediately. He shows us where the outdoor kitchen was that his family shared with four other families. He shows us where their shared outdoor bathroom was, where they'd squat over a hole and where, once, my dad looked down and saw someone stealing his shit for fertilizer as it was coming out.

There's a human-sized hole blasted into the concrete wall outside of where the kitchen used to be. Dad, the consummate storyteller, launches into one for his family. We finally are ready to listen. "In 1972 when they bomb, everybody go in here. Right here," Dad climbs in, showing us how he and his family would crouch in the hole. He's sixty-five and has returned to the place where he used to cower and shake as a frightened child. "When they bomb, you can see the walls shake. *Boom, boom, boom.* You could see the bombing from here."

While Dad tells his story, I am amazed that the building continues to stand, that it withstood so many violent forces seeking to destroy it. I am amazed that my father and mother are still here, too. Their memory and legacy lives on in these walls, streets, and friendly strangers.

The man who led us here has to leave shortly afterwards to work and Dad presses 500,000 *đồng* in his hand. The man resists, but my father is stubborn and resists his resistance. It's the least he can do to thank the person who made it possible for my dad to do what he's always wanted: show his children where he came from, and by extension, where we come from, too.

We spend hours sitting at Dad's old neighbour's food and drink stall. She and her friends make us tea and corn. My parents reminisce, brag about their children, tell stories about their life in Canada. Random strangers show up periodically to join in on their conversation.

When Michael and I visited Sài Gòn a few years prior to this trip, back in 2018, we befriended our seatmate on the plane. Upon landing, he offered to have his mother pick us up, treat us to dinner, and drive us to our hotel. He said that taking care of your fellow villagers is a core tenet of Vietnamese culture. Even though we were strangers, we were part of his village.

That's the beautiful thing about Vietnam. The sense of community is unlike anything I've ever experienced. People float in and out of conversations, restaurants, and streets like old friends. The common language fosters familiarity between my parents and these kind strangers. Even though we are foreigners and interlopers, no one objects. Everyone welcomes us into the village, no questions asked. It fills me with an overwhelming sense of belonging, of coming home somehow. Of being able to better answer the question, "Who are you and where do you come from?" Up until this trip, I had never felt a connection to Vietnam. I had never claimed it as being a part of me. That's changed now.

I end the day feeling closer to my parents than I could have ever imagined. I expected to learn who they are in dribs and drabs but have been blessed with a deluge. It's a day I'll cherish for the rest of my life.

There are moments of tenderness between my parents throughout the trip that, at first, feel so surreal because of how unexpected and unfamiliar they are. Each time, I'm prodded with what feels like a thread and needle to the chest. Each moment tying me closer to my parents. Each thread forming a new, stronger connection with them.

It's looking over to my parents on the plane and seeing their heads tilted together like teenagers sharing a secret, Mum's head on Dad's shoulder and her hand on his arm. They're laughing and smiling.

It's watching Mum and Dad dancing to "Gangnam Style" in a bamboo basket boat in Hội An, their faces split in half by their goofy grins and their Vietnamese conical hats slipping off their heads from the force of their pumping fists.

It's Dad spelling "LOVE" on the beach in Đà Nẵng and looking up at Mum.

It's my parents riding on the backs of motorbikes in Sài Gòn and Dad shouting to Mum, "You look beautiful!" when we're stopped at a traffic light.

It's Dad reaching for Mum's hand when we try to cross the chaotic streets full of swarming motorbikes or when we walk up and down slippery steps.

As the days and weeks unfold, I hoard these memories in my heart. I'm grateful for every second they're smiling and for each reminder that there is love between them. After everything, they're still here. It's not all bad.

As the minutes tick by, we learn each other's rhythms and idiosyncrasies. We learn how to be together. We learn how to navigate treacherous terrain—that is, our mood swings. The answer is almost always food and a nap.

In truth, although this is the most concentrated time we've ever spent with Mum and Dad, the roles here aren't so different from back home. Dad is the provider who thrives when telling us where to go and what to eat.

Mum takes care of Dad, making sure he takes his daily medication and reeling him in so he doesn't give away all their money.

Linh wrangles Mum and Dad, making sure they're awake on time and where they need to be since neither of them has a cell phone or watch.

My husband, Michael, takes care of me. He's joined by Dad, Mum, and Linh in doing so.

I am coddled. When we eat, my parents heap my plate with fish they've deboned for me, crab they've worked hard to crack open, fatty pork belly with the fat carefully peeled off. Wherever we go, they love asking people to guess how old I am, howling with every audible gasp they elicit when they reveal my real age. I am their baby, and they delight in the fact that I am still so fresh-faced and youthful. They are more tactile with me, grabbing my hand, teasingly pinching my cheek, giving me hugs before we go to bed. They tell me I'm cute and pretty and beautiful. They brag about me to others, saying I'm smart and successful.

This is what I've been missing my whole life.

—⁓—

Over the weeks, I observe some of the people we encounter—their lined faces, sun-damaged skin, gnarled, shaking fingers. I see an alternate reality where my family wasn't forced to leave. We meet countless people who are younger than my parents in age but look so much older. My parents are spry and energetic. They have meat on their cheeks.

"Thank God Vietnam kicked us out. If we stayed, maybe I'd be a garbage man or selling lottery on the street," Dad says after we pass a handful of elderly women baking in the sun, trying to sell "lucky tickets" for a few cents' worth of profit. Most of these ticket sellers are unable to work because of old age or disability.

In this life where my parents weren't forced to flee, I probably wouldn't even exist. They may have never met if they hadn't been stuck in a refugee camp in China together. And if they had met and gotten together, would they have had enough money to feed a fifth mouth?

In the alternate reality where I do exist, I wonder how different my life would be. I take to observing restaurant kids in Vietnam. Some are impossibly young, maybe five or six, and helping out at the restaurant. For many of these families, their restaurant is a multigenerational endeavour. I watch as grandparents, parents, and grandchildren all work together to satisfy customers. I wonder how many feel like the restaurant is their only option.

In Huế, we go to a restaurant where two restaurant kids are shrieking at the top of their lungs and chasing each other, but their parents ignore them, too focused on getting five bowls of *bún bò Huế* out to our table. "That would never fly at our restaurant," I say. Dad laughs, "Yeah, we'd send you to the kitchen!"

In this universe where we stay in Vietnam, life is still hard but in a different way than it is in Canada. I don't know whether to be grateful for it. Maybe in Canada we have endless opportunities and the big Canadian Dream. But here, in Vietnam, we'd have our language, our culture, a place to belong without so many conditions. Either way, we win. Either way, we lose. Isn't that just life?

—⁓—

Because I always thought I was either an accident or my parents' attempt at having another son, the feeling of being unwanted always nagged at me in the deep recesses of my heart. On the trip, I ask Dad for the truth.

"You weren't an accident," he says, surprising me. "My father and your mother's father, their generation always had at least a half dozen kids. Once things got settled, we knew we wanted another kid. It didn't matter if you were a boy or girl."

He repeats it again. "You weren't an accident."

It's reassuring to hear I had been wanted from the very beginning. I finally put that long-held insecurity to rest.

—⁓—

In Vietnam, I finally understand the way our parents love and care for us. Although Mum and I have grown closer over the years, Dad remained just out of reach to me. He's always been the distant figure looming large and imposing but never nearby. In Vietnam, he becomes a real three-dimensional person to us. The way he loves us becomes obvious.

After Mum carefully peels jackfruit seeds and boils them for us to eat, Dad doesn't eat any. "Save them for Rachel," he tells my sister. "Maybe she'll want some when she comes over."

He wakes up at five in the morning every day in Hải Phòng to grab us freshly made *bánh cuốn* and *bánh khúc* for breakfast because he knows the ladies who sell them sell out fast, and his family loves to eat them as much as they love to sleep in.

They both want to cook for us even on vacation. Mum makes a delicious vegetable soup when we say we're craving greens, and Dad is struck with the desire to make us a crab noodle soup. He and Michael walk an hour to a market to buy two crabs and carry them all the way back to the hotel, where Dad carefully makes the broth with a whole chicken butchered by Mum. When he serves the soup, he spends almost the entire meal cracking open the crab and making sure we all have heaps of the delicate meat in our bowls.

At restaurants, Dad orders the dinner courses for us because we can't speak or read the language. He serves us the food even though custom dictates that the youngest should do the serving. They always ask if we're okay, if we want anything more. When we say we're full, they sneak more chicken legs onto our plates.

In his quest to try new experiences with us throughout the trip, Dad's the reason our entire family goes to a spa to get pedicures—he's never had one—and the reason he and Michael end up shooting AK-47s together on a whim. He's the reason we order an expensive type of sturgeon fish he's always wanted to try. My entire life, I've always said my dad was allergic to spending time with family, yet here he is, proving me wrong. If nothing else, I now realize Dad's absence wasn't because he didn't want to spend time with us. He just needed time away to decompress from the restaurant.

Because we're not fluent in each other's primary languages, conversations with my parents often lack nuance. This inability to fully understand each other with words makes the little moments of tenderness so much more significant. Food and keeping us fed and eating well has always been my parents' love language. Leaving everything they knew behind so we could all have a chance at a better life is part of that love language. Busting their asses day in and day out well into their sixties is part of their love language. Not pursuing their own dreams and slowly losing bits and pieces of their language, culture, and themselves so their kids could have everything—that's their love language.

I think about the way Mum would take time after closing up the restaurant to clean my freshly pierced ears or comb through my hair the two times I was unlucky enough to get lice. I think about how she came running up the stairs to the apartment on a muggy July night because I was eleven and there was blood on my underwear and I was worried I was dying. I think about how Dad spent so many evenings in a car with his lead-footed daughter, teaching me how to drive. I think about how Mum would put money in my bank account every week because my first adult job paid me only $40,000 a year in expensive Toronto.

I think about my childhood and how they've always supported my dreams and celebrated my successes and never once forced me to be or do anything I didn't want. I think about how they gave me a blank slate, not because they didn't care, but because they wanted me to have everything they didn't when their own slates were destroyed. I think about how when I go home, Mum prefers that I surprise her, and how every time I do, she screams with so much joy, I can feel how much she loves me. I think about how, when we visit, my parents make us at least three courses for dinner every single night after they've already spent twelve hours cooking for everyone else. I think about the bowls of carefully peeled fruit, the giant vats of *tong sui*, the family photo that my mother carries in her wallet.

For my entire life, my parents and I have danced on the peripheries of each other's lives, never knowing each other and being too afraid to ask. On the trip, I ask questions and they answer, even though it's painful. This is another way they love me: they let me in.

The pure affection and deep love I feel for my parents grow each time I recall one of these not-so-small moments in time. It blossoms and blooms and takes root, slowly dislodging the pain and resentment that have festered there for decades. Although we still don't speak the same verbal language, I'm finally fluent in their love language. I finally see what I've always missed. I finally understand that this is what Mum and Dad do. They take care of us. They've always taken care of us.

My worries about us fighting and the Black Blood of the Phans raining down on us all never come true. We only have a handful of disagreements the entire four weeks we're together. Instead, I learn that my parents are fun and funny. We have inside jokes now. I just love being with them.

When the trip ends, I am hit with a wave of grief knowing that I'm going back to a reality where I won't see them every day. I want to travel with them again and look forward to our next trip together. I want to make up for all the lost time our circumstances and the restaurant took from us.

"This was beautiful," Dad says on one of our final days. "Thank you, Rachel. This was my dream. A great adventure."

A week after we return from the trip, I'm on the phone with my parents. I talk to my dad for longer than two minutes this time. "I miss you too," he says. "A whole month together and now I'm missing something."

All of us feel it. A deeper connection with each other, long-standing questions answered about our past, a tie to our homeland and culture that didn't exist for me before. It feels a lot like coming home. It feels like I can finally say I know my parents and we belong to each other. They are as much mine as I am theirs.

12

"THERE ARE LOTS OF THINGS I WANT TO TELL YOU."

We're still marked as foreign, even in Vietnam.

In Hải Phòng, there's the lady selling *bánh cuốn* who tells my dad, "I heard your voice and I know you're not from around here." When Dad, incredulous, tells her he was born there, she shrugs. "I can still tell you're not from here."

There are other markers, too. There's the fact my parents are travelling with a tall white man, my husband, and that their two daughters have flawless English but are clueless when spoken to in Vietnamese. A more unexpected marker arises at a restaurant, in the men's washroom of all places. A man asks Dad where he's from after Dad declines using a grubby hand towel that's been pawed and defiled by who knows how many men before him. Dad's hygiene apparently isn't from around here either.

It strikes me then that we are doomed to be forever foreigners wherever we go. In Canada, we're subjected to constant questioning about where we're *really* from. The COVID-19 pandemic revealed how easily we can become villains and scapegoats, no matter how long we've lived there or even whether we were born there. Long before that, I was a high schooler being told I should be deported. We're either not Canadian enough or we're simply not the right kind of Canadian, period.

The stench of foreignness follows us even here, in the land where my parents breathed their first breaths. The question of identity hangs over me the entire trip. *Who are we? Are we Chinese? Are we Vietnamese? Are we Canadian? Can we really claim any of those countries as our own?* Each has laid claim to us at one point or another and has felt like home, but generations of my family have learned just how conditional those claims can be. My family knows all too well how easily belonging can be revoked.

It's startling to accept that no matter how we identify, we never quite belong anywhere. We're always marked as Other, as people from elsewhere. In turn, I become more possessive and protective of my relationships with my family and the connections we've cultivated on this trip. Suddenly, the truth is stark. In this world, the bonds we have with each other are often all we really have. Borders and language and citizenship shift and evolve, are lost and taken away, but this—each other—is completely ours.

———

My whole life, Dad has told us stories about his life and the war, but I didn't have the ears to listen. In Vietnam, I pay attention. I take it in. I learn. One of the biggest lessons is how tenuous belonging and home can be.

Before the cancerous infection known as World War II metastasizes across the world, it has its unofficial start in Asia in 1937, when the Japanese invade China. What would transpire between then and 1945 would one day be described as "the Asian Holocaust" because of the sheer scale and heinousness of Imperial Japan's war crimes against Chinese civilians. This is when the Rape of Nanjing occurs, which sees more than 300,000 murdered, 80,000 women raped, and 40,000 executed. And that was just *one* event. Although precise figures are challenging to determine, some sources estimate around ten to twenty million Chinese are massacred and countless tortured in one of the bloodiest world conflicts in history.

The Japanese decide the land is not ours. They decide our own bodies are not our own. They decide our lives are not worth living. We have to leave.

So we do. My grandparents flee to neighbouring Vietnam not long after the invasion.

Not even two decades later, a civil war breaks out in Vietnam between the North and the South. In 1955, the Americans get involved. They do this to save South Vietnam from falling to communist North Vietnam. They fear that if one country falls to communism, the surrounding countries will also fall, like dominoes. Thus begins the so-called Vietnam War, or as it's known in Vietnam, the Resistance War against America.

My dad, Poon Hy, is born three years later in 1958. My mother, Hoang Thieu Tran, is born three years after him in 1961.

The war rages on. Once again, another country has decided that the land is not ours. They decide our own bodies are not our own, that we cannot be trusted to make our own decisions. They decide our lives are not worth living if it keeps the dominoes from falling.

To go to school, Dad sometimes has to walk for two hours through the mountains and rice paddy fields. He loves learning. His mind is a sponge. But when he's in the middle of third grade, the war forces him out of his safe haven. He and his siblings are evacuated to the mountains.

They hide there for five years. At night, they're plunged into complete darkness because any light would alert bombers of their location and of the army camped there. Every time the Americans come to bomb Hải Phòng or Hà Nội, which is often, they have to fly over those mountains. If they see any lights below, they'll bomb.

Some bombs are dropped and don't detonate. Brave souls try to use the bombs to their advantage, attempting to take out the explosives and using the remaining parts of the bomb—particularly the metal casings—to make cooking pots and other tools. Many do detonate, of course, causing the destruction they were created for. Cluster bombs release their shrapnel. To this day, Dad has friends with shrapnel still in their legs.

Dad passes the time by making money. He walks through the mountains to Hải Phòng to pick up cookies, sugared peanut candies, cigarettes, and grenadine. It sometimes takes a full day of walking, less if he can borrow *ah yeh*'s bike. Then, he returns to the mountains to set up a little tent on the side of the road to sell his goods to the men in the army.

He is young and so are the North Vietnamese soldiers. Some were in training for only three months, Dad says. They're like babies. Eighteen, nineteen, twenty. And they're just as broke and hungry as everyone else. For their bravery, Dad says they're paid the equivalent of $5 a month.

When Dad tries to sell the peanut snacks, smokes, and grenadine to make sugary drinks to the young soldiers, he's disheartened to discover they don't have any money. But he's already stubborn as an ox. A compromise is struck. The soldiers will give Dad an AK-47 for three days and just ten bullets in exchange for one cigarette. Dad agrees, thinking the gun will help him hunt for food to feed his starving siblings. The soldiers make the exchange and share one smoke, each person taking a few drags before passing it on. This is what my dad is doing at twelve years old.

By the time he returns to Hải Phòng in 1973, Dad is too old to resume school. He can't be a fifteen-year-old in a third-grade class. The opportunity to receive the education he so desperately wanted has been taken from him. His childhood has been lost, stolen. Did he ever even have one?

The Americans bomb Hải Phòng repeatedly and heavily. The bombing campaigns are so extensive and span so many years that it's impossible to give an exact number of how many times my parents' hometown has been bombed during the war. Estimates are in the hundreds.

As a major port city and industrial powerhouse, Hải Phòng is aggressively targeted by the Americans, whose aerial bombing campaigns during the war are some of the most intensive and destructive in history. The United States wants to disrupt North Vietnam's supply lines, infrastructure, and industrial capabilities, including their weapons and ammunition factories, to weaken the communist forces. They want to break the North Vietnamese.

In 1965, when Dad is seven and Mum is four, the Americans launch a three-year campaign called Operation Rolling Thunder. Targeting various locations in North Vietnam, including Hải Phòng, it is one of the most significant bombing campaigns of the Vietnam War, killing an estimated tens of thousands of North Vietnamese soldiers and civilians.

ABOVE: Five-year-old Rachel clings to her mother at the staff table in the first May May Inn, with a pile of her library books behind them. In the background sits John the Tailor, a familiar face in the early years of the family's restaurant. BELOW: Five-year-old Rachel cracks open a fortune cookie while seated next to one of the many waitresses who came and went through the doors of the May May Inn.

ABOVE: Rachel wrapped in her mother's embrace on Mother's Day, a day when the restaurant gave red roses to customers. BELOW: Rachel, aged seven, hugs her brother, John, tightly in the kitchen of the first May May Inn.

Rachel clutches her cherished pink Power Ranger toy while posing in front of Niagara Falls—a rare family trip on one of the few occasions her parents closed the restaurant.

The newspaper announcement of the Phan family's big move: relocating their restaurant to a new, larger location just a few blocks from the original.

ABOVE: Ten-year-old Rachel beams beside her older sister, Linh, on the night of Linh's prom in 1998. BELOW: The Phan family poses for a picture in the second May May Inn on the night of Linh's prom in 1998.

ABOVE: Thirteen-year-old Rachel poses in the restaurant on the night of her eighth-grade graduation. BELOW: The Phan family, joined by Rachel's partner, Michael, pose for a photo together in their restaurant, China Village, in 2017. Taken just moments before the start of New Year's Eve dinner service—the busiest night of the year for the restaurant which is now located in Leamington, Ontario—it captures a brief calm before the chaos.

Rachel and Michael pose with their dog, Ivy, right after their elopement in 2019.

Rachel and her husband, Michael, serve tea to her parents during the Chinese tea ceremony at their wedding reception in 2021.

Rachel, centre, wearing her red *cheongsam*, poses with Michael and her family at their wedding reception.

Rachel, centre, regularly travels back to see her parents and spend time at the family restaurant. She poses with her parents in front of their beloved aquarium—they discovered expensive fish during the pandemic.

ABOVE: Rachel, centre, poses with her husband, sister, and parents during their big family trip to Vietnam in 2024. Here, they are in Hà Nội, with Rachel's dad wearing dress clothes to honour Hồ Chí Minh. BELOW: Rachel poses with her sister and parents on a beach in Đà Nẵng.

Tran and Hy Phan are all smiles in Đà Nẵng.

Rachel and her mother hold on to each other as Rachel's mum points out a banana tree.

Hy and Tran Phan jump for joy in Vietnam.

Rachel poses with her family at the tomb of Emperor Minh Mạng in Huế. Linh holds a small illustration of their brother, John.

Khu dân cư Hạ Lý (Hải Phòng) bị máy bay Mỹ ném bom
liên tục 3 ngày từ ngày 29/7/1972.
*Ha Ly, a densely populated area in Hai Phong was bombed
for 3 consecutive days from 29 July, 1972.*

ABOVE: At the War Remnants Museum in Sài Gòn, an image shows two people wearing conical hats pushing a cart along a dirt path, surrounded by destruction and rubble. The placard reads: "Hạ Lý, a densely populated area in Hải Phòng, was bombed for 3 consecutive days from July 29, 1972." This was where Rachel's father lived. BELOW: Rachel and her family sit on the backs of motorbikes in Sài Gòn alongside their food tour guides. Though hesitant at first, Rachel's mother overcame her fear and, by the end, was the only one riding confidently without holding on for dear life.

ABOVE: Rachel's parents and brother pause their busy kitchen routines to prepare a meal for her and her husband, Michael, during a weekend visit. BELOW: On their day off, Tran and Hy Phan, both in their sixties, dedicate hours to making hundreds of egg rolls in preparation for another busy week at the restaurant. They usually make around 700 egg rolls on Mondays.

Tran Phan meticulously layers egg roll wrappers one on top of the other. A brace supports her right arm, offering small relief from the chronic arthritis pain she developed after three decades of working in the restaurant.

Hy Phan fills each egg roll wrapper with bean sprouts, cabbage, chicken, and celery before stacking the finished egg rolls on a tray.

Rachel and her husband, Michael, pose with their yellow lab, Elm.

A few years later, a B-52 bombing of Hải Phòng on April 16, 1972 kills thousands of people in one night. In the same year, the Americans launch two large-scale bombing campaigns: Operation Linebacker I, which lasts for six months, and Operation Linebacker II, which lasts less than two weeks. Known to many as "the Christmas bombings" or "the 11-Day War," Operation Linebacker II has Americans dropping more than 20,000 tons of ordnance in both Hà Nội and Hải Phòng and killing at least 1,600 civilians. It will be the United States' final major military operation of the Vietnam War and the largest campaign of heavy bomber strikes since World War II.

In total, the Americans and their allies drop more than 7.5 million tons of bombs on Vietnam during the war.

When my dad isn't in the mountains, he has a front row seat to these horrors. He and his family cower in their makeshift bunkers, which he showed us in Hải Phòng. "We ran and pretended we were safe. But how could this hold up against a bomb?"

Once, a bomber hits the entrance of a large bunker, not far from Dad's house, with three hundred people inside. When it's over, Dad sees the bodies. He remembers how some of the bodies looked plastic. Others, like Jell-O.

In the present day, Dad stops and starts to cry while he tells his stories. "There are lots of things I want to tell you about, but I don't know how to say it."

He wipes at his eyes, continues to talk.

"My parents didn't teach us anything," he says. "That's why I teach you guys nothing. I got that from my family."

As a kid, I hated how absent my parents were. But as an adult, I see how the loss of their own childhoods made it impossible for them to know how to parent. How could they when they didn't even know what childhood looked like, having never experienced it themselves?

—~~—

When Dad is ten years old, he gives himself his first tattoo. Two older guys are burning bicycle tires and mixing the resulting liquid with whiskey to form the ink. They tie three needles together and dip them in.

They tell Dad to go away because they think he'll be afraid. Dad, always stubborn, always brave, asks for the needle. He's ten, so of course he doesn't know how it works. He goes too hard and blood gushes out. But he persists. He tattoos his birth year on his wrist.

A few years later, in 1975, Dad tries to enlist in the army at the age of seventeen. He wants to serve his country. He's seen what the Americans have done to his neighbours, to women and children, and wants to fight back.

He's denied because he's Chinese. It will not be the last time his being Chinese is seen as a problem, as a reason to deny him full acceptance as a Vietnamese citizen.

As a young child, Dad is teased for being Chinese. He's told to "get the fuck out of my country."

How fitting that his youngest daughter will one day hear the same words, in a different time, in a different culture, in a country so far away.

Unable to join the military, Dad picks up odd jobs. One is working a large cart with a friend—Dad would push from the back while his friend pulled. They'd find and transport dirt to fill bomb holes around town. Some of the bomb holes, Dad says, were so big that he swam in them when it rained. He does that for two years, his feet hitting the hot tar road every day. The only shoes they have are makeshift ones made from old bike tires. Another job has him carrying 220-pound bags of rice from boat to land in Hải Phòng's port. One hand carried the bags while the other carried a bamboo stick used to track the number of bags he'd carried that day.

Dad tells us more details about his jobs and the gruelling work, but my head swims with the details. He must sense I'm losing focus, so he sums it all up for me in a perfectly succinct, heartbreaking sentence.

"Don't forget, your daddy have very hard life."

I want to forget because it hurts and breaks my heart. I want him to stop talking. I want to ask for a break because I can't bear to hear the pain in his voice or see the tears in his eyes. But I owe it to him to remember, to write it down, to share it. I know hearing these stories secondhand is nothing compared to having lived it.

—※—

Mum's memory is fragmented and comes to us in bits and pieces. Unlike Dad, who's a natural storyteller and wants his stories to be known, Mum carefully guards her pain and trauma. She pushes it deep down, so deep she might forget. I can tell she's trying hard to remember so she can answer our questions. She's trying the best she can.

This is what we know.

Mum is the second youngest of six children, not including her dad's family with his second wife. As the first girl, she's expected to work hard from a young age, cleaning the house, washing clothes, taking care of her family, working at the store. It's a primer for a lifetime of back-breaking manual labour. As she gets older, her responsibilities grow to include babysitting her eldest brother's children every day. It's a grind under any circumstance, but extra stressful during times of war.

"I always have to work hard," she says to me and Linh on a rooftop patio in Hà Nội. "And I still have to work hard." The three of us start to cry, thinking about Mum as a young girl with all the responsibilities of a grown woman. She shrugs, wills her eyes to go dry, and says, "That's my life." It shears me in two. This is why my mother doesn't know how to rest and relax. In her tumultuous life, the one constant has always been work.

We hear how her early life is one of restrictions. As the eldest girl, she's expected to stay at home to take care of the house and sell beer. But she's still a young girl. One night, she goes out with friends and stays out a little too late for the liking of one of her brothers. When she comes home, he hits her and cuts her hair. He assumes that without her beautiful hair and with the memory of his hands striking her, she won't want to go out again.

It wasn't enough for Mum to be suffering because of the war. She was also deeply controlled and cruelly punished for stepping out of line. Home was no safe haven for her.

She vaguely remembers being sent with her sister and one of her brothers to China to escape the war. Here, her memory is hazy. She is maybe twelve. She remembers there being so much dirt and mud. She's pretty sure she's there when she starts her period. The tiny shack they live in is essentially one room. There is a hard surface they share for sleep, and the kitchen is a stone's throw away. There are no soft comforts here.

At some point, they go back to Hải Phòng, only to have to evacuate to the mountains. There, *ah po* weaves silk. There is no power, no lights, just each other and their fears. And the work.

When I push for more details, Mum gets frustrated. Her face pinches as she tries to pull at the loom of her memory. She can't. She's so sorry. Her stories shift and change. I know her spotty memory is a coping mechanism—how else can one endure the trauma of living through such horrors?

Later, I look into how traumatic experiences can impact a person's memory and find that it's common for one's memories to become altered, fragmented, and distorted. Memory gaps surrounding traumatic events are normal. Avoidance and suppression, too.

I see it all in my mother. I tell her it's okay, there's no need to apologize.

When my husband, Michael, and I first travelled to Sài Gòn, we visited the War Remnants Museum. The horrific images haunted me. Babies with enlarged heads and deformed limbs from the toxic Agent Orange chemical used by the American military to clear foliage and destroy Vietnamese livelihoods. An American GI holding the pieces of a man's body and proudly looking down as if staring at a lion's pelt. Bloodied children's bodies and tangled limbs splayed in a pit. Although haunting and traumatizing to witness, it felt like a period of history that was removed from my life. This was the past. A moment in time. I stupidly didn't think too deeply about how my own family history is marked by this same blood. When I return with my parents five years later, I see that our family's history is dripping with it.

I am thirty-five years old and at the War Remnants Museum once again. The museum, once known as the Exhibition House for U.S. and Puppet Crimes—a more fitting name, I think—looks more or less the same. It's still full of tourists and way too hot. The photos are still devastating and unbearable to look at.

The difference now is that I'm with my parents and my sister. I'm unprepared for how radically it changes the experience.

As we move through the museum, my sister cries, but my parents are unmoved. This information, although jarring and fucking awful for us, is not new to them. There is a picture from 1972 of a destroyed and bombed out Hạ Lý, the same ward my father grew up in. The placard underneath the image says that Hạ Lý, a densely populated area in Hải Phòng, was bombed for three consecutive days.

"Yes, I lived through that," he says. "We saw that in real life." He doesn't say it with emotion. He says it matter-of-factly. It just is.

Mum tells us about having to take shelter in crudely made bomb bunkers. Dad tells us how, after bombings, he and his family would sort through the piles of dead bodies, looking for gold teeth. "That was how we could afford to feed ourselves," he says.

If I was haunted by the atrocities I saw when visiting the museum in 2018, I can't bear to imagine how haunted my parents are. Us looking at pictures for a few seconds is nothing compared to the horrors my parents lived through in real time, and later, in their memories.

The American War in Vietnam officially ends in 1975 when the communist North captures Sài Gòn in the South.

In the end, between two and four million people are killed because of the pointless war. More than half are Vietnamese civilians. These were people just unlucky enough to have been in the wrong place at the wrong time. These were people just trying to live. My parents could have easily been among the casualties.

Even though we are from the winning North Vietnam side, my family quickly learns that it's not enough to be born in a country and to speak its language, eat its food, and be ingrained in the culture. My dad learns this firsthand.

After we leave the War Remnants Museum in Sài Gòn, our tour guide raises her voice. "Hey, your dad has a story he wants to share." We stop and circle around my dad, who is visibly shaking and emotional. The story spills out of him.

"When I'm sixteen or seventeen, me and my friend were working but didn't have money to eat outside. We had to walk home an hour and a half to eat lunch. I was starving, my stomach growling *be-ba-la-bum*, so I was rushing home," Dad begins.

On his way home, an unfamiliar woman stops him and accuses him of stealing her purse. The police come. They don't ask questions. His haste and her accusations have already rendered him guilty. Dad immediately gets arrested while his friend runs off to alert my *ah mah*. As he's telling the story, his face goes ashen.

"They tortured me," he says. He wears an expression I've never seen before. The pallor of his face makes me wonder if this story is draining him of his life force.

"They put me in jail where two men punched me and beat me," Dad says. "I couldn't fight back or I would get killed. I had no chance to protest or call a lawyer."

As they pummel his scrawny body with their fists and feet, they tell Dad they'll stop if he'll just admit he stole the woman's money. In the hallway, my *ah mah* has arrived and is wailing for her son's release.

"I refused because I didn't do it!" Dad says. "I say, 'I didn't do it. I won't admit it!'"

His mum howls more loudly in the hall, each shriek a sharp knife to my dad's chest. The beating continues for what feels like hours.

Eventually, his accuser comes back, says she found her purse with her money. But the police have already written Dad's name down, convicted him, listed him as a criminal. When he's released to his mother, his body is broken and already blackened from the bruises, which will get worse before they get better.

"That's why I hate communists," Dad says on the sidewalk, tears streaming down his face. "Everyone talks about what the South Vietnamese and Americans did, but we don't trust communists either because they also tortured and killed people. Look what they did to me. And the worst thing is that they didn't even say sorry."

Dad blinks, looks at us like he's seeing us for the first time. The cloud clears from his face. "I've never told that story to anyone before. Only my mum, your grandma, knows."

When we ask him how he feels, he releases a deep breath. His shoulders loosen. "I feel relief now. I feel lighter."

—···—

After Sài Gòn falls in 1975, there are two major waves of refugees who flee Vietnam to seek refuge in neighbouring countries. They're called "boat people" in reference to the often barely seaworthy vessels that hundreds of thousands take in the hopes of finding a better life.

In the immediate aftermath of the war, those fleeing are primarily people from South Vietnam who fear persecution under the new communist regime.

In 1978, there is a second, much larger, wave. This one is primarily made up of people who are of Chinese descent. Two of those people are my parents.

After the war, tensions between Vietnam and China escalate for several geopolitical and ideological reasons. One is Vietnam's alignment with the Soviet Union, who helped fund and arm North Vietnam's war efforts. This is met with disapproval by the People's Republic of China, further straining the Vietnam-China relationship with its already long history of conflict, rivalry, and territorial disputes.

In the late 1970s, Vietnam implements several socialist economic reforms, including the collectivization and nationalization of industries. Those policies disproportionately affect the ethnic Chinese, many of whom are business owners or involved in commerce. People of Chinese descent living in Vietnam, also known as Hoa people, are a minority in the country but play significant roles in Vietnam's economy, controlling much of the retail trade in Vietnam. They are capitalists in a country that is now firmly communist. The Vietnamese government look at the Hoa and see a potential fifth column. The Hoa are looked at with suspicion. Their loyalty is questioned. They are seen as a security threat. Having even a drop of Chinese blood is enough to be perceived as traitorous. The Hoa are marked as Chinese spies.

Then, China invades Vietnam in 1979, and all hell breaks loose.

The Vietnamese government decides it is time for the Hoa to get the hell out of their country. A strategic campaign to persecute the Hoa and expel them from Vietnam during the late 1970s and the early 1980s is kicked into high gear.

One of the ways my dad's family tries to hide is by changing our last name from the Chinese *Poon* to the Vietnamese equivalent, *Phan*. A Chinese last name would lead to persecution, a heavy fine, the loss of opportunities, the loss of Vietnam.

Our own names don't even belong to us. This is how tenuous belonging is and how quickly and easily one's identity can shift, change, and be erased.

My mother's family runs a successful business, making them the rich business owners that are so despised and mistrusted by the communist government. It doesn't help that Vietnam is destitute, having had so much of its infrastructure, coffers, and land demolished by the war.

To encourage them to leave, the government levies Hoa-owned businesses like ours with taxes and restrictions. They confiscate money and valuables. The cries of "you're not from this country" and "get the fuck out" are increasingly lobbed at the ethnic Chinese. Hoa business owners, like my mother's family, are told they cannot work at their own businesses. Students of Chinese descent like my cousins are barred from going to school. The Hoa lose their jobs. Curfews are imposed on Chinese neighbourhoods. Vietnamese citizens are banned from being friends with anyone of Chinese descent. Rice rations are cut off. Hoa are detained by police and given two choices: leave the country or report to rural resettlement zones, which were described by refugees as concentration camps.

On my dad's side, my *ah yeh* retires at sixty-five after working in the harbour for thirty years. Not even a month later, the Vietnamese government kicks him out without any benefits.

The second wave of boat people is about to begin. This new wave is between 60 and 70 percent Chinese. The Vietnamese government is happy to see us go. It's an effective money-making venture for them since police can collect ten taels of gold from each Hoa adult being forced to leave. One diplomat in Hà Nội estimated that these funds made up "the largest single export commodity of Vietnam's threadbare economy." The gold is melted down and shipped to Moscow as repayment for their support during the war.

People, like my mother's eldest brother, have to rely on bribing government officials to ensure safe passage and protection for their families. Freedom, it turns out, isn't really free. It, too, has a price tag.

Anyone with a Chinese connection is forced out. There are stories of even loyal communists and former Viet Cong being expelled for having a single Chinese ancestor. So deep is the suspicion cast on the Chinese.

My family has no chance of making it in Vietnam. Stripped of opportunity, dignity, and community, my family knows the government will not stop until they go. If they stay, the only future they can look forward to is one begging for money and mercy on the street.

The Vietnamese decide the land is not ours. They decide our businesses and our livelihoods are not our own. They decide our lives don't matter. We have to leave.

Throughout our trip, Dad tells strangers we meet why we had to flee. Several times, he is met with adamant insistence he is wrong. "Vietnam didn't kick you out," they say. "You left on your own." Four decades later, we are denied even the right to our truth.

My parents and their families flee to camps in China. It is at one of these camps that Hy Phan and Tran Hoang meet while they're picking potatoes and peanuts for a paltry salary of the equivalent of $29.50 a month.

Dad says, "She looked at me. I looked at her and I thought, 'Ooh la la.'" They started talking and checking each other out. Mum says she thought Dad was cute. He made her smile. He made her happy. The physically demanding work of farming—my parents' other duties included riding a water buffalo to till the land and spreading dung on the ground to fertilize it—is made bearable by stolen glances at each other and the thrill of secret touches.

Every night, they go out to the bamboo grove to talk for hours while staring up at the moon and counting the stars. They fall in love in these fields, working long hours together.

"I feel very lucky to have her," Dad says. "I feel so happy. I remember seeing my friends and talking about my girlfriend. And your mum loved me so much back then. She said I was like a gold mine!"

To Dad, it almost feels like paradise. He and Mum have found each other and started their whirlwind romance in China, which, in his eyes, initially welcomed the refugees warmly and took care of them. "Holy shit. We find a spot!" Dad remembers thinking. They're put up in what feels like five-star hotels and fed more food than they ever remember seeing.

Still, there are cracks in the facade. Mum's family hates Dad because they think he's a criminal. They don't know that Dad was falsely accused. Like the police, they're quick to condemn him. All they see is a bad boy from Hạ Lý.

One of Mum's brothers follows my parents during their courtship. He hides amongst the bamboo while Mum and Dad talk and throws rocks at Dad until he hits his mark. Mum is used to his overprotectiveness and control. Dad, as the eldest in his family, is not.

He stands up to my uncle, puffing up his chest and issuing a stern warning. "Don't fuck around. I love her for real. If you throw more, I will hit you."

When Dad tells us this story in Sài Gòn, he's pragmatic about the incident. "Your uncle was trying to protect his sister and didn't know I love her very much," he recalls. "They thought I was just fucking around. He didn't know I was in love for real."

It's the first time in my entire life I've heard my parents say they were "in love." After the horrors of war and having to flee home, their love must feel pure, refreshing, like a cool stream in a desert. I can see how they found refuge in each other.

But as we know, nothing ever lasts. "We couldn't stay because we didn't trust them," Dad says about China. "Because they're communists." They were right to be skeptical. After a few months, the refugees are moved to another camp, where they're used as even cheaper labour to grow rice or fruits. This is where Mum works the rice paddy fields non-stop, working every day, bent over, planting seeds, throwing grains. They know they have to leave.

My parents become two of the many people fleeing war-torn Vietnam who look to Hong Kong, which was then under British rule, as the promised land. More than 200,000 Vietnamese seek asylum in the city. Thousands die trying to make the journey.

Dad tries twice to get to Hong Kong.

He goes with four of his friends. He takes rice and mashes the grains into balls, shoving them in his pockets to have just in case the journey is long. His buddies say this is his only chance. He has to take it.

"Me and your mum were already in love," Dad says. "When I left for Hong Kong the first time, we cried all night and held each other and made love all night."

The next night, under the cover of darkness, Dad decides to take his chance and leaves with his friends. They wait until only the light of the moon hangs overhead to lower their chances of getting caught. They walk up and down mountains with only a compass in hand and rice balls in Dad's pocket. That first time, they get painfully close to the Hong Kong border. Dad can almost taste freedom.

But freedom is taken away with a few shots of a policeman's gun. Dad and his friends, traipsing stealthily in a field, are shot at by cops. They run. The cops run, too. They shoot at the sky, screaming, "Stop!" Dad and his friends try their best to hide in the rice field, praying for mercy among the tall plants. They're caught anyway.

Their greatest sin in Vietnam turns out to be the most welcome blessing in China. When the cops learn they're Chinese, Dad and his friends are treated like old friends. "You're Chinese? Welcome home!"

The cops boil water for them so they can take hot baths. They bring Dad and his friends out for *dim sum*. They send them back to the camp in a cab afterwards with a friendly warning not to try again. They tell my Dad that hardly anyone makes it to Hong Kong alive.

Dad doesn't listen. He can't afford to. He tries a second time. He and Mum hold each other and cry and say goodbye again. Dad knows the chances are low—maybe 10 percent—because once he gets close, he'll have to swim. "If ten people got there, maybe one would survive because there were lots of sharks," Dad says. "And if you got there, police could send you back." But he, and so many others, decide it's worth it.

The second time the cops are less nice. They don't crack open the champagne and roll out the "Welcome home!" banners. They beat Dad with a wooden stick. Put him in the police station. Let him go and put him on a bus back to the village in China, where Mum is worrying herself sick over whether he made it.

From there, the only course of action for Mum and Dad is to find any kind of vessel that will take them to Hong Kong.

People will sell gold, jewelry, anything and everything they have, to secure passage on a small wooden boat. Most are old and falling apart. Dad has only one gold ring and a watch in his possession. It would grant him a spot, but not my mother, and by this point, he is unwilling to leave her. The people running the boats want more, sometimes up to ten rings. Mum and Dad start looking for passage on smaller, less reliable wooden boats that would be more dangerous but cheaper.

According to the International Red Cross, as more refugees set out to sea, the likelihood of them reaching a foreign shore declines dramatically. The odds are not in my parents' favour. The number of people drowning or dying of exposure, hunger, or thirst at sea rises from 50 to 70 percent because more people are taking to the water in these old, rickety, crudely made boats.

"We'd have accepted anything that floated," Dad says. "We knew there was a high chance we could die. But we took a chance. The boat could bring us somewhere we could have hope."

While Mum and Dad desperately try to formulate a plan in China, they get word from her eldest brother that he's secured a twenty-six-metre fishing boat to take to Hong Kong. All it took was selling everything he had.

The journey is horrific. Dad estimates there were one hundred people crammed on that boat. They sleep huddled together, holding each other. There are no showers.

The Office of the United Nations High Commissioner for Refugees estimates that 200,000 to 400,000 boat people perished at sea. Other organizations estimate that up to 70 percent of Vietnamese boat people died on the waters. The conditions are brutal. Women are raped or abducted, and boats are picked clean by pirates.

Mercifully, my parents' boat journey is spared these horrific fates. But Dad still recalls the suffering he witnessed around him. "There were many small boats next to us, and the people, they call for help, but who's going to help them? No one's helping me. Children and women are crying for help—and we just kept going."

The trip takes longer than expected because neither my uncle nor any of the other passengers are experienced sailors. At one point, the boat hits a large rock, and they have to stop in China for repairs. Dad remembers how people in China tried to make a buck by offering them bamboo-enclosed showers—and how the people covered in sweat and grime from weeks on the boat lined up to enjoy the sheer bliss of hot water and clean skin.

But the Chinese authorities are firm. None of the passengers can stay. Here is another country, the original motherland, that has closed the door on this land being ours. They know that death beckons those that take to sea, but they decide our lives don't matter. We have to leave.

Mum and Dad are on that overcrowded boat for one month.

When they get to Hong Kong, they find themselves crammed yet again into detention camps in large warehouses. The government is overwhelmed with refugees they don't want. They treat the refugees like pond scum.

Because the camp has no facilities, a big ship with showers and toilets is brought in. Every morning at seven, everyone lines up to enjoy just five minutes to shower and shit. The police kick the door when your time is up to make you leave and make space for the next person.

Seen as parasites by the Hong Kong authorities, the refugees are beaten and monitored. At midnight, the police come through and count everyone to make sure no one has left. They can't risk refugee vermin fleeing to the city and mixing with their citizens. Children are assaulted. People are harassed. The United Nations has to step in and intervene. Hong Kong is browbeaten into treating us like human beings.

Hong Kong decides their land will never be ours. They decide we are not worthy of respect or dignity or thoroughly cleaned bodies. They decide our lives don't matter. We have to leave.

My *ah yeh* has a sister in Hong Kong who picks Dad up from the camp. At first, the guards don't want to let him out, but they eventually relent. My parents are overjoyed to leave the miserable camp.

Dad finally sells his gold ring and buys new clothes and shoes. His uncle finds him a job making and selling parts for cargo ships. Since he's responsible for watching over the store at night, he sleeps in a crawlspace there. It's a job he desperately needs because he's just found out he's going to be a father at twenty years old.

My seventeen-year-old mum is pregnant. She's thrilled by the news. "I was young, but I just felt happy."

Despite being refugees and not having a home, Dad remembers it as one of the best times of his life. He's in love. There's no war. He's going to have his own family. His boss loves him because he can write orders in Chinese. When his boss discovers Mum is pregnant, he offers her an "easy job" being his live-in nanny, taking care of his kid and cleaning his house. "It was a great time in our lives," Dad says. "We had money, we could go anywhere we wanted. We could hold hands and walk around. It was such a difference from the camp. It was like we hit the jackpot." They marvel at all the city lights in Hong Kong—a luxury they were denied in Vietnam, where there was no hydro and so many bombers overhead.

Like I learn in Vietnam myself, it's the little things that count most, especially after a lifetime of having many nothings.

When it's time to explore their options, my parents consider Canada, the United States, and Australia. England is already out because Dad heard the weather isn't great.

Of course, the best option is the United States. *Mei gwok* is what we call it in Cantonese. *Beautiful country.* Why wouldn't we want to go to the beautiful country with its limitless opportunity and clear pathways to the great American Dream?

We say, yes, we want to go to the States.

But the United States doesn't want us, at least not yet. To qualify, my family would have to spend a mandatory six months in a camp in the Philippines to learn English. Dad says no because he heard the conditions in those camps are terrible. They can't live through that again.

Our second choice beckons. Canada. It's 1979 and Canada's sponsorship program is up and running. Canadian immigration officials meet refugees and interview potential candidates for admittance to their country. My parents and mum's family, including my grandparents, aunts, uncles, and cousins, are accepted. A promising new life awaits.

—⁂—

It's easy to forget how young my parents were when all of this started. They were just teenagers.

And yet. . . .

They survive bombs.

They survive starvation.

They survive disease.

They survive the cruelty of multiple powerful governments.

They survive Mother Nature and the punishing South China Sea.

They survive giving up everything and starting over with nothing in a foreign country, surrounded by people who speak a strange language.

They survive starting their own business and fumbling their way to success.

They survive.

"We're lucky to be alive," is all Dad says.

Canada becomes home. For me, it *is* home. But sometimes it doesn't feel like it. Not when someone's yelling "fucking Chinese" at me on the street or telling me to "go back to where you came from."

I know my place is tenuous here, that at any moment, Canada could decide we don't belong. We're not Canadian enough. Our lives don't matter. What then? Will we have to leave?

I think about how incredible it is that, despite all the horrors, Mum and Dad are still the way they are. Dad could have become angry and violent. Mum could have become sullen and impossibly sad. But they're still capable of so much joy.

In a world that has sought to destroy, take, and erase, we're still standing. We're not leaving.

13

"THANK GOD I HAVE TWO DAUGHTERS."

I know what people picture when they think of Chinese children. I know the stereotypes. We care deeply about bringing honour to our families. We're always striving, always achieving. We're docile sons and daughters who abandon our own emotional fulfilment to satisfy our parents. If our parents throw the alley-oop to us, we dunk the ball. We are the manifestation and realization of their greatest dreams. We summit on the mountain of the Canadian Dream.

In my family, I see how the stereotypes play out, become flesh and bone. Linh has always been the obedient eldest daughter and my pseudo-mother, while John has put his dreams on hold to stay and help out at the restaurant, the reluctantly dutiful son. I play my role, too, as the pampered baby.

After Vietnam and connecting with my parents on a level that would have seemed unfathomable to me before the trip, I start wondering if I could deepen my relationships with my siblings, too. Who are they beyond the flattened stereotypes of birth order? What secret feelings do they keep buried, undisturbed by the light of awareness and acknowledgement?

I was three years old when we opened the restaurant, but my sister was turning twelve and my brother was ten. Their lives were uprooted in a way that mine wasn't. Unlike my memories of the time, which are hazy as if floating in a dream, theirs are clear.

Linh is forced to start over at a brand-new school in a brand-new town in her final year of elementary school. So great is her despair that she prays to a God our family doesn't believe in that we won't move. But clearly, our family restaurant was divinely ordained.

John is also starting over but dealing with a spate of health issues that has him out of the classroom and in the hospital. The restaurant's impact on our family is immediate. Weekends, which were once spent with my *ah po* and cousins or Mum's friends at the mushroom farm, are now spent working. There is no free time for anything. Social lives are a frivolity sacrificed at the restaurant's altar.

However, the restaurant brings each of us into closer proximity with each other. It means we actually see our parents on a regular basis. Our dad becomes a living, breathing person who really exists. He is no longer the spectre floating in and out of our lives between shifts in the wee hours of night. Seeing him is no longer like spotting Nessie in the murky depths.

All our lives become more structured, revolving solely around the restaurant and its demanding, needy schedule. At the age of twelve, my sister is working every night and weekend, making drinks, changing the daily specials signs, answering the phone, working the cash register. My brother, age ten, is in the kitchen doing the dishes. As he grows, he learns how to cut chicken, man the deep fryer, make rice, throw out the garbage.

When my sister isn't helping Mum and Dad, she takes care of me. "That was just another one of my responsibilities," she says. Even before the restaurant, she was already shouldering my care, taking me to daycare while Mum worked the morning shift at the mushroom farm and Dad slept after working all night.

So much of my childhood is spent watching and mimicking my sister. She is the best role model I have.

I observe the books and magazines she reads and follow suit. I listen to her music—alternative rock like Our Lady Peace and Smashing Pumpkins—and lord it over my childish classmates who are still listening to kiddie music. I watch her do arts and crafts in the restaurant dining room when it is slow. She shows me how to use a hot glue gun and tells me to be careful so I don't accidentally burn myself.

I happily let her practice her speeches and presentations for school on me. That's how I learn about *The Great Gatsby* and *The Wizard of Oz* and *Rebecca*. She shows me that doing your homework and getting good grades in school is important. I strive to be as studious and excellent at school as she is. I never question her or the example she sets. She knows everything. She is the smartest person in the world.

As a kid, I am thankful the restaurant keeps us tethered together. Although other teenagers my sister's age are sneaking shots of vodka at bush parties and feeling each other up—the things I am doing once I am that age—she is always within arm's reach, working the cash register and showing me how to be a good girl, the best daughter. She is there to shower me with love and attention when I ask for it. I grow and thrive under the light of her gaze.

Across cultures, birth order often carries significant symbolic implications, which in turn influences familial roles, expectations, and responsibilities.

The eldest child is naturally thrust into a leadership role, and the expectations foisted upon their shoulders are immense. They often feel significant pressure to succeed academically and professionally since their achievements are seen as a reflection of their family's honour and status. They typically act as caregivers and mentors to their younger siblings and feel a strong sense of responsibility for their siblings' well-being. As the firstborn, these children are expected to pave the way for their younger siblings while also facing expectations to mature, take on adult responsibilities, and contribute to the household. The pressure is multiplied in immigrant families where parents often work long hours to secure financial stability in their new land. Traditionally, the oldest son is expected to take over the family's business if there is one.

Middle children have more flexibility than their older siblings. They likely enjoy increased independence because they're subjected to less parental scrutiny. They may engage in attention-seeking behaviours because they feel overshadowed and pursue activities that distinguish them from their siblings. Some suffer from "middle child syndrome," which causes them to feel lost, neglected, and ignored in comparison to the younger or older children. They may act out and become the family's "wild child." Unsure of their place in the family, they may place a higher value on friendships, finding camaraderie and support outside of the family unit.

The youngest child, the "baby," tends to be spoiled, receiving extra attention and indulgence from their parents and their older siblings. The baby of the family may become less independent compared to their older siblings because they're accustomed to relying on others for support. They're more likely to be carefree and easy-going since they've grown up in an environment where their needs were often catered to by older family members. They can be more relaxed and less burdened by the responsibilities levied on their older siblings. As they get older, though, they may be expected to take on the care of their elderly parents if their older siblings are unable or unwilling to do so.

These are generalizations, of course. But in my family, they all turn out to be true.

Linh knows the role she plays in our family and falls in line without question. Saying no is not an option. "That's just what was expected of me," she says. "I had no choice. I always tried to be a good girl." It is the same sense of responsibility Dad has as the eldest of seven in his family.

My sister's need to be good and pleasing is intensified by the fact that she is also the healthiest of the three of us. Both my brother and I are sickly children, and to compensate for us stressing out our parents, Linh puts her head down, works hard at school, and never makes a fuss. She gives Mum and Dad zero reason to worry about her. As the eldest child, she is cursed with relatively fresh parents who haven't yet been beaten down by life. They are strict with her in a way they aren't with me. The message from my parents to my sister is clear: "be good or be punished."

"The way they treated you was totally different," my sister says. "They were way more relaxed with you. I couldn't do anything. I couldn't go to parties or go on dates. They wouldn't let me have a boyfriend." Our mum, who will one day let my guy friends sleep over at our apartment, explicitly tells my poor sister that she isn't allowed to have a boyfriend until she finishes school. "And she meant university!" my sister wails.

It's not like my sister ever has the time to have a life outside of the restaurant anyway. She misses out on pivotal childhood moments like sleepovers, movies, and first dates with crushes. It is both a blessing and a curse.

"The restaurant served a dual purpose. It was nice to have the restaurant because if I didn't have plans, I always had an excuse." She pauses. Her face turns contemplative. "But the restaurant was also a handcuff because I couldn't go to parties or sleepovers. I always had to wait for the restaurant to close, so by the time I could go, I would have missed the entire thing."

Linh's friends would have already eaten dinner together—communal hands grabbing for pizza, mouths wide, with food and funny stories—and watched the movie. By the time Linh could make it to the sleepover, she would have missed all the fun and made it just in time for bedtime, the least exciting part of a sleepover.

My sister was desperate for these experiences and wanted to be like everyone else. While other kids in our town spent their summers detasseling corn, she hated being confined within the restaurant's walls. "I'm not working at the restaurant this summer! I'm going to pick corn!" she threatened every year. But every summer, without fail, she could be found at her usual spot behind the bar at the May May Inn.

I love that my sister is always near, so I don't see how much it eats at her. I don't know that resentment is taking root within her, growing and twisting, and becoming an internal infection that leaves no mark on the outside.

At first, the restaurant is novel and exciting to her. Our family is all together! We can see Mum and Dad! But it doesn't take long for the cracks to appear. There is the fighting in the kitchen, of course, the tension of my parents' fraying marriage casting a putrid black cloud over everything. Then, there is the inexplicable pain of always being around our parents but being strangers to them, like satellites floating around each other.

"The restaurant was the thief of Mum and Dad," Linh says plainly now. "They couldn't do things like parent-teacher nights because evenings were always busy. They never saw me in plays or in the fashion show. I'd have to go to these things and see my friends and all their parents, and I would have no one." The only concessions our parents could make were big events, like graduations. They could spare closing just once every four years.

There are less obvious pain points, too. In the dining room is an unspoken stressor for a young girl: the mortification of seeing people you know from school. "The restaurant was a source of embarrassment because my friends or teachers were coming in for food," Linh says. "It was so cringey seeing my teachers coming in for dinner on weekends!"

Once, my sister's favourite teacher comes to the restaurant. Out of embarrassment, Linh pointedly averts her gaze. She doesn't make eye contact or exchange a single word with her teacher.

"It was like I was pushed onto a stage that I didn't want to be on. None of my friends had the same opportunity to have their family seen in action like ours was. None of their families were open to critique," she says, putting into words a feeling I've felt my whole life. "What if there was criticism of the food? What if they heard Mum and Dad yelling at each other? It was always something I was embarrassed about."

It's the same reason why I don't tell my friends what the name of our restaurant is. It's why I avoid reviews like the plague. It's why I feel a hot rush of anxiety when a friend from Toronto tells me they're passing through Essex County and want to go to the restaurant. It's not because the food isn't delicious or that I'm ashamed of my family. It's something else entirely. My parents work so hard and put so much of their love and themselves into the food they make. What would it mean if someone rejected that? It would feel personal, like an affront to my whole family. Better to be avoided altogether.

As Linh grows older and her social expectations change, the resentment she feels toward the restaurant grows into pure hatred. The handcuffs become tighter, the life they deny her so much more tantalizing. In the age before smartphones, Linh's only consistent window of time to socialize is between three and five o'clock, when the restaurant is dead. Our landline is her social lifeline, her fingers mindlessly twirling the spiral cord of the phone. For a too brief moment, she is like any other teenage girl.

But she soon learns how not-enough it is. She is curious about boys, wants to know what it's like to be chased and desired, to interlace her fingers with those of someone who loves her. To be able to say, "I'll see you at the party?" and actually show up. To be free.

When Linh moves out at eighteen to go to university, I am devastated, but she couldn't be happier. I have no clue because I am only nine and I wouldn't have understood anyway. *How could she be happy to leave me?* But she is. She's outgrown the town, its people, her circumstances. She is eager to leave Kingsville.

"I could not fucking wait to get out of there," she says.

The moment she moves out, Linh intentionally disentangles from our parents.

Over the next ten years, Linh calls home maybe once or twice a year. She isn't great at keeping in touch with Mum and Dad because she doesn't want to. She gave them her childhood and teenage years. She was always their reliable and dependable helper, an extension of themselves. No more. This is her time.

She relishes in the luxurious splendour of doing whatever she wants on the weekend. She finds out what it is like to get drunk and sleep in. As the years pass by, she moves farther and farther away from home. First, Toronto. Then, England. Now, Germany. She places a premium on her freedom and independence, choosing not to get married or have kids. Having successfully raised me, she feels she can mark "parenting" off her to-do list. "You turned out great! I did an amazing job with you," she says. She got that life accomplishment out of the way early.

It's not until she's older that Linh starts to fully process why she kept our parents at arm's length for so many years. "They were not a source of love to me," she says. "They were always a source of conflict for me because they were fighting a lot. It took me a long time to understand what love was for them."

She admits, too, to running away from knowing them as people and being unwilling to confront the full magnitude of our parents' difficult lives. "That would make them human, and it would make me sad for them or guilty about how much better my life was," she says. "All the sacrifices and the things they had to go through so I didn't have to deal with that myself. It was just easier for me to not know them as people. Knowing them as people meant I would have to acknowledge their pain and I wasn't ready for that."

For a long time, she stays away and finds freedom in not knowing. It is less painful that way. After the childhood she had, she is already used to the distance.

Still, it's impossible to free ourselves of the restaurant's powerful pull entirely. Every holiday, my sister comes home without fail because our hands, minds, and bodies are all needed for the busiest time of year.

"Everything is so tied to this restaurant," she says. "We opened the restaurant when I was twelve and now I'm forty-four. In all that time, I've only missed New Year's Eve twice—that's all." My brother and I have each only missed it once. ("Do you know how amazing it felt to actually be able to enjoy that day and spend it outside of work?" my brother asks later.)

It's an unspoken rule in my family, along with all the other expectations placed on our shoulders. We'll be there on New Year's Eve, no matter what. While the rest of the world celebrates, we're miserable and depleted. But that's restaurant kid life.

When I ask my sister to share her happiest memories of the restaurant, she gives it to me straight.

"This is a tough one, sis," she says. "I don't have happy memories there. Nothing like having a sleepover with friends or after-parties. It was always work and stress for me."

Well, *shit.*

When I think about my sister and our childhood, I don't see any of her pain. I just see her smile. The steady smile she gave a customer when they paid for their order was the same one she gave me when I proudly showed her my completed homework. She was always there for us: when I was confused about a passage I'd read in a book, when Dad needed her to call a customer back to confirm an order, when someone asked which noodle dish was better. She was everything we'd ever needed her to be. She was the quintessential eldest child, expected to take on the thankless work of parenting while she herself was left parentless.

I hate that I'm only now realizing the toll it's taken on her and how many pieces of herself she must have lost as a young child and woman, having to put us and the restaurant ahead of her own needs. I wonder if we'll ever be able to wrap our heads around just how much the restaurant has taken from us, how much of a sacrifice it's demanded and continues to demand, and how we continue paying the high price. But what can we do about it now? The price has already been set.

In the fourth grade, I am tasked with writing about "my hero." I write about my brother.

John is seven years older than me, but he always feels more like my peer than my wise, mature sister does. We play *Super Mario World* and *Mortal Kombat* and watch hours and hours of TV together. We are adopted into the *Full House* family—John loves singing along with Uncle Jesse—and walk the halls of Bayside with the *Saved by the Bell* gang. John gets me into sports, and I happily watch even the most boring ones, like golf, if it means my cool older brother lets me hang out with him just a little bit longer. We watch wrestling together, and with our cousins, play-wrestle as our favourite characters: Chyna, the Undertaker, Kane. If someone is mean to me at school, John volunteers to give them the People's Elbow like he's The Rock. "Do you want me to beat them up?" he asks, earnestly, angrily.

When I get scared, which is often, my brother teases me but lets me sleep in his room on the floor. He knows I am afraid of the dark and that I hate sleeping alone, so we make a blanket nest on his floor and he turns on his lava lamp to bathe us both in warm light. I always have the best sleeps during our sleepovers.

There is no part of me that ever doubts that my brother will do anything for me. As a child, I feel protected by him. Simply knowing that he is at high school and not that far from me, in elementary school, soothes me. When I muster up the courage to sing in my school talent show in sixth grade, it isn't my parents in the seats cheering me on, but my brother—who probably skipped class—sitting in the back. It's no small deed to have someone show up for you. It feels like the best thing in the world. It's what my sister always wanted when she was in school, and it is a gift my brother gives me.

These are all heroic actions to me. My brother earns his title as my hero.

―⁓―

Over time, my brother changes, bit by bit.

Maybe it is because the expectation to be a good, dutiful son rankles him. Maybe it is because he hates school and is painted as a "bad kid" by his teachers because of it. Maybe it is because his two sisters are bookish nerds and he wants to set himself apart from us. Maybe it is because Asian boys are too often seen as effeminate and undesirable laughing stocks, and he doesn't want to be another submissive goody two-shoes. Maybe it is all of the above.

Whatever the reason, he becomes rebellious. He yells at my parents. He steals booze and fortune cookies from the restaurant and sells them at school. He graduates to selling mushrooms and weed. He gets his tongue pierced.

The tongue piercing is the final straw for my dad, whose red-faced rage is a terrifying thing to behold. When he takes his belt out, we cower and shake. But he doesn't hit my brother. He coolly tells him to get out.

After getting kicked out, John calls the house when he knows Mum and Dad are working. "May May?" his voice sounds so impossibly far. I don't like it. "I forgot some stuff because Dad kicked me out so fast. Can you bring it outside in five minutes?"

I tell him yes because I desperately want to see him. I meet him outside by the gate and hand him his things. My eyes rove over his face, trying to decipher whether he is okay and where he might be staying. Does he look clean? Has he been sleeping?

"Dad's just being a prick, that's all," he says when he catches me looking at him like I am studying a map. "Don't worry about me, okay? Just go to school, listen to Mum and Dad, and try to help out if you can."

I think it's odd he advises me to do the things he himself resists doing, but I don't say that. I nod in solemn assent and tell him to take care of himself. He gives me a brave smile and says, "Of course!" Within two weeks, he is back home, as he should be.

John learns his lesson after that.

When he starts smoking, he makes sure our parents don't find out. He's so good at it that when my husband mentions John's smoking many years later, Dad asks, "John smokes?" My husband backtracks when he sees my mother's wide eyes and my grimace. "I mean . . ." He splutters. I quickly change the subject.

When my brother gets his first tattoo at twenty-two on his bicep, he makes sure to wear t-shirts so Dad can't see. He adds to the ink over the years and religiously wears compression sleeves over his arms to hide the truth written on his skin. He's in his thirties when he finally stops caring. By that point, the poisoned barbs of my dad's tongue are gone. He's too tired to police his children. If he's old, we're old, too. When I get my first tattoo, my parents coo and love it. It's not the first time I notice how differently they treat me compared to my siblings. I must be profoundly annoying to them sometimes.

———

As we get older, my brother gets angrier. He's yelling more often than not. The Phans are mercurial, unpredictable, and prone to intense mood swings and horrific tempers. Our Black Blood has trickled down through the generations, and John's moods have become the blackest of all. To me, it seems he stops maturing, becoming a classic case of arrested development.

My brother tries to move out a handful of times. First, he moves to an apartment a few minutes from ours. He lives there for two years before he moves back. As time meanders on, he moves to Windsor. Then, London, Ontario. He comes back on weekends to help out at the restaurant. When I ask him why, all he says is, "Someone had to help Mum and Dad." When they call him, they don't come right out and say it, but the words they do say are enough to make him feel guilty for not being there to help. They tell him how busy the restaurant is, how sore their wrists are, how stressful dinner service was. He feels the pressure.

In London, he works as a security guard at a bar for eight months. "That's the only actual real adult job I've had," he says. It's hard to get into the groove of a new job when he's driving back and forth to work at the restaurant. It's hard to give your all to a job when your old one is still calling you every day.

For some people, it's also hard to really let yourself be free when you know you have a safety net waiting for you back home. It can be scary to be unchained and to know you can do whatever you want. To know you can fail. Although some people, like my sister, thrive on the thrill of freedom, others like my brother keep their wings clipped. It's safer this way.

It doesn't help that my mother's voice rings loudly in his ear. "I don't think you can do it," her voice says. My brother, who so often doesn't listen to my parents, listens to this. He inevitably always moves back home.

Because of that, John never really had to grow up and leave the nest. While many of us move out, go to school, start our careers, progress, my brother is fixed. Stuck.

It's a quagmire that's all-consuming, undeniable. I experienced it briefly myself.

Growing up, I never had a real job. I never had to. Linh envied how other kids spent their summers detasseling corn, but not me. I was a free bird. I did my short stints here and there in the kitchen, but never consistently.

Still, I've felt how easy it is to fall into the trap of the restaurant. It offers security and leniency—you can fuck up, be a menace, and still have a job. It's run by our parents, who are willing to overpay and accept bad behaviour a real employer wouldn't. With our parents as our bosses, shoddy performance, being late, talking back, and not working full-time hours aren't causes for termination. If you're lucky, you'll get the silent treatment. If you aren't, the worst you can expect is a few minutes of yelling and cursing.

It's why I didn't have a real job until I moved away to school. The restaurant and our parents cast a wide safety net, one that told us it's okay if we don't grow up as long as we come home and work.

It's how I come to work my first shift as an overpaid waitress for my parents at the age of nineteen. I am a working-class nepo baby. I am all nerves and inexperience and shaky fingers.

When I hear the chime of the bell over the door, my heart immediately starts hammering percussively in my chest. *Ba-dum, ba-dum, ba-dum.* My armpits are sweat-slicked. My mouth bone dry.

"Rachel, customer!" my mother calls to me, just in case I didn't get the memo from the bell. The smile on her face is probably in reality warm and encouraging, but all I see is something sinister behind the uplifted curl of her lips. *This woman is feeding me to the wolves! How could she do this to me?*

When I leave the safe haven of the sticky, hot kitchen, I find myself face to face with my own personal nightmare: customers I have to charm and serve and *oh my God, I really can't fuck this up.*

The customers are kind, patient. I hate it all the same. After waitressing for one day, I tell my mum I don't want to do it anymore. I hate when people look at me. I hate the sound the bowls make against the plates because my hands are shaking so badly.

Mum lets me stay in the back after that. She pays me $20 an hour to wash the dishes and make wontons while she tends to the customers I begged to leave behind.

Her leniency allowed me to stay undisturbed in my comfort zone. I can see how it's done the same for my brother.

———

Eventually, my sister and I go off to university. We're both good students who have been supported and encouraged to chase our dreams by teachers and guidance counselors.

My brother didn't enjoy the same treatment. As a fellow member of The Sick Kids Club, John missed so many days of school in first and fifth grade that he was held back and had to repeat both grades.

It must fuck with you so deeply to have that happen, not once but twice, and to be sandwiched between two overachieving, keener sisters: Linh, the model responsible, smart daughter, and me, the overindulged baby who coasted at home but made up for it by working three times as hard at school. Although I endured racist bullying at school, I could at least seek comfort in my academic achievements. My brother could not do the same. His challenges at school were twofold: he had to navigate the harmful words and expectations of others while struggling academically.

I get why he becomes so deeply angry as the years tick by.

As Linh and I leave home, gain life experiences, and explore new identities and possibilities, my brother sinks deeper into the roles he's always known: black sheep, stereotypical middle child, restaurant kid. He must feel so trapped in these roles that feel so fixed. The chip on his shoulder calcifies.

It's awful being in the kitchen with him. He rages and rampages. While my parents have mellowed out as they've gotten older, my brother is in the prime of life. His rage is visceral, ugly, easily thrown your way. Five minutes in his presence and I forget that there are other words beyond "fuck."

He doesn't care that customers can hear him through the swinging kitchen doors. He doesn't care that his words lash like whips against my exhausted parents' spirits. He just doesn't care.

He threatens to leave. He moans and wails about the unfairness of his life. When he says, "Fuck my life," our dad visibly flinches. Dad, who lived through the horrors of war, displacement, and working himself to the bone, cannot believe his only son has become so ungrateful that he casually curses his own life.

Sometimes Mum will call me crying because John's upset her. "He yells at me all the time," she says. Her voice quivers and I want to simultaneously wrap my arms around her and slug my brother in the face. "He says he hates his life. I tell him, 'Mum and Dad, we do everything. You just come in and deep fry for a few hours and then you leave.'"

They're at a loss, Mum and Dad. "What can we do? Fire him? Then he won't have a job."

To calm herself down, she says, "Thank God I have two daughters." She says it often.

I nod. A crack grows between me and my brother. He falls spectacularly from the pedestal I placed him on all those years ago, when he was my hero and he still felt like he had a wide-open future just for him.

There are so many "maybes" that run through my head. Maybe, if my parents enforced rules, curfews, and limits, things would have been different for my brother. Maybe, if he felt supported and capable and allowed to leave, he wouldn't feel so stuck and angry. Maybe, if my parents didn't let my brother live with them for decades and support him financially, he'd be more independent and inclined to save money—and earn it honestly, too. Maybe, if my father wasn't so absent and neglectful, my mother wouldn't feel so bonded with my brother. Maybe, she would have pushed harder for him to leave.

Maybe, maybe, maybe.

But what good does it do to ask difficult, impossible questions? It doesn't change our reality now.

The thing is, I understand my brother. For a long time, I pulled away from him because I resented the way he treated my parents. My frustration with him grew as I waited for him to take responsibility, to help make our parents' lives easier.

But as I get older, the lens through which I look at him has changed and softened.

How must it feel for him to see his two sisters being free to live their own lives away from home while he's caught in the restaurant's net? Although it's true that he's never had to get a "real" job because he's always been able to run back to Mum and Dad's kitchen, it's also true that he's never felt like he could actually leave.

These are the prospects for restaurant kids like us. This is the cautionary tale. For every Linh and Rachel given everything they need to be their own people and forge their own paths, how many Johns are out there, saddled with the responsibility of carrying on the family business and never knowing what it's like to be their own free person?

The pressure must be suffocating. It's easy to see how someone can just stop moving under the weight of it.

—⁓—

When I ask my brother whether he resents me because I never had to work as hard at the restaurant as him or my sister, he doesn't miss a beat.

"Yes, I hate that you didn't," he says.

"Oh yeah, absolutely," my sister chimes in.

The weight of their resentment is a heavy thing. It's palpable, even if it's clothed in love. Even though they've spent their whole lives babying me, too.

"There's nobody to blame but Mum and Dad because they didn't make you work," my brother says. "Because you were the baby and you weren't a boy." My brother pauses. We never talk about feelings, so it feels like we're approaching icy waters. He might shut down at any moment. Tell me to fuck off. Walk away.

Instead, he tears up. Soldiers on. "They wanted you to have a better life, I think."

"You don't think they wanted the same for you?"

"I don't think they really cared what I did because if I failed at life or succeeded, I always had the restaurant," he answers. "Linh got away after university. I fucked around and stayed around, which I regret. I didn't get away."

I ask him if our parents ever explicitly told him they wanted him to take over the restaurant. He says no, but with a caveat. "Deep down, I had a feeling that was their end goal, for me to carry on the tradition."

Lately, my brother seems to be coming around to the restaurant. I don't know if it's genuine affection or if it's much-delayed resignation. Either way, he's slowly accepting his path and settling into it. He's started social media pages for the restaurant, grown a loyal following, and shown off his entrepreneurial spirit with restaurant giveaways and contests. He's given back to the community by running charity car washes at the restaurant and giving meals to healthcare workers during the pandemic. He covered the meals with money from the paycheque he gets from my parents. He's modernized the menu by creating his own innovative dishes, from the popular *soo guy* poutine to a creamy, spicy, breaded shrimp dish he calls "General Phan shrimp." He's started to express an appreciation for my parents and how hard they work.

In 2023, the restaurant's landlord tells my parents he's going to increase rent, nearly doubling it. My parents are crestfallen. When they signed the agreement in 2003, he promised he would never do this, but verbal promises are not binding. With the new rent, my parents won't turn a profit. Suddenly, they feel forced to court prospective buyers. Some even come down from Toronto to view the restaurant.

After a few showings and offers, John steps in and tells them to stop. "I want to take it over." He's firm about it. For the first time, he's clear-eyed about what he wants from the future. None of us can believe it when we hear. But none of us can deny the shift we've seen in him.

"I just care so much for Mum and Dad," he says, tearing up. "I know I can be an ass. There's just a lot I do for them and I feel they don't appreciate it, know what I mean?"

Of course I know what he means. Our parents, who have given everything and sacrificed so much so we could live our dreams, are not the most forthcoming when it comes to saying "thank you." Why should they? Us taking care of them is what's expected. It's our duty, not our gift.

"You guys are my everything. I know I can be difficult at times, but in the end, I'm there one hundred percent if you guys need anything." It's true. My brother's ride-or-die nature and protectiveness is why he was my hero all those years ago. Here he is, doing the same for the restaurant, our most annoying family member. The source of so much of our ire.

"Growing up, I hated the restaurant so much. I still do at times. I still don't feel like I can ever be free," John says. "But I don't ever want to be free. I'll always be there for our parents. Free from the restaurant, maybe. But it's what I do and what I enjoy doing."

He adds quickly, "For now."

My parents, who have never hired anyone long-term to help in the kitchen, have relented and let my brother hire a friend to work the deep fryer. My brother admits it's nice to have his friend in the kitchen. I think about how frustrating it must have been when it was just him, Mum, and Dad, day in and day out, without any relief. His friend working also means John can get away occasionally, too.

It's a look at what the restaurant under his control might look like: fun featured dishes born of his own mind and creativity, and the ability to press pause and take a break. Unlike my parents, he doesn't want the restaurant to be his entire life. Once again, my brother's future is wide open, just for him.

14

"THAT'S WHY WE HAVE YOU, RIGHT?"

The restaurant in Leamington is still kicking. In fact, it's thriving. China Village is experiencing greater success than ever before after COVID-19 saw the closure of two other Chinese restaurants in town. My parents, who are now in their sixties, are working just as hard as they were in those early days of the May May Inn three decades ago.

Although some things are still the same, others have thankfully changed. Mum and Dad are more chill now. They have fun. They laugh more. They sit more. They take breaks.

They still fight, of course, as all couples do, but now, after decades of pressing on the same bruises and screaming the same Chinese epithets at each other, the fighting has changed shape. Gone are the days of impassioned chicken ball throwing—more evidence of how bone-tired my parents have become. When they fight now, it's through icy silence.

"Your dad was cranky and hasn't talked to me since Friday," Mum will say on the phone. "Can you tell him we should close next Sunday?" I'm thirty-six and live four hours away, but I'm still expected to defuse the tension, just like little Rachel did when she begged them to stop fighting for China's sake.

But this is the choice they made all those years ago when they caught a glimpse of life without the restaurant, without each other. It was so unbearable to them that they immediately surrendered, called a truce, got the band back together again.

Could any of us have foreseen that they'd still be at it, with the same intensity, twenty-two years later? On one hand, it's not surprising—what else would they be doing?—but it's disappointing all the same.

"I hate my job, Rachel," Mum says to me out of the blue. As always, an ache tugs at my heart, but the sharpness of the pain has long been dulled by years of hearing her utter this exact same phrase.

My parents are slowing down physically and we all know it, but no one seems prepared to do anything about it. Working all day, every day, is still the norm for them.

It's strange to think that they're old. Dad now qualifies for senior discounts, and Mum isn't far behind him. In Vietnam, they kept up with all our walking, but they were still ten feet behind us. I got accustomed to stopping every few minutes to look behind me to make sure they were okay. There are moments when Dad looks impossibly shrunken and aged, like when he's unwell and huddled so small under a duvet. The hairs on their heads are turning shades of grey and ash.

Throughout our trip, Dad is repeatedly called *Bác,* an honorific you only use on a person you think is older than your parents. He's shell-shocked when he first hears it. "I'm old," he says, his face frozen in a mask as he comes to grips with what this means. The term is a mirror reflecting his own mortality.

It shifts how he treats the trip. Although we're worried about how much things cost, Dad is happy to spend lavishly and to rack up as many new experiences as we can together. "This might be the last time we can do something like this," he says. "You guys have a longer future than me."

For the first time, we're starting to think about that future and life after the restaurant. My parents are starting to say the big "R" word—retirement—and mapping out what that might look like for them. The giant question mark overhead casts a shadow over all of us.

With their retirement imminent, I suddenly feel like the clock is ticking too fast. I'm only starting to get to know who my parents are. We've wasted so much time being strangers to each other. Instead of confronting the uncertainty ahead of us, I look back and reflect. I silently pray that we can right the many wrongs and pain points of the past. I hope that will be the map that guides us forward.

For now, retirement is no longer a thing my parents dread or resist. They're counting down the days. When we're in Vietnam, my parents repeatedly say they don't want to go back to Canada because they don't want to go back to work. For decades, the restaurant has been all they've known. It's been the very centre of their lives and they're sick of it.

"At work, I stand for ten hours. I get tired," Mum says. "In Vietnam, I can walk for eight hours and no pain!" She's starting to see what she's been missing from life all these years. Bit by bit, we can start to give her the opportunities that have always been out of reach for her. I'm surprised by how protective I am of my mother the older she gets. Suddenly, it feels like my purpose is to make sure she's happy.

My mother isn't like my father. She was raised with a completely different set of expectations. She's not the eldest, so she wasn't expected to take control and make decisions. She was expected to be controlled, to be a follower. She must do as she's told and take care of the family. It's only now as an adult that I can see how lonely and isolated her life has been. In Asia, she was denied choices and agency. In Canada, she is surrounded by people who don't speak the language she dreams and thinks in. Because she's always working, she's had few opportunities to make friends. Dad was always able to socialize because he could go to the coffee shop to play cards after work or when it was slow. But Mum either had to stay at the restaurant or go home to take care of us.

She speaks enviously about how Dad has had big parties for his fiftieth and sixty-fifth birthdays, but she's never had a special day just for her. For her sixty-second birthday, Michael and I go home to surprise her. I take her out for a massage at the spa, and we plan a family dinner. But she wants to know what Dad must have felt like being surrounded by so many people wanting to celebrate just him. She asks to invite friends, but in lieu of her own, she invites my dad's.

I observe her at the dinner, the way everyone talks to each other but not to her. I see how conversation passes her by and wonder what it must be like for her to feel so left out of everything because of something as annoyingly pervasive as language. No matter how hard she tries, she can't grasp the nuances, the meaning, the words all around her. Language is like the slipperiest of eels, evading her whenever she reaches to grab it.

How isolating, how alienating. My mother has paid for her circumstances every day of her life in Canada. When they first landed here, Dad went to English school, but Mum couldn't follow because she had to stay home to take care of Linh and John. That was what was expected of her, so that was what she did. To this day, Mum can't just relax. She's lived a life where she's had to care for others, get stuff done, put her own needs last. The language of doing is one she's fluent in.

Recently, I've noticed how limited her life is and how much she relies on Dad to filter information to her. How frustrating it must be to not be able to read menus and to have to depend on others to tell you what your options are, or to not understand what tour guides are saying and needing your husband to translate for you. Of course it's easier to just say, "I'll have what you're having" or "Just order for me." You can't know what you want when you don't even know what the options are. Mum is prone to mood swings and lashing out in high-stress circumstances, but I can't blame her. Her whole life has been a series of frustrations. No one's fucking listening.

It pains me to see how she has so little sense of self. The way she defers to my dad and what he wants. The way she babies him, making sure he takes his medicine, adjusting his clothes before photos, wanting to find him weed and risk getting arrested in Vietnam.

She's a woman whose needs have always been put last. When we ask a hotel if my parents can change their room because Mum is uncomfortable in it, she lights up. "Thank you so much," she says, beaming. An hour before, she had resigned herself to staying put because Dad said so. "I'm tired. I don't want to fight with your dad right now. I can't say no when my boss said yes." The last part is said as a joke, but we know it's the truth.

This is who my mother is. She takes care of others. She puts us first, ahead of herself, and she does it all without really, truly being heard or known.

When we're in Vietnam, I often feel lost because I don't understand the language. People laugh and I miss the joke. But this is just a fleeting vacation. I know it will end and I'll go back to a place where I'm not a fish out of water. Since moving to Canada, this has been my mother's entire life.

I look up and notice how refreshing it is to see her laughing and understanding the punchline. I wish more than anything she can experience years of this to make up for all the time she lost when life passed her by because she was too busy working.

But that day still feels so achingly distant. Even now, my mother works harder than anyone I've ever met or will ever meet. At sixty-two, my mother knows the luxury of only one day off a week. This one day isn't nearly enough to offset the other six days, when she gets to the restaurant before 9 A.M. and leaves at 10 P.M. She spends her day off thinking about all she has to do the next day and the day after that.

"I'm so tired, Rachel," she says to me every week. She just wants to rest. She's exhausted. Her wrists hurt. Everything hurts. But she keeps going because it's all she knows.

A few years ago, when Mum had carpal tunnel surgery on her left wrist, she was ordered by the doctor to stop working for three to four months. "Just relax and rest," he told her. *A dream*, I thought. *My mother can finally take a break.*

She lasted four weeks.

"I'm so boring!" she said in her broken English. "There's nothing to do!" At first, she started small—slipping into the kitchen just to say hello, pouring wonton soup here, throwing an egg roll into the deep fryer there, answering the phones—as if she could pretend she wasn't really working at all. But we knew what she was doing.

Since she never made it to the full three months, her wrists still kill her.

A few years ago, Dad convinces her to go on a cruise. She dreads it. "I don't want to go! I just want to stay home."

They go because Dad wants to and that's the end of that. But Mum ends up feeling grateful, changed. "I felt so light," she says, smiling wide, showing off her tan. She relished going to endless shows, lounging on the beach, and eating surf and turf every night. She wanted adventure. She wanted something that was so much more than the stifling walls of the restaurant. Her body could do way more than labour over a wok and stove. She could snorkel! She could dip her toe in the ocean and feel the lapping water on bare skin. She could finally truly live!

My mother has more than earned a future where she can seek all the marvellous things she never experienced as a child in war-torn Vietnam, or a refugee in a crowded camp, or a worker at a mushroom farm, or the person in charge of a busy restaurant, or an immigrant mother. This woman, who has given so much to everything and everyone around her but has received precious few morsels back, is long overdue for an easy retirement. My dream is to have her and Dad move in with me so I can wrap my arms around her whenever she needs the reminder that she's so much more than just someone who works slavish hours in a restaurant kitchen. She's so much more than just forced resilience—she can be loved and cared for, too.

I want her to know there is a world outside of the restaurant kitchen, a world her children have been able to savour and capture on film and share on social media platforms. A world brought to us by her and Dad's sacrifices.

She dreams of retirement. She dreams of stopping and living. She dreams of moving back to Vietnam. She and Dad look at property while we're there "just for fun," but the idea is tantalizing to them both. They talk about it with certainty now. For six months of the year, they want to be there.

———

But before my parents can retire, they still need to work. After Vietnam, my parents decide to reopen on Tuesdays. Before, they were closed on Mondays and Tuesdays. "I have to make money," Mum said on the trip. "We're closed for a month. You know how much money we're losing?" The change means they'll be working seven days a week, since Monday, their one day off, is actually spent making egg rolls.

The decision is a knife to every tender part of my body. At an age when my parents should be winding down and treating their ailing bodies with care, they're ramping things up again. They're working just as hard.

It makes me feel like shit that I'm living the life of my dreams off the backs of their endless hard work. I wish they didn't have to do this. I wish I could tell them, "Yes, I'll take this on for you."

In actuality, I have conflicted feelings about their retirement. I don't want my parents to work so hard. I don't want them to have to work at all anymore. But I know that when they do retire, their financial care will fall on me and my siblings.

Taking care of your elders is seen as an unshirkable responsibility that's been a tenet of our culture for thousands of years. This expectation is rooted deeply in Confucian values, which emphasize filial piety—one of the eight fundamental virtues in Chinese culture—and respect and duty towards one's parents and elders.

Traditionally, it is the responsibility of adult children to show their filial piety by assuming their elderly parents' care. Parents are to be supported emotionally, financially, and physically as they get older. This includes but is not limited to providing financial assistance, helping with daily tasks, ensuring their well-being, and honouring their wishes. The expectation in return is that parents will provide wise counsel and care to their children throughout their lives.

As the child with the most financial stability and security, I feel the stress of this looming reality profoundly. My parents have increasingly made comments to me about their life as seniors. "I'll live with you and you'll take care of me!" Mum says to me often.

Their impending retirement and golden years fill me with equal parts relief and dread. The burden hasn't been fully placed on my shoulders yet, but it already feels unbearably heavy. A not-so-small part of me resents that I have to take care of them when so many of my needs went unmet while I was growing up. Guilt grows in the fertile soil of these thoughts and strengthens my resolve to be fully present with them in a way they never were for me. "Of course, Mum, I won't put you in a retirement home. You can live with us forever!" I say through clenched teeth. Although I genuinely want to do this, the prospect still feels like a bitter, unfair weight on my shoulders. *Where were they when I needed them most?* I ignore these secret internal cries and force the cycle of obligation and resentment and guilt to begin anew.

Maybe this is my comeuppance. The restaurant took so much from Linh and John early in their lives, while letting me off the hook. It feels like fate—it feels like justice—that now the financial burden should fall on me. It's my time to put in the work I was too lazy to do as a kid.

―――

What do we owe our parents? It's the question I, and so many other children of immigrants, have to wrestle with constantly.

I know the terrors my parents have lived through and how they've clawed tooth and nail to survive horrors I am lucky to only know secondhand. They did that and succeeded, against all odds, to give us a chance at a better life. Yet the suffering still didn't end. They've spent almost their entire lives being chained to the restaurant and going through the motions of a job that stresses them out and wreaks havoc on their bodies. So much of their lives have been tinged by grief, loss, and misery, while mine has been abundant with joy and opportunity.

It's impossible not to play the comparison game. I compare my soft-bellied life to theirs. I think about how I would have no idea how to survive the circumstances they were forced to endure. The Rachel of today would not be able to live in their shoes, and because of everything they've done for us, I mercifully don't have to.

Because of that, how can the answer not be "I owe them everything"? And now that it's almost time to pay up, who am I to complain?

The guilt of having so much when my parents didn't and knowing that everything I have is thanks to their tenacity and resilience is enough to push me into one more rigid box. I'll be the dutiful daughter now.

But truthfully, I'm already buckling under the weight of the pressure. I don't know how to deal with the expectations and obligation I feel to give everything back to them and more, while also navigating the bitterness and guilt I feel. I don't know whether I'll be able to handle this pressure and the reality of *finally* having them all to myself.

I just don't know. All I know is that the guilt I feel for even thinking these shameful thoughts, and then putting them down on paper, is all-consuming. What is this compared to everything my parents have been through? Will I ever not be such a horrible and ungrateful daughter?

"John jokes that he'll put us in a retirement home," Mum says when I bring up, once again, how they should be saving more. My tone is harsh, even though I know this conversation stresses us both out.

"But you know those are expensive, right?" I say. I know she knows, but I can't control the words coming out of my mouth. "And who has to pay for that? Me."

"I know you're going to take care of me."

"It's so stressful though."

"But I don't eat a lot. I don't spend a lot of money. It'll be okay."

"Yeah, but you could live a long time and I'll have to pay for you." What I mean to say is *I hope you live a really long time*, but it comes out all wrong.

She scoffs. "Well, I don't know! Mummy might not be here in two years!"

That shuts me up. We drop the subject and talk about something else, something safer.

When I scold my dad for not saving enough, he doesn't look chastised in the least. He looks me straight in the eye and says, "That's why we have you, right?"

It's such a simple, bare-bones statement. He says it so matter-of-factly, it's insulting. It makes me recoil to know I am my parents' retirement plan. All those years of them gambling and buying fucking horses and giving us all the money we could ever ask for has led to this. I try not to think about how that money could have been squirrelled away as savings. Invested. Grown over time.

I try not to think about how the money they pissed away at card tables and slot machines could be used in their retirement to lighten the burden that will fall on our shoulders to take care of them.

I can't think about that. These thoughts just squeeze the closed fist of anxiety I feel whenever I think about their lack of savings and the expectations they've placed on us to rectify their mistakes. If I didn't already hate the casino for taking my parents away from me all those years ago, I definitely hate it now.

I hate how angry it all makes me. I hate how ungrateful it makes me feel. But I just nod and start putting away as much extra cash as I can for my parents' retirement fund on top of my own.

During the pandemic, my parents have dinner with my *ah mah* and her friends. One of the ladies is younger than Mum and already retired. She buys Mum—a virtual stranger—earrings, a necklace, and a purse. It's a blatant show of wealth.

Mum tells us afterwards how jealous it made her. How sad she felt because she was never able to save money, only spend it as it came in.

"Before, Mummy messed up. Didn't save. We gambled . . ." Her voice trails off and I am suddenly filled with so much grace for her. When would she have learned financial literacy? When she was fleeing to the mountains? On that overcrowded boat? Working dusk 'til dawn to make it in this stupidly expensive country? Feeding three always-hungry kids?

"It's okay, Mum. I'll take care of you." I don't say it through clenched teeth this time. I browbeat my guilt and stress down. I push it into deep, dark corners, where everything else I'm ashamed to think and feel and remember lies infectious and reeking. I try to exercise patience. It's a work in progress.

It sometimes comes back unbidden, all the things I did as a little shit to break my parents' hearts.

Not calling enough.

Breaking the dishes at the restaurant.

Not helping out enough.

Demanding that they speak to me in English.

Losing my Cantonese.

The guilt adds up, spirals, consumes. Taking care of them in their old age is the least I can do. I can repent and make things right. I can right my own wrongs.

Of all the sins I've committed against my parents, it's the loss of Cantonese that causes the most soul-aching pain. I'm cruelly reminded of my failure every time I talk to them.

I can't remember it now, but there was a time when I dreamed and imagined in Cantonese. It was the first language I learned—the only language I shared with my parents at my birth.

I remember bits and pieces, snatches of time when the words that flowed from my lips were in six distinct tones. When I called my dad *"Baba"* and could carry a conversation with my *ah mah* and my *ah po* without turning to my parents in shame and confusion because our words failed to reach each other.

But the change happened so gradually, so naturally, that I can't pinpoint the moment I lost my mother tongue. I feel the loss acutely now, but as it was happening, I cared not a whit for this deadweight language that was useless at getting me anywhere at school or in town. What good did knowing how to speak Cantonese do when I desperately wanted everyone to forget that I was Chinese in the first place? My first language slowly became a party trick, an ability I reluctantly pulled out when someone inevitably asked me how to say this or that in Chinese.

As time wore on, my ability to speak Cantonese became nothing more than the names of my favourite dishes and foods or simple phrases that children learn when they're toddlers and so little is expected of them. But I didn't care. I saw the way my mother struggled with the English language, the way she and Dad stumbled over their words. The way people sometimes looked at them with pity, like they were stupid and slow. The way their speech marked them as different, inferior, shameful. I didn't want that for myself.

I read constantly and pushed myself to do well in school so my English would be clear and accent-free. I stopped watching Chinese movies with my dad and started watching cool Canadian shows, like *Breaker High*, *Student Bodies*, and *Ready or Not*. Mum and Dad wanted so badly to fit in and learn the language that they never made a fuss when we responded in English to their Cantonese. Eventually, facing the pressure to learn English themselves to better converse with their customers, my parents started speaking to us primarily in English, too. Mum needed to understand what customers said when they talked about their food allergies, their aversion to MSG, their questions about whether the meat in the fried rice was *really* chicken.

It was so easy to lose. Like nothing at all. In a small town with no Chinese community and no option to go to Chinese school on weekends, I was inundated with English all the time. I saw it as my ticket to true Canadianness. Surely, if I could speak in perfect English, that would be my protection, my cloak of acceptability, my badge of honour.

My success at playing the assimilation game didn't make me more patient or sympathetic to my parents. It made me feel even more disconnected from them. It made the gulf between us bigger and amplified my angst over feeling nothing like them. It made me cruel.

I was always a sensitive child, afraid of things like the dark, the Unabomber, Hitler. One night, afraid of these monsters of past and present,

I refused to shower for longer than a minute, terrified that drawing the shower curtain might compel the spirit of Adolf Hitler to visit me, naked, in the bathtub.

"Get back in there!" my mother hissed in Cantonese, her tired legs propped up on the couch and her hand massaging her temples. "You were only in there for one minute."

I refused. I could have told her I was scared, and she probably would have just called me *so zyu*, or "silly pig," a Cantonese term of endearment. But instead, I chose insolence. "You don't even care that I shower! You don't care about me at all. The restaurant is more important to you."

It was like a storm cloud descended on my mother. She calmly got up, walked down the hallway to the bathroom, and came out with a hairbrush. It was ordinary and unremarkable, curved plastic and pokey bristles. But it felt like searing, shocking pain when she walloped me across the bottom with it. Once, twice, three times. It was the only time I can remember my mother hitting me. When she finished, I went to my room in a pained, aching rage, my hair just slightly damp from the rapid-fire shower that started it all. Instead of a dresser to hold my clothes, I had a giant cardboard box that once held Styrofoam takeout containers. On the side of that box, I wrote in furious red nail polish, "I HATE MY MOM. I HOPE SHE DIES."

For years, those ugly, awful words—my open rebuke of her—stayed there for all to see. My siblings, my friends when they came over, me.

Everyone but my mother. I knew she couldn't read those violent words. They were in English, out of her reach, out of her realm of comprehension. The cruel taunt remained right under her nose for years, but to her, it was never anything more than stark red lines on a piece of cardboard. I'm grateful for that now.

I couldn't see it when I was growing up and desperate to fit in, but my mastery of the English language pulled me further away from the things I hold most dear as an adult: my parents, my first language, my culture.

In my weekly phone conversations with Mum, she'll say a word or phrase in Cantonese and we'll go back and forth on what she might mean. "I don't know how to say it in English," she'll say, frustration in her voice. I'll start guessing, and more often than not I'm wrong. We frequently end the call never truly getting on the same page.

In the moments of levity, when I do allow myself to speak a minor, trivial thing in Cantonese, Mum will stop and squeal, "You're so cute when you speak Chinese! *Hou duk yee!*" But these moments are few and far between. My shame and insecurity constrain my tongue, making it that much more impossible to speak a language that has an absurd number of tones. I give up before even trying.

When I talk to my parents about the language barrier between us and whether my inability to speak Cantonese makes them sad, they both say the same thing: "It's our fault."

"I was supposed to send you to Chinese school, but there's no Chinese school here," Dad explains. "The closest was in Toronto, so why would I get sad? It's my fault, too. Sometimes I wish we could talk in Chinese together. It would be better. But it's okay. I know the situation."

Mum echoes his statement. "If I'm sad about it, what can I do? We have no choice. You were born in Canada and speak in English. It's my fault, too. If I talked to you more in Chinese . . ."

Her sentence trails off and I fill in the gaps. My parents could have spoken to us in Cantonese, but they didn't because they wanted to do everything "right." They wanted to excel at the assimilation game—and they did. So why, then, does it feel like I'm the biggest loser of all whenever someone tells me, "Wow, your English is so good"?

There's a feeling I can't shake that my loss of language makes me somehow less Chinese than my peers who can speak Cantonese fluently. But when I ask my parents, they both answer without skipping a beat. "No, you're still Chinese."

Their words feel like the most soothing of balms. For a brief moment, the gulf between us feels smaller, and I feel fully, proudly Chinese—just like them. How funny that I spent an entire childhood trying to be anything but Chinese, and now as an adult, I claw desperately at any semblance of Chineseness I can reach. Perhaps the greatest irony of all is that I wrote this book as a love letter to my parents, yet they may never be able to read it due to the very language barrier that has shaped so much of our lives. How funny, how heartbreaking.

———

As I contemplate what life would be like if Mum and Dad lived with us in retirement—and how I should take Cantonese lessons sooner rather than later—one possible future has started to take shape.

When we're in Vietnam, John decides to open the restaurant for a few weekends. He often sends me and Linh messages because neither of our parents has a cell phone. He asks for their guidance on how to make sweet and sour sauce, *soo guy*, and one specific customer's shrimp dish. He seems keen to learn. He expresses interest in making this his baby. He starts to appreciate how much blood, sweat, and tears have gone into the restaurant over the years.

"It's so early and I'm already here at the restaurant," he says one morning while we're gallivanting on the other side of the world. "I don't know how Mum does it every day. It's crazy how much work there is to do to run the restaurant. Mum does so much every morning—that woman is a superwoman."

He's finally starting to get it. He's seeing just how much Mum and Dad have done for the restaurant, and by extension, for us. Rather than being angry and resentful, he's showing gratitude and a desire to continue their work.

It's poignant to think about how my parents' legacy may continue under my brother. It's almost comical to think that the restaurant, our cockroach of a family member, may survive a change in management and stick around. We just can't get rid of it.

If this is the path forward, it's a welcome one for my parents, not only because it would take care of their son, but because it would give them a chance to ease into retirement. Mum, who has worries that retirement will be boring, and that all she'll do is "eat and sleep and get fat," thinks about how she and Dad could still help John when it's busy.

"But that's not real retirement, Mum! You're not going to do that!" I protest.

At first, I'm adamant about it and angry. I blame my brother for expecting Mum and Dad to work for him in retirement. But lately, I've come to terms with the fact that, after three decades, my parents need the restaurant. It's wrapped so tightly around their fixed identities. It's been their whole world as adults. They can't just go cold turkey and suddenly stop. They'll need to be weaned off it.

"Okay, you can ease into retirement," I acquiesce later. "You can start slow and learn how to relax." She laughs. It's a compromise. It's a partial, temporary answer to the question of what retirement might look like for them.

―――

Later, Mum tells me they might still sell the restaurant. She and Dad are having second thoughts about burdening John with it. It's a constant back-and-forth, an open-ended question. All she knows for certain is that she's ready for her role in it to end. "I very want to get out of here."

―――

We're working at the restaurant again. It's New Year's Eve, 2023. Michael and I are making wontons in the dining room with my brother's girlfriend, Sabrina. Since the restaurant pivoted to being takeout only during the pandemic, it's less stressful than previous years, when people would line up out the door and dishes would pile high. It gives us a chance to breathe. It gives me a chance to actually talk to the customers who come in to pick up their eagerly awaited orders.

One man comes in and says he met my dad when he first came to Canada. "George isn't in the back, is he? He's not still working hard, is he?" He's flabbergasted when I confirm that, yes, George is in the back and he's still working very hard. The man is long retired and enjoying life. He expected my dad to be doing the same.

At one point, three different customers are in the dining room, waiting for their orders. My belly flips and warms when I hear them gush about us. It feels special, being able to facilitate these warm interactions between strangers who bond over their love of our food and everything my parents have worked so hard to achieve. It feels even more meaningful knowing that the restaurant's days, at least under my parents, are numbered.

A few weeks later, I ask my brother to post a question on the restaurant's very active Facebook page: "What does our family restaurant mean to you?"

The responses pour in. One is from a friend from elementary school: "Aww best memories with Rachel. I loved going with her after school, dropping our backpacks and sitting at the bar with a pop."

"Your family has been a staple in the community for a long time! China Village has the best food in our area."

"It's exactly that: a family restaurant. You guys put so much love into everything you do and you can see how close you all are. It reflects in the excellent food you continue to make every day."

"To us, China Village means family nights. It means that everyone is gathering at someone's house to enjoy their favourite takeout meal of the week. China Village feels like laughter, love, and most recently, recovery. It's knowing once the rest of the family finds out you're having China Village, you're ordering for more people, or calling back to add on to the order. China Village means that our family is coming together to enjoy dinner and always needing the extra chicken balls because the kids will eat ten apiece. China Village means family. We are so thankful for you and your family. Your family brings our family together."

Their words warm my heart and soften the sharp edges that have crystallized after so many years of hating the restaurant for everything it's taken from us. What remains is pure pride. I'm proud of my parents for building something out of the destroyed ruins of their lives. I'm proud to be their daughter. I'm proud to be their forever restaurant kid.

This is their legacy and the culmination of all their painstaking hard work. This is their crowning achievement. This restaurant is our family's resilience made brick and mortar.

Not bad for two teenage refugees from Vietnam.

When I ask my parents what they're most looking forward to in retirement, I expect them to say something like being able to relax and sleep in, or enjoying life at a slower pace, or not having clothes that smell of oil and grease, or tending to their expensive pet fish, or travelling the world.

Instead, the first thing Mum says is, "Maybe I go find a part-time job to work two days a week, make a little bit of cash."

Dad's the same. He says, "Maybe still do a little bit of work on the side."

I resist the urge to facepalm and I tell them to try again, gently reminding them that retirement isn't about more work. They both pause and think. "Maybe I'll get a small puppy and go for a walk every day," Mum suggests.

"If I stay home, I don't think I'll feel good," Dad admits. "I have to find something to do on the side, maybe go on a trip."

Even though the question mark still looms large over us, I'm starting to lean into it. My parents have too often been denied the chance to make their own choices. So much of their lives have been spent reacting, pivoting, and bending without breaking. Retirement will be their chance to finally do whatever the hell they want.

I can live with that for now. I look forward to pulling my parents out of the rigid boxes they've been put into—restaurateurs, hard workers, refugees, immigrants, Chinese—and tease out something new. I'm ready to welcome them as whole, complex people. We have so much lost time to make up.

ACKNOWLEDGEMENTS

Writing a book—especially a memoir—is emotionally, physically, mentally, and spiritually taxing. I could not have done it without the love, care, and encouragement of the following people:

My heartfelt thanks to Chris Casuccio at Westwood Creative Artists for seeing something special in my story from the very beginning and for your patient guidance throughout the writing process. (And a special thank you to Tamara Baluja for introducing us!)

My eternal gratitude to Anna Comfort O'Keeffe at Douglas & McIntyre for taking a chance on a first-time author and for being such a wonderfully kind and patient person. To my team at D&M: Claire Lin, Ariel Brewster, Corina Eberle, and Luke Inglis, thank you for making my life's greatest dream come true.

To write this book, I received grants from the Ontario Arts Council recommended by ECW Press and Hamilton Arts & Letters. For that, I am deeply grateful.

All my love and thanks to Ishani Nath, who was the first person to tell me I should write a book about being a restaurant kid and provided gentle, thoughtful feedback as one of my earliest readers. I'm indebted to

Deb Aguillon and Scott Fowlie, who always keep me emotionally fed and hydrated with their daily love, support, and silliness. Special mention goes to Mikey Franklin and Kyron Wong, who have supported *Restaurant Kid* in various capacities over the years.

A heartfelt thank you to all my friends and in-laws—the Eastman, Mac-Donald, and Anderson families—for your support and love throughout this journey. Your encouragement and enthusiasm have made all the difference.

This book would not be possible without Kim Abrahamse, Mari Mendoza, and the entire Firefly Creative Writing team. The earliest excerpts of *Restaurant Kid* were written in your workshops and nurtured through your one-on-one coaching. Thank you for facilitating such safe spaces for writers.

To my Deeper Waters Still friends, Sofy K and Treasa Levasseur, thank you for showing up every Monday night and creating with me. I can't wait to support you on your respective publishing journeys one day!

I've learned that publishing is not for the faint of heart and that it's as opaque as it is confusing, so I'm grateful for my author friends who are always generous with their time and wisdom: Alexandra Posadzki, Jennilee Austria-Bonifacio, and the many lovely, talented people in my 2025 Debuts, Small Press Debuts, and Bi+ Book Gang groups.

Thank you to Alison Byczok and my team at CNIB for giving me the time and space I needed to focus and pursue this dream I've nurtured ever since I was a little girl.

Thanks to Tanjim for helping me navigate social media back when I didn't have a clue, and to the many online book besties I've made throughout this journey so far. I write for lovers of words and critical thinkers like you.

To the people we met in Vietnam: your generous spirits, kind hearts, and community care made our once-in-a-lifetime family trip back to my parents' homeland that much more meaningful. I learned so many life lessons by being in your warm and welcoming company.

A special shout-out to every waitress who has worked at May May Inn and China Village, and to the people who have stepped in to help out at the restaurant over the years: thank you for your hard work, years of service, and care for our family.

To our loyal customers and regulars over the past three decades: we'd be nothing without your support. You've made my parents' dreams come true and we're forever grateful for you.

To Michael—my love, my unicorn, my partner in life. I am blessed beyond measure to call you mine. This book is only possible because you took care of the dogs, the house, and me. Thank you for nurturing my dreams as if they are your own. You are my life's greatest answered prayer. I love you.

Our perfect pups, Ivy and Elm: thank you for making sure I move away from my desk throughout the day and for bringing *me* out on walks. Ivy, I miss you.

My brother, John, my childhood hero: thank you for always showing up for us and for everything you do for Mum, Dad, the restaurant, and the community—I see you and I appreciate you. Thank you for ensuring my childhood was full of fun and joy, and for always being my protector.

To Linh, my sissyduck, my best friend, and my soulmate. There is no me without you. Thank you for raising me when you were just a child, and for being the reason why I love books and dirty jokes. From the very beginning, you've been my confidant and greatest supporter, and your unwavering belief in me has always been my lifeline. I couldn't have done any of this without you.

Mum and Dad: I owe everything to your courage, sacrifice, and hard work. You've endured and overcome unimaginable hardships to give us a life filled with opportunity, and the countless hours you've worked to build a future for our family are a testament to your strength and love. You've shown us what true resilience and dedication look like—and the life I am blessed to lead today is because of everything you've done to get us here. This book is my love letter to you.

All glory to God.

ABOUT THE AUTHOR

Rachel Phan is a Toronto-based Chinese Canadian author. A graduate of Toronto Metropolitan University's Master of Journalism program, she's shared her stories on CBC, *HuffPost*, the *National Post*, and *Maclean's*. You can follow her on Instagram at @rachelmphan.